Urban Geography

URBAN GEOGRAPHY

Girish Chopra

Commonwealth

Urban Geography

Edition : 2024

ISBN 81-7169-992-8

Published by :
COMMONWEALTH PUBLISHERS PVT. LTD.
4831/24, Prahlad Street,
Ansari Road, Darya Ganj,
New Delhi - 110002
Ph. : 23272541, 23257835
Fax : 91- 011- 23257835
e-mail : commonwealthbooks@gmail.com

Laser Typesetting by :
Dimple Computers
Delhi

Printed at :
Roshan Offset Printers
Delhi

Preface

Urban geography is the study of the history of urban settlement, the development of cities, urban structure, spatial patterns that occur within the city, as well as urban problems and policies. It forms the theoretical basis for a number of professions including urban planning, retail store site selection, real estate development, crime pattern analysis, logistical analysis, among others.

Urban planning and regional planning use the science of geography to assist in determining how to develop the land to meet particular criteria, such as safety, beauty, economic opportunities, the preservation of the built or natural heritage, etcetera. The planning of towns, cities and rural areas may be seen as applied geography although it also draws heavily upon the arts, the sciences and lessons of history.

This book addresses the changes in the nature and outcomes of urbanization processes as well as the development of new ways of thinking about urban geography. Its most distinctive feature is a dynamic approach to the study of urban geography: unravelling the interlocking processes of urbanization to explain constantly changing urban geographies. This work will serve as a highly useful reference tool for all who concerned.

Girish Chopra

Contents

1

Growth Patterns of Urbanisation

For most of human history, people have lived and worked mainly in rural areas. In 1900, just 14 per cent of the world's population lived in cities. But during the twentieth century, rapid population growth and other demographic changes meant that the number of people in cities grew quickly. In 1950, it was 30 per cent, and now more than 47.5 per cent of all the world's people live in cities or urban areas. Within 20 years, another1.5 billion people will be living in the world's cities. Meanwhile, it is predicted that total rural population will stay roughly stable with very little increase.

There are several reasons why urban populations are growing. Partly it is because of natural population growth occurring within cities. Rural-to-urban migration also plays a part. Country dwellers move to cities in pursuit of a better life including.better employment, to be closer to services, to join family, or to flee confl ict or disasters. Outlying rural areas near cities also become urbanised as population increases and cities sprawl outwards due to the need for land.

Patterns of urbanisation tend to vary from country to country. Currently, of developing regions, Latin America has the highest concentration of people living in urban areas. However, the greatest growth for the next 30 years is expected to be in South and East Asia. Not all urban dwellers live in large cities with millions of residents. Many live in much smaller urban towns or cities. But as world population grows, it is expected that more and more people will live in very large cities. By 2015 it is forecast that 23 cities will have populations of more than 10 million people each. All but four of these will be in developing countries.

Urban Poverty

Understanding urbanisation is crucial to understanding poverty. Often it is believed that with better access to services and employment opportunities, city dwellers are better off than people in rural areas. But much of the increase in urban population tends to be in poorer areas. Large numbers of poor people are concentrated in overcrowded neighbourhoods, often in makeshift houses without proper services. In Africa, 40 per cent of urban households have an income below the locally defi ned poverty line.

The urban poor often face a very different set of problems to the poorest people living in rural areas. Poverty is generally measured according to income: an income of US$1 a day or less is accepted as a global benchmark for absolute poverty. But this ignores the fact that poverty is not just about how much a person earns. The proportion of their income they must spend on basic services is also relevant, particularly for urban dwellers. For instance, someone living in a slum who pays high prices for water and food and has many health-related costs because of widespread disease, may be worse off than a rural dweller who has ready access to water, grows their own food and has low health care costs – even if the latter has a lower income.

It is often assumed that the benefi ts of economic growth driven by urban development will accrue evenly, making the rich richer but also lifting the poorest out of poverty as well. However, urbanisation has often led to sharp divisions between rich and poor in urban areas. While those benefi ting from the economic development in cities are becoming wealthy, millions more are being left out of the very economic processes that their cheap labour is driving. Instead, they are falling more deeply into poverty.

Housing

Access to adequate housing is a problem for many urban dwellers. Prices are often higher in cities than rural areas due to higher land and labour costs. The poorest people, including many who migrate to cities from rural areas, are unable to fi nd affordable housing. Instead, they set up illegally on vacant or unused ground, often on the outskirts of cities, constructing makeshift houses for themselves and forming slum areas. They are often in dangerous locations, such as close to train lines or in areas prone to fl ooding. At least one billion people worldwide live in slums.

Slums are generally cramped areas lacking adequate sanitation. Houses are small and tightly packed together, often made out of cardboard, tin, plastic, wood or other scavenged material. Many governments and local authorities view slums as illegal settlements, and refuse to take responsibility for providing services. Slum dwellers are left with no clean running water, electricity, sewerage systems or garbage collection. Because they are set up without any formal planning, slums also lack adequate roads, public land like parks or playgrounds, schools, health centres and drainage. Garbage piles up around the slums or else is burnt, causing smog and air pollution.

While slums might seem like temporary constructions, often they become permanent homes for thousands of people, who establish houses, raise families and run businesses like food stores, bars or hairdressers there. Although neglected by authorities, they can be very vibrant and active communities. Resourceful residents will often fi nd ways to supply essentials, for example by piping in water and selling it to other residents. The failure of governments to recognise slums as legitimate settlements often means that residents have no permanent ownership over the land they live on, even when they have been there for many years. This makes life very precarious. Without warning, slum dwellers can have their houses bulldozed or be evicted if governments sell off land or crack down on 'illegal' settlements.

Health

Limited access to basic services causes health problems everywhere, but these are compounded in overcrowded urban areas. The lack of proper sewerage or drainage systems leads to disease, which spreads quickly in cramped conditions. Pollution and sewerage can contaminate what little clean water there is. Mosquitoes, which spread malaria and other diseases, breed in stagnant drains. Air pollution is also a problem in many large cities, due to emissions from vehicles, burn-off of waste and industrial activity. Many people suffer from respiratory illnesses, and worldwide, about half a million people die prematurely each year as a result of urban air pollution5. The urban poor usually live in marginal areas far from health services, making it diffi cult for people to seek treatment. Even those close to medical help often cannot afford to pay fees or buy medicine.

EMPLOYMENT

The greater employment opportunities in urban areas are a major reason for migration to cities. Although the urban poor are often persecuted, in fact their presence is vital to the economies of many countries. They provide the cheap and plentiful labour that is vital for industry, which in turn drives economic growth.

Many people in urban areas work in informal jobs like street vending or casual labour, which are unregistered and not protected by any labour laws or safety legislation6. Consequently, such workers generally don't have any job security, often don't have a fixed wage, and may have to work in unsafe conditions. Those without work permits or licences are vulnerable to harassment and blackmail by authorities. Although wages may be higher than in rural areas, living costs for things like food, housing, fuel and transport can also be much higher in cities. For those who can't find work, there are little or no social services such as income support available.

SOCIAL CONDITIONS

Urbanisation can bring major social change, as people move from their home communities to cities where they may have no family or connections. Often there is less social support available in a large urban community than in a small rural village. Children and young people are especially vulnerable in cities, where they may be exploited or abused. They risk ending up living on the street, or being used for child labour, because of their need for income and the many employers willing to take advantage of children.

Urban areas tend to have less conservative values than rural areas. Traditions that are prevalent in small rural communities can become diluted by the wide range of social and cultural infl uences in a city environment. This can have positive and negative effects. Groups such as women may fi nd greater freedom in urban areas, breaking out of traditional roles. But social mores and customs that have held families and communities together can disintegrate, leading to increased family breakdown.

Cities generally have higher crime rates. Slum areas are often a maze of dimly lit alleys and dwellings, which can be a haven for criminals who are able to escape easily. With the police sometimes avoiding slums because of the danger, residents are at risk of attack or burglary. Urban poverty means that many people turn to crime just to survive.

Responses to Urbanisation

Urbanisation is offering major challenges for governments and city authorities, who struggle to provide services for rapidly increasing city populations. Growing urban populations bring a critical need to look for new ways to tackle poverty. Many strategies to combat poverty tend to focus on rural poverty, ignoring the differing needs of poor urban dwellers. The need to improve the lives of urban dwellers has been recognised in the United Nations Millennium Development Goals, which pledge to achieve signifi cant improvement in the lives of at least 100 million slum dwellers by 2020. It has been estimated that this will cost US$70–100 billion, requiring a signifi cant increase in support from international donors including Australia. Governments also need to work to change attitudes towards urban residents, particularly the poorest people.

As citizens, the urban poor have the same rights to services and affordable housing as other residents. Yet they are consistently denied these rights. Their homes are labelled as illegal and they go without basic services. Rather than being victimised, poor urban dwellers need to be recognised as making a vital economic and social contribution to city areas through their labour and communities. Those governments that are working to improve urban conditions are often constrained by a lack of resources.

There is a need for poor urban dwellers to be supported in their efforts to improve their own lives. Slum dwellers in cities around the world have mobilised themselves and set up community organisations that provide services including credit facilities, education, social support and representation for residents. For example, in Thailand, community networks have formed in slums to address housing problems. They have worked to resolve land disputes and helped people secure housing rights and improve their living conditions. If the world does not fi nd the will and the resources to address the needs of a rapidly urbanising world, the number of the poorest people living in urban areas will continue to rise.

Urbanization has two general definitions in the geographical and environmental literature:

— It often refers to the movement and concentration of humans from rural areas and their villages to towns and cities.

— It can also be defined as the transformation an area on the surface of the Earth to an urban pattern of land-use.

People living in rural areas depend on agriculture or other means natural resource harvesting for their survival. Rural populations can sometimes organize themselves into villages. A village is a small number of rural households linked together because of culture, customs, family ties, and an association with farming land or harvesting resources. In urban areas, the majority of the people living here do not directly depend on farming or natural resource harvesting for their livelihood. Urbanites can often have jobs in education, commerce, industry, science, and the arts.

Towns are defined as human settlements that are larger than a village but smaller than a city. Towns generally have centralized areas within them where commerce and business are the primary activities of the residing citizens. A city is a complex human settlement with built areas that specialize in particular types of industry, commerce, and residential living. Cities with populations greater than 10 million are called megacities.

Humans began organizing themselves into villages about 10,000 years ago with the dawn of agriculture. The domestication of plants and animals allowed populations of people to settle down in one location instead of relying on a nomadic hunting and gathering lifestyle for survival. With the advent of agriculture, the food producing activities of a portion of the settled population yielded enough surplus food to support parts of the human population that were engaged in other activities.

Some of the early settled villages grew to be towns and small cities as populations increased because of the site's proximity to rich farming land, natural resources, and trading routes. In these early towns and cities, a number of specialized jobs were created dealing with commerce and trade. The concentration of people into towns and cities also had a profound effect on the development human society and culture. Urbanization allowed for the rise of commerce, politics, organized religion, education, technology, the arts, and science.

Ever since the beginning of the Industrial Revolution, the rate of urbanization has been increasing more rapidly. Industrialization, the mass production of goods, and the development of commercialized commerce had a great effect on the movement of people from rural areas to urban areas. In 1900 about 15 % of the human population lived in towns and cities. By 1990, about 45 % of the Earth's human population were concentrated in urban areas. Demographers estimate that in the year 2025 about 60 % of the world's population will be living in urban communities.

Urbanization in MDCs is now beginning to level off. Most MDC urban areas underwent dramatic urban growth during the nineteenth and early twentieth centuries. Today, many urban areas in developing are experiencing similar demographic expansion. In 1995, the percent urban share of total population in Asia and Africa was about 35 %. By the year 2025 the percent urban population is expected to rise to about 55 % in these regions. Table 1 lists top ten urban regions in the world for 1900, 1950, and 2000. The data in this table illustrates the different timing of urban expansion in LDCs and MDCs.

Table 1: Ten top urban regions for 1900, 1950, 1992, and 2010 - projected (population in millions of people).

1900	1950	1992	2015*
London 6.6	New York 12.3	Tokyo 25.8	Tokyo 26.4
New York 4.2	London 8.7	Sao Paulo 17.0	Bombay26.1
Paris 3.3	Tokyo 6.7	New York 16.2	Lagos 23.2
Berlin 2.4	Paris 5.4	Mexico City15.3	Dhaka 21.1
Chicago 1.7	Shanghai 5.3	Shanghai 14.1	Sao Paulo
20.4			
Vienna 1.6	Buenos Aires 5.0	Bombay 13.3	Karachi 19.2
Tokyo 1.5	Chicago 4.9	Los Angeles11.9	Mexico City 19.2
St. Petersburg1.4	Moscow 4.8	Buenos Aires 11.8	New York 17.4
Philadelphia1.4	Calcutta 4.4	Beijing 11.4	Jakarta 17.3
Manchester1.3	Los Angeles 4.0	Rio de Janeiro 11.3	Calcutta17.3

* United Nations - World Urbanization Prospects: The 1999 Revision

URBANISATION AND ECONOMIC GROWTH

Urban economies are the backbone and motor of the wealth of nations. As countries become more reliant on manufacturing and services and less on agriculture, urban areas are more likley to become important for fostering marshallian externalities, nourishing innovation, providing a hub for trade, and encouraging human capital accumulation. Such economies should be particularly important for developing countries since trends in urbanization show that the share of the urban population has increased substantially in these since the 1950s. For example, between 1950 and 2000 urbanization, defined as the share of urban to total population, increased by 124 per cent in developing countries compared to 38 per cent in the industrialized world, so that the gap in relative size of the urban population between developing and developed countries has narrowed substantially. At the same time one has not witnessed a similar convergence in economic growth rates between these two groups.

Although this discrepancy between the rates of urbanization and economic growth rates in developing countries has long been recognized, it has only recently again come strongly under the limelight. Subscribing to the over-urbanization hypothesis argued that developing countries' rates of urbanization are higher than that of today's developed nations compared to when these were at the same stage of development (i.e. in the 19 century) and hence are above their optimum level.

In contrast, opponents of this view have questioned the implicit assumption underlying this 'over-urbanization' hypothesis that the course of industrialization and urbanization in developing countries should conform to the path taken by today's industrialized countries. Instead, it has been argued that a more satisfactory approach would require analyzing whether less urbanization in developing countries would have indeed favored greater growth and development. Although important, this traditional debate has probably missed an essential point, namely to take account of the distribution of the population across cities, i.e., the degree of urban concentration.

As a matter of fact, there is a large literature that demonstrates both theoretically and empirically that there are increasing returns at the city level, thus suggesting that urban concentration may be more important than urbanization per se; see Duranton and Puga for a theoretical survey on the micro-foundations of urban agglomeration economies and Rosenthal and Strange for a review of the empirical evidence. Examining patterns of urban concentration in developing countries, one finds that, along side increases in urbanization, developing countries have also experienced sizeable growth rates of urban concentration over the last fifty years.

Specifically, whereas the growth of large cities (more than 5 million inhabitants) has been slow or even zero in the industrialized world, developing nations are experiencing ever greater population concentration in large urban agglomerations and in mega-cities (defined as cities with a population greater than 10 million). For example, between 1975 and 2000 the number of mega-cities increased from 3 to 15 in developing countries, compared to a rise from 2 to 4 in developed countries. In seeking econometric evidence, one discovers only a few econometric studies that have attempted to highlight the impact of urbanization or urban concentration on economic development.

Moomaw and Shatter regress different measures of urbanization and urban concentration on growth and find that metropolitan concentration has a positive while urban primacy, defined as concentration of urban population in the largest city, has a negative impact. McCoskey and Kao using panel cointegration techniques find that long-run effects of urbanization on growth cannot be rejected. More recently, Henderson has identified a non-monotonous impact of urban primacy on economic development, thus suggesting a (broad) range of values of optimal primacy levels, below which urban concentration fosters rather than deters economic development.

There are, however, two compelling arguments for examining developing countries separately. Firstly, developing and developed countries may be on different paths of development. Secondly, cities are likely to be very heterogeneous across these two broad economic groups even after controlling for city size. For example, using information from the Global Urban Indicators Database for cities of under one million reveals that water, telephone and electricity access are significantly higher in cities of developed than developing countries. Moreover, infant mortality rates in cities in developing countries are several multiples of the ones that can be found in similar sized cities in developed countries. A similar pattern can also be gauged from limiting the sample to cities greater than one million inhabitants.

Finding of Henderson focus on allowing for potential non-linearities in the relationship by utilizing semi-parametric estimation techniques. This proves to be a fruitful exercise as results support a U-shaped relationship between two different measures of urban concentration and growth. This suggests the existence of an urban-concentration trap where marginal increases in urban concentration would reduce growth for about a third of the countries in the sample.

Estimation Methodology

To estimate the impact of urbanization and urban concentration on growth, Henderson assume that there are only two factors of production, physical capital (t) and labor (t) so that the production function is given by:

$$Y_{it} = F[K_{it}, L_{it}, A_{it}] \tag{1}$$

where Y_{it} is the flow of output produced in country i at time t. The production function also depends on $A_{ip'}$, to reflect the effects of technological progress. Assuming a Cobb-Douglas constant returns to scale technology, first differencing and normalizing by labor, the production function in (1) becomes:

linearity. Specifically, we can use the semi-parametric Kernel regression estimator proposed by Robinson, which does not restrict the non-linearity to take on any specific functional form, but still allows the use of other conditioning variables.

One can consider the following equation to be estimated:

$$\tilde{y} = \alpha + g(X) + \delta Z + u \tag{4}$$

where Z=(Z′ | Δ log*k*) are a set of explanatory variables that are assumed to have a linear effect on $\tilde{y}$ (which stands for Δ log *y*), g() is a smooth and continuous, possibly non-linear, unknown function of X, and *u* is a random error term. A common used non-parametric estimator of an unknown function like *g*(X) without allowing for the effect of other conditioning variables is the well-known Nadaraya-Watson estimator:

$$\hat{m}_h(X) = \frac{n^{-1}\sum_{i=1}^{n} K_h(X - X_i)\tilde{y}_i}{n^{-1}\sum_{i=1}^{n} K_h(X - X_i)} \tag{5}$$

such that *i=1…n* are the *n* number of observations, $K_h()$ is the shape function, commonly referred to as the Kernel, that is a continuous, bounded and real function that integrates to one and acts as a weighting function of observations around X and depends on the choice of bandwith *h*. The appeal of this estimator lies in its very flexible approach to non-linearity by allowing the relationship of $\tilde{y}$ with respect to X to vary over all values of X. Specifically, this technique corresponds to estimating the regression function at a particular point by locally fitting constants to the data via weighted least squares, where those observations closer to the chosen point have more influence on the regression estimate than those further away, as determined by the choice of *h* and *K*.

An additional appeal of this sort of technique is that it avoids any parametric assumptions regarding the conditional mean function $m(X)$, and thus about its functional form or error structure. Allowing for the linear effect of other explanatory variables only slightly complicates the estimation of g(X). Specifically, Robinson showed that in controlling for other conditioning variables the (semi-parametric) Kernel regression estimator for $g(X)$ simply becomes:

$$\hat{g}(X) = \hat{m}_{\tilde{y}}(X) - \hat{\delta}\,\hat{m}_{X}(X) \qquad (6)$$

where $\hat{m}_{\tilde{y}}$ (X) and $\hat{m}_{x}$ (X) are the (non-parametric) Kernel regression estimates of E($\tilde{y}$ /X) and E(Z/X) and $\hat{\delta}$ is the OLS estimator of:

$$\tilde{y} - \hat{m}_{\tilde{y}}(X) = \delta(Z - \hat{m}_{X}(X)) + \varepsilon \qquad (7)$$

where ε is a random error term. Intuitively, $\hat{g}$ (X) is the estimate of g(X) after the independent effect(s) of Z on Y has been removed.

Given that the estimate of $\hat{g}$ (X) is at least in part based on non-parametric estimation techniques, one cannot subject it to the standard statistical type tests (e.g. t-test) that economists have grown so accustomed to using in parametric regressions. One can, however, relatively easily calculate upper and lower pointwise confidence bands as:

CI =

g (X) +/- $(c_\alpha c_K)^{1/2}$ η' (x) / [h $$CI = \frac{\hat{g}(X) \pm (c_\alpha c_K)^{\frac{1}{2}} \hat{\eta}(X)}{\left[\sum_{i=1}^{n} K_h (X - X_i) \right]^{\frac{1}{2}}} \quad (8)$$

where $c_\alpha c_k$ is a kernel specific constant corresponding to the α quantile of the distribution and $\hat{n}^2$ is defined as:

$$\hat{\eta}^2(X) = n^{-1} \frac{\sum_{i=1}^{n} K_h (X - X_i) \tilde{y}_i}{n^{-1} \sum_{i=1}^{n} K_h (X - X_i)} \quad (9)$$

One should note that (6) ignores the possible approximation error bias of $\hat{g}$ (X) Including this in (6) would complicate the expression considerably since the bias is a complicated function of the first and second derivatives of g(X). This bias tends to be highest at sudden peaks of $\hat{g}$ (X) and at the necessarily truncated left and right boundaries of the data.

However, if h is chosen proportional to $1/n^{(1/5)}$ times a sequence that tends slowly to zero then the bias vanishes asymptotically for the interior points. For all the estimations use a Gaussian kernel for K_h and an optimal bandwidth h such that:

$$h = \frac{0.9m}{n^{1 \cdot 5}} \quad (10)$$

where m =

$$(\hat{\sigma}^2(X) \times (\text{interquantile range})_X / 1.349)$$

One should also note that the size of $\hat{\sigma}^2$ (X) at any point of X will depend proportionally on the marginal distribution of X. In other words the accuracy of the estimate of g(X) at X is positively related to the density of other observations around that point. In order to visualize this effect suggested by Haerdle, calculate the pointwise confidence bands at points chosen according to the distribution of X. Specifically, we can chose points so that five per cent of the observations lie between them.

Urban Concentration

Since the semi-parametric methodology allows the link between economic growth and the urban variable to vary over the entire observed range of urban concentration/ urbanization, results are, as is standard when using this estimator, depicted graphically. As stated earlier, this also allows one to link the statistical accuracy of the results with confidence bands and the distribution of observations. More precisely, single depicted points below and above the continuous line constitute lower and upper confidence bands. The horizontal distance between each set of confidence points on the confidence bands indicates the distribution of the observations across the indicated range of X, where five per cent of the sample lie between each set of points. One should also note that, do not report the actual estimates of g(X) on the vertical axes, just graph the relationship between X and the dependent variable. The primary reason for not reporting these is that the estimates of g(X) are predicted values from which the influence of the other control variables have been purged, and hence, cannot be directly linked to the actual range of observed $\tilde{y}$. Moreover, the predicted absolute levels of g(X) cannot be strictly compared across graphs. Instead one should use the figures to gauge the estimated slope of the relationship in question.

In Figure 1, the first graph estimates of g(X) using urban density. As can be seen, while the general shape suggests a U-shaped relationship between urban concentration and growth, this link is not very smooth near either end of the curve. However, as can be gauged from the horizontal distance between the confidence band points at the ends, the estimate of g(X) in these areas is based on relatively few observations. For example, only one per cent of the observations lie between the last set of confidence band points and the end of the curve.

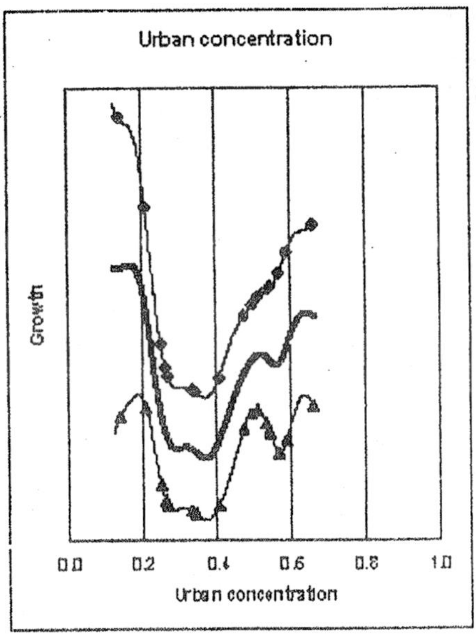

Figure 1. GDP growth and primacy

We can use these results to separate the sample into countries that are on the left or right side of the turning point value of urban density, which is estimated to be 0.36, according to their actual observed level of urban density at the beginning and end of the sample period, 1960 and 1990. This is shown in the first two columns of Table 2. Accordingly, in 1960, 12 of 39 countries had urban density levels below the threshold value and thus were in an urban-concentration trap. This figure was only reduced by 1 by 1990, although comparison across time for individual countries reveals that there was more movement across categories than the aggregate numbers suggest.

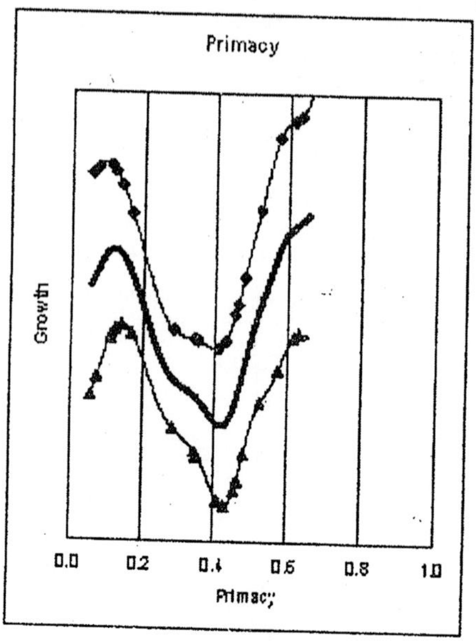

Figure 2. GDP growth and urban concentration

In particular, while the urban density in Indonesia and Tunisia fell to such an extent that these two countries fell into the urban-concentration trap, growth in urban density pushed El Salvador, Myanmar, and Nicaragua into the upward sloping part of the estimated curve. In Figure 2, the relationship between urban primacy and growth is depicted. Again, a U-shaped curve, but much smoother than for the case of urban density, is apparent.

Specifically using this semi-parametric estimate suggests that there is a negative relationship between primacy and growth, up until primal cities have less than 41 per cent of the urban population (compared to 36 per cent for the urban concentration case), thus leaving nearly three quarters of the countries considered in an urban-concentration trap - as shown in the last two columns of Table 2. Moreover, by 1990, only Chile and El Salvador managed to escape levels of urban primacy that are associated with negative economic growth.

Table 2: Distribution of countries above and below the estimated threshold levels

Country	Urban Density 1960	Urban Density 1990	Primacy 1960	Primacy 1990
Algeria	0.25	0.15	0.23	0.12
Argentina	0.57	0.53	0.45	**0.40**
Bolivia	0.40	0.46	**0.28**	**0.29**
Brazil	0.53	0.46	**0.15**	**0.14**
Cameroon	0.37	0.39	**0.23**	**0.22**
Chile	0.39	0.42	**0.39**	0.42
Colombia	0.42	0.48	**0.16**	**0.20**
Costa Rica	0.63	0.55	0.63	0.56
Dominican Republic	0.59	0.63	0.46	0.59
Ecuador	0.51	0.46	**0.29**	**0.26**

El Salvador	**0.31**	0.43	**0.25**	0.46
Ghana	0.25	0.27	0.25	0.27
Guatemala	0.41	0.50	0.41	0.50
Haiti	0.43	0.56	0.43	0.56
Honduras	0.30	0.35	0.30	0.35
India	0.39	0.41	**0.07**	**0.06**
Indonesia	0.48	**0.32**	**0.19**	**0.14**
Iran	0.45	0.41	**0.25**	**0.20**
Jordan	0.30	0.30	0.30	0.30
Malaysia	0.16	0.13	0.16	0.13
Mali	0.26	0.35	0.26	0.35
Mexico	0.47	0.50	**0.29**	**0.25**
Myanmar	**0.29**	0.39	**0.23**	**0.33**
Nicaragua	**0.33**	0.36	**0.33**	**0.35**
Pakistan	0.45	0.46	**0.17**	**0.21**
Panama	0.61	0.66	0.61	0.66
Paraguay	0.47	0.45	0.47	0.45
Peru	0.37	0.39	**0.37**	**0.39**
Philippines	0.30	0.30	0.27	0.27
Senegal	0.36	0.48	**0.36**	0.48
South Africa	0.49	0.56	**0.14**	**0.14**
Sudan	0.30	0.29	0.30	0.29
Thailand	0.65	0.57	0.65	0.57
Tunisia	0.38	**0.33**	**0.38**	**0.33**
Turkey	0.48	0.38	**0.21**	**0.19**
Uganda	0.41	0.41	0.41	0.41
Uruguay	0.57	0.46	0.57	0.45
Venezuela	0.51	0.45	**0.28**	**0.18**

Zambia	0.16	0.34	0.16	0.34

There are two different measures of urban concentration one should note that countries that are on the right segment of the urban density curve, but on the left part of its primacy counterpart, are mainly large countries, such as Brazil, India, and South Africa. How the two measures can potentially present different pictures concerning a country's level of urban concentration, in that large countries tend to have much smaller levels of urban primacy than small countries.

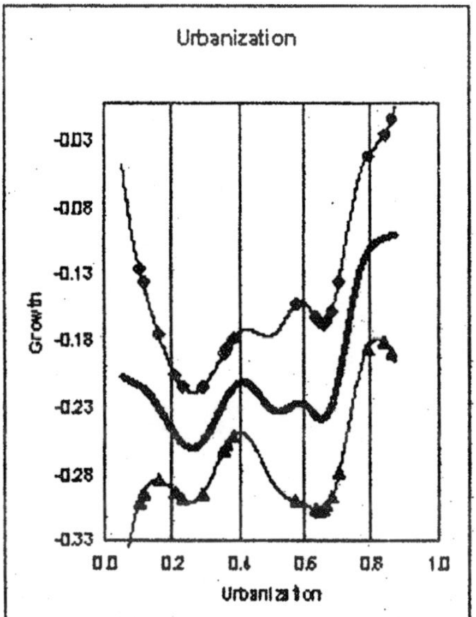

Figure 3. GDP growth and urbanization

For instance, in 1990, Brazil had an urban primacy level of 13.6 per cent, whereas its urban concentration was 46.3 per cent. On the contrary, Uruguay, which is almost fifty times smaller than Brazil, had a primacy level of 45.2 per cent, and an urban concentration level of 46.3 per cent. The lack of a linear relationship between urban primacy and growth has already been highlighted by Henderson, although, he, in contrast, finds a bell-shaped relationship, thus suggesting the presence of an optimal urban concentration level above which primacy deters growth. However, the results do not necessarily refute those of Henderson. Specifically, it must be pointed out that Henderson's result is based on a sample of about 70 countries, of which approximately a third are high-income nations. Thus any optimal urban concentration levels will not be driven by already developed nations.

Trends in Urbanisation and Urban Growth

Urbanization is regarded as a complex process. It leads societies towards the industrial and technological enrichment and thus is an epitome of a society. The understanding of the growth dynamics of urban settlements at different levels becomes the primary requirement for any explanation of this emerging pattern.

The importance of such an endeavor lies in its relevance for scientific analysis of data on host of socio demographic and economic variables. It provides the necessary background for understanding the processes of demographic, social and economic changes operating in spatio-temporal context leading to an uneven pace of urban development in different part s of the country. Often, it is possible to find faster pace of growth of a few urban centers on the one end and stagnation or decline of others on the other end. As because it is a complex process impacting changes with respect to socio economic and socio cultural parameters and thereby their relationships, hardly there can be a single definition of the concept of urbanization that can be applicable to all situations. Demographic approach of urbanization defines it as a process that makes the proportion of the total population concentrated in urban settlements or increases the proportion of urban population to total population over a period to time.

However, the concept of urbanization as a process of change and transformation is yet in the stage of evolution throughout the world and more so in the developing countries. The fact that in India the definitions and attributes of urban area, which provide basis of all quantitative analysis of urbanization, have undergone several changes and modifications over time validates the authenticity of the above statement. In 1901 census, the definition adopted for an urban area was as follows:

— every municipality of whatever size;

— all civil lines not included within municipal limits;

— every other continuous collection of houses, permanently inhabited by not less than 5000 persons, which the Provincial Superintendent may decide to treat as a town for census purposes.

Evidently, in the above definition administrative setup and size was the basic consideration for deciding the status of any settlement as urban or rural and not necessarily the economic parameters. Many of the places, which thus had been treated as towns were in reality nothing more than overgrown villages. The same definition of town continued up to the 1951 census.

A more realistic and meaningful definition was adopted of urban entity was adopted for the first time in the census of 1961 primarily to avoid the anomalies to the earlier definition. This definition brought under its fold considerable economic characteristics in addition to the other administrative and demographic criteria. The definition adopted in 1961 was as follows-

— a place should be either a municipal corporation, cantonment board, notified town area committee etc;

— I. a minimum population of 5000, II. a density of at least 400 people per sq. km., and III. at least 75 per cent of their male labour force in non-agricultural occupations.

It therefore, becomes obligatory on the part of any researcher to first understand the above limitations while analyzing any data pertaining to various aspects of urbanization in India. Keeping in mind the aforesaid points we would now seek to analyze the trends in urbanization and urban growth in the three states of northeastern India.

The Northeastern Region of India comprises eight sister states namely, Arunachal Pradesh, Assam, Manipur, Meghalaya, Nagaland, Sikkim and Tripura. The region forms the eastern part of the great Himalayan Range and thus is endowed with enumerable natural resources. The region is mainly hilly is character excluding the Brahmaputra plain of Assam. Urbanisation in this region has a long history that started before the advent of the British.

The earliest urban characters were mainly the capital cities built by different rulers. They were essentially rural in character made up mainly of the palaces, high walls, temples, pavilions etc. With the advent of the British and subsequent colonization of the India soil, centers for collection and other related activities started along with the development of administrative activities. Partition of India affected the towns by changing the population size and area of the towns. In the post independence era under the planned effort of development decentralization activities started and administrative units were reorganized.

The second half of the 20th century saw tremendous pace in the level of urbanization in this so called backward region. Although there are states, which are still struggling in this regard, states like mizoram are witnessing urbanization above the national average. Between 1981 and 1991, against the average urban growth of 36.09 percent in India, the seven northeastern states notched 49.79 percent, despite the relative backwardness of the region in terms of economic growth, communication and health services.

The most spectacular growth was in Mizoram where the urban population has almost doubled and the number of towns almost quadrupled from six to 22 during this period. The explanation, during the 1980s, the federal government carried out a large-scale administrative re-organization of the districts of Mizoram as part of a bid to sharpen counter-insurgency operations. This saw several villages being regrouped into urban centres. However, mention should be made that even in 2001 the level of urbanization in the northeast India is less than 20%, far less than that of the national average.

The demographic transition in northeastern India is unique in that it was brought about by settlement policies begun by the colonial British rulers in the last century, which has seen the northeastern states swamped by "outsiders." From less than one million people 150 years ago, northeast India's population had swelled to nearly 30 million by 1981. All this is closely linked to the political problems in the region. The most dramatic transformation was in Tripura where the tribal people had shrunk from 64 percent of the population in 1874 to 29 percent in 1981. "The impact of this phenomenon on the society, polity and economy of the region has naturally been very significant.

The migrant communities have gained control over land and secondary sources of livelihood. The widespread identity crisis in northeast India has been caused by large-scale migration of population from outside the region during the past one hundred years.

TREND IN THE PATTERN OF URBANIZATION

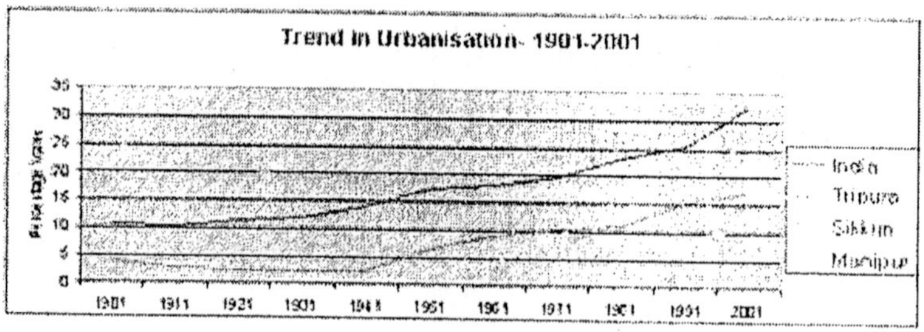

Figure 4. Trend in Urbanistation- 1901-2001

A cursory glance of the figures throws ample light that in 1901 Manipur had a highest share of the urbanization with 25% of its population living in the urban area. Tripura was in its infant stage of urbanization with only about 4% under its share while Sikkim was then a rural state. A century later the situation is not very different in the two states of Tripura and Sikkim. As of 2001 Mizoram has still been crawling in 17% while the Sikkim has just stepped in its teenage with 11% of its population living in towns and cities. Situation is, however, different in Manipur 100 years down the line. Surprisingly, the state has witnessed about 2% decline in its urban population in the last one century.

Moreover, the rates and levels of urbanization differ between the states over the years. For example, Tripura saw increase in its share of urban population with increasing trend till 1961 both in terms of decadal and annual growth rates and constant trend between 1961-81 before registering a fluctuating trend or rather declining trend in the decades that followed. Sikkim right from 1961 has been having fluctuating growth trend of its urban population. Moreover the state saw negative trend between 1981-91. Exceptionally, the state of Manipur experienced steady decline in its growth rate of urban population till 1941 and abysmal fall in 1951 when it recorded only 0.54% of its population as urban.

The decadal growth rate plunged to -97% during the decade. However, in the very next decade i.e. in 1961 the state registered a sky reaching growth of more than 2000% while the annual growth rate climbed to about 32%. The urban population rose to about 9% in the same decade. The decades that followed experienced declining growth rates in its urban population, however. Some of the possible forces that might have marred the urban situation in Manipur may be put forward as below -

— Rural-urban growth differential (URGD), which are also applicable in case of other two states under the examination.

— World War I & II, Independence movement during the first half of the century - the state borders Burma and was very active during Indian Independence Movement.

— Large-scale illegal immigration in the rural areas from Bangladesh and other sister states.

— Frequent ethnic clashes - as the state is ethnically one of the most diverse states in the Northeast.

— Fragmentation of the state.

Urban Growth by Size Class

Having analyzed the trends in urbanization it is now appropriate at this stage to examine the pace of urban growth in the states under study in terms of (a) the growth of towns by size class and (b) growth of population in different size class of towns and cities.

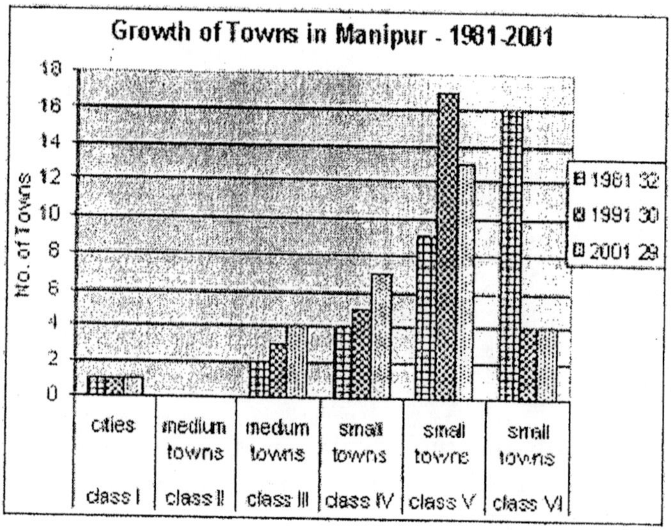

Figure 5. Growths of Towns in Manipur- 1981-2001

Growth of Towns: The figure along side highlights the fact that the state of Manipur registered uneven urban growth both across the towns and between the years. First of all the state has seen a negligible increase in the numbers of towns in the last twenty years from 32 to 33. Secondly, class III and class IV towns have been increasing at a constant rate (there are no class two towns in the state), while class V and class VI towns have shown declining trend over the years, although, still, appreciable share of towns fall in these categories. The state has maintained one city in the last 20 years and there has been no increase in the number, so far.

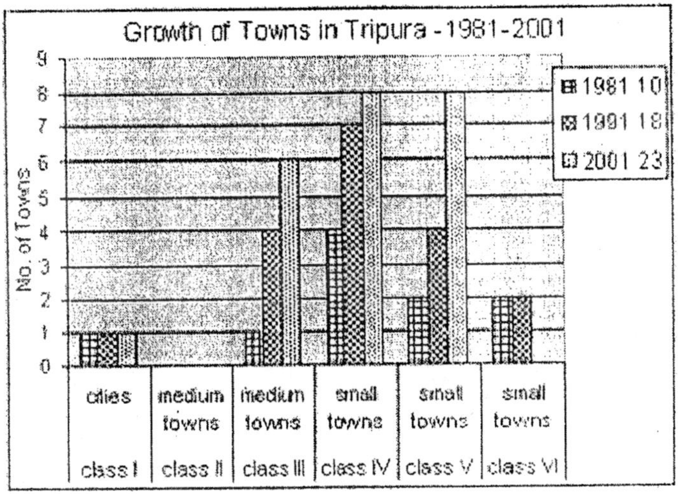

Figure 6. Growths of Towns in Tripura- 1981-2001

Considerable similarities can be observed between Tripura and Manipur with respect to the growth of their towns across the size class. The state, however, witnessed appreciable increase in the total number of its towns from 10 in 1981 to 23 in 2001.

Moreover, across the towns, class II and III towns registered their growth in increasing rate in the first ten years i.e. between 1981 and 1991 while their growth slightly slogged in the 1990s. As against this, class V towns gained tremendous momentum in the 1990s. The worst suffer in the state has been the class VI towns which after stagnating between 1981-91 are out placed in 2001. There are no more class VI towns in the state. The state has maintained one city over the years.

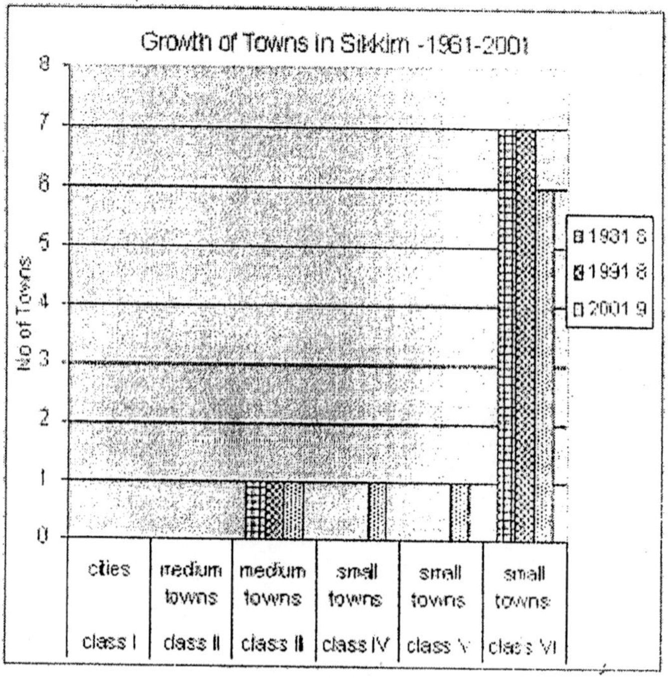

Figure 7. Growths of Towns in Sikkim- 1981-2001

The growth of towns in Sikkim is very different to the above states under examination. The state as a teenager in the field of urban environment is devoid from class I and II towns. It moreover had no class IV and V towns under its share till 1991 before adding one each under these categories in 2001. Most of the towns in the state are small towns falling in class VI category. They too are witnessing declining trend over the years. The state has maintained one-class III towns in the last 20 years.

Growth and distribution of population by different size class: It is evident from the figures attached herewith that as against the main stream urban concentration in cities the urban environment in the northeast India is different. Despite the fact that the majority of the urban population still resides in the cities their share has been either declining or has become stagnant over the years.

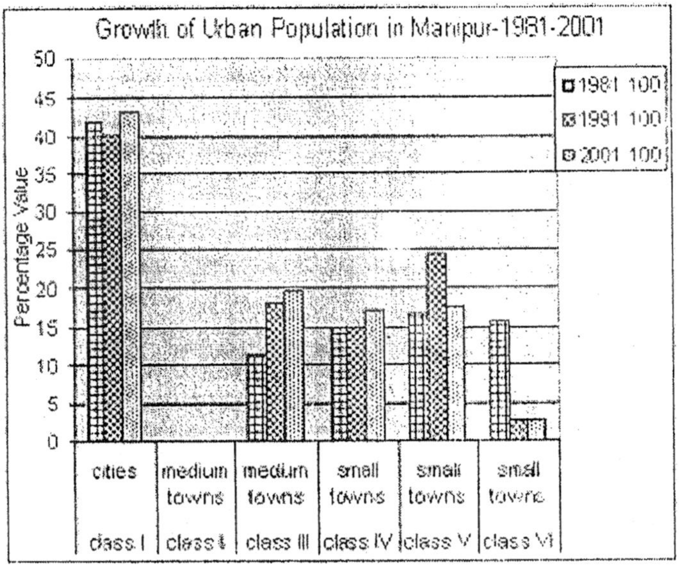

Figure 8. Growth of Urban Population in Manipur- 1981-01

In case of Manipur the share of population saw fluctuating trend in class I towns between 40 and 43% in the last 20 years. As a result there has been considerable rise in the proportion of population residing in the medium and small towns (excluding class VI towns). The proportion of population living in class III, IV and V towns rose from about 36% in 1981 to over 51% in 2001. Nevertheless, contiguous to the mainland scenario the worst sufferers are the class VI towns where the share of population is declining with time.

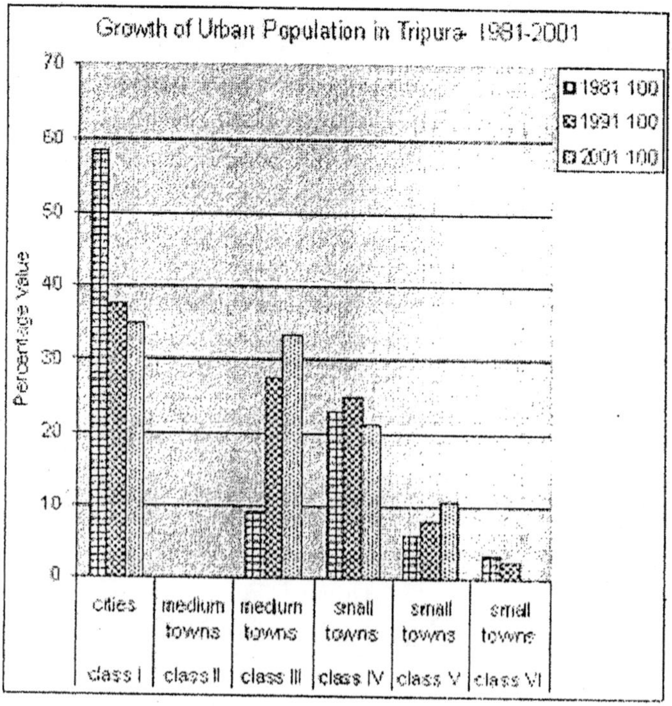

Figure 9. Growth of Urban population in Tripura- 1981-01

Situation of urban population in Tripura is to a large extent similar to that of Manipur. The state bore a notable fall of about 28% of the population living in class I town between 1981 and 2001. On the other hand population in the medium and small towns excluding the class VI towns gained tremendous momentum over the years registering a rise from 34% in 1981 to 61% in 2001, of the total urban population in the state. Surprisingly, the year 2001 saw no population in its class VI towns because of their conspicuous absence from the scene. The state had seen about 3% of its urban population residing in class VI towns in 1981.

The state of Sikkim has been an exception within the northeast. The state is devoid from class I and II towns. Gangtok is the only class III town in Sikkim. All the towns beside Gangtok are small towns in the state. The share of population residing in class III town registered appreciable fall, from 72% in 1981 to 49% in 2001. The rest of the urban population in the state resides in the small towns. Even within the small towns the share of population declined in class VI towns between 1991 and 2001.

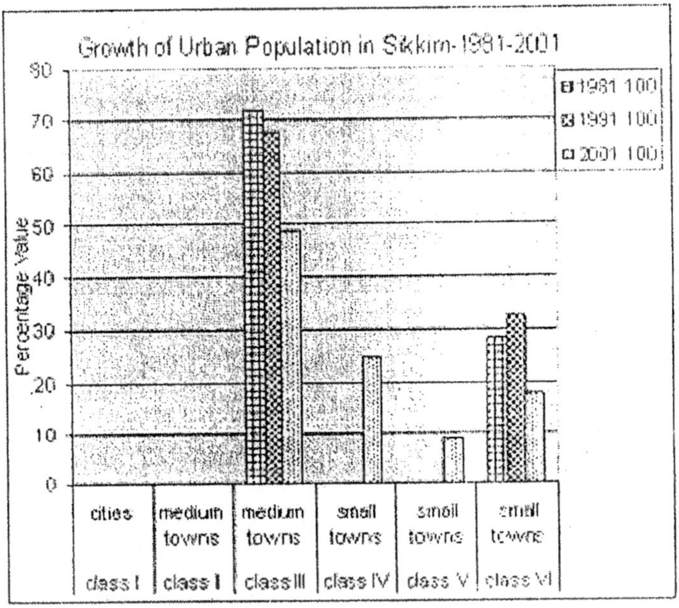

Figure 10. Growth of Urban Population in Sikkim- 1981-01

On the whole, the picture that emerges from the analysis indicates that there has been increasing intensity of spatial concentration of population in medium towns over the years probably at the cost of the small towns. Although this may not be true as far as Sikkim is concerned which is still to come a long way in the field of urbanization. Moreover, it is to be remembered that the northeast India is mostly a hilly region, excluding the plains of Assam, and hence do not have enough scope for the expansion of large towns.

Level of Urbanization in 2001

The morphology and structure of urbanization of population in the three states of northeast India according to the provisional figures of 2001 census comprises sixty-two towns/urban agglomerations and a population accounting for 17% to the total population, which is appreciably below the national average. Similarly, at a state level Manipur comprises of 29 towns (including one UA) and about 24% of the urban population while Tripura and Sikkim have under their folds 23 (including one class I town) and 9 towns and 23% and 11% of urban population as of 2001, respectively. It reveals that urban population is unevenly distributed among different states in the northeast depending upon the physiographic, economic, social and political set up of the respective states.

Moreover, large chunk of population still resides in the medium and higher order small towns even today. Hence, as in mainland India, distribution of urban population is not top heavy. The distortion in urbanization and urban units are not of uniform nature across the districts and as well. Towards this end the table below highlights the situation of urban units in different districts of the states under study.

Table 3. Number of Towns- 1991 and 2001

State/District	1991			2001		
	Statutory	Census	**Total**	Statutory	Census	**Total**
SIKKIM	8	-	**8**	8	1	**9**
North	1	-	**1**	1	-	**1**

West	2	-	**2**	2	-	**2**
South	2	-	**2**	2	-	**2**
East	3	-	**3**	3	1	**4**
TRIPURA	12	6	**18**	13	10	**23**
West Tripura	4	6	**10**	5	8	**13**
South Tripura	4	0	**4**	4	-	**4**
Dhalai Tripura	-	-	-	1	2	**3**
North Tripura	4	-	**4**	3	-	**3**
MANIPUR	28	ß	**31**	28	5	**33**
Senapati	-	-	-	-	-	-
Tamenlong	-	-	-	-	-	-
Chuchandpur	-	1	**1**	-	-	-
Bishnupur	7	-	**7**	7	-	**7**
Thoubal	9	-	**9**	9	-	**9**
Imphal West	8	2	**10**	8	2	**10**
Imphal East	3	-	**3**	3	3	**6**
Ukhrul	-	-	-	-	-	-
Chandel	1	-	**1**	1	-	**1**

Note: 1. Where the town is spread over more than district census has counted its number in the district in the bigger portion of the town felled.

3. For the purpose of size classification an urban agglomeration is treated by the census as one town whereas for the purpose of the total number of towns each constituent town is counted as separate towns.

Source: Census of India, 1991, DCH of the states under study; Census of India, 2001, Provisional Population Totals, Rural Urban Distribution of the states under study.

The table presented in the previous page reveals some important points of note. First, towns are not uniformly distributed across the district and hence across the space. Secondly, there is a tendency of the urban units to concentrate in and around the state head quarters. The districts with majority of the towns and cities in the states under study are also the districts with chief administrative center, that is the capital city of the respective states. Due to economic and administrative reasons many medium and small towns tend to come up around such centers. On the other hand, there are district, for instance in manipur, which are still without single urban unit and hence are rural in character.

Figures in the next page highlight a clearer picture of the towns and population in different districts in 2001. It is evident that in Tripura only West Tripura district comprises relatively uniform distribution of urban units and the population there in. It is also the district with administrative headquarters of the state. The adjoining South and North Tripura follow the West Tripura in this regard. On the other hand Dhalai, which was a rural district till 1991, has concentrated its 100% urban population in class V towns.

Similar is the case with Manipur. Imphal West where most of the administrative activities of the state are located has led to the emergence of almost all categories of towns and thus has relatively fairer distribution of urban environment. The districts closer to this district tend to follow the line. However, the districts that are relatively away from the administrative head quarters of the state have either concentrated urban environment in one particular category or they are rural in character.

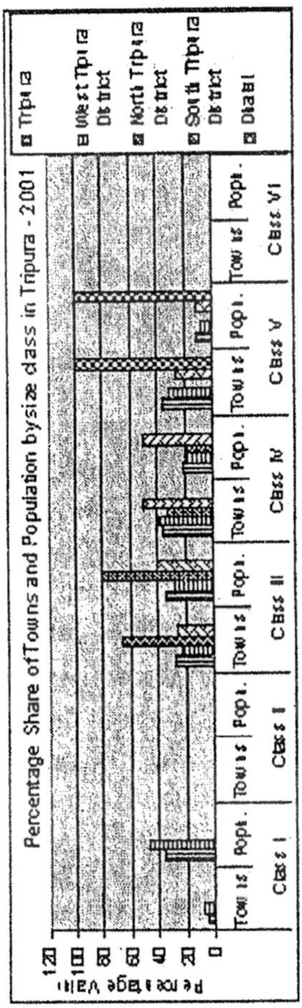

Figure 11: Percentage Shares of Towns and Population by Size Class in Tripura -2001

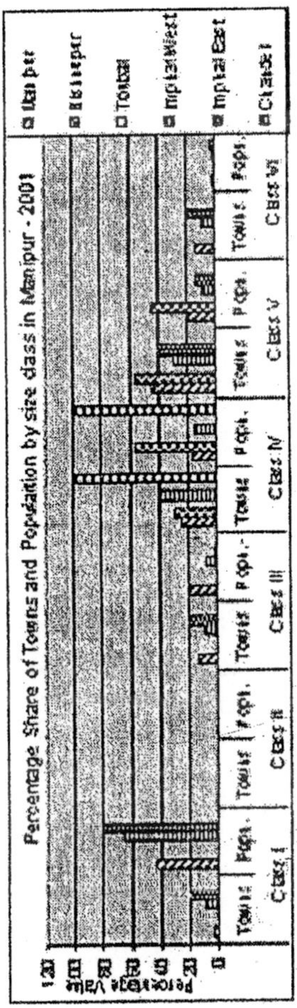

Figure 12: Percentage Shares of Towns and Population by Size Class in Manipur -2001

2

Changing Patterns of Urban Land-Use

Metropolitan areas in the United States are growing at unprecedented rates, creating extensive urban landscapes. Many of the farmlands, wetlands, forests, and deserts that formed the America of 1900 have been transformed during the past 100 years into human settlements. Almost everyone has seen these changes to their local environment but without a clear understanding of their impacts. It is not until we study these landscapes from a spatial perspective and the time scale of decades that we can begin to measure the changes that have occurred and predict the impact of changes to come.

The U.S. Geological Survey's (USGS) Urban Dynamics Research (UDR) program studies the landscape transformations that result from the growth of metropolitan regions over time. Using sources such as historic maps, aerial photographs, and Landsat satellite data, USGS scientists first assemble retrospective urban land use databases that reflect several decades of change. These databases are then used to analyze the effects of urbanization on the landscape, and to model urban growth and land use change under alternative growth scenarios.

Most major metropolitan areas face the growing problems of urban sprawl, loss of natural vegetation and open space, and a general decline in the extent and connectivity of wetlands and wildlife habitat. The public identifies with these problems when they see residential and commercial development replacing undeveloped land around them. Urban growth rates show no signs of slowing, especially when viewed at the global scale, since these problems can be generally attributed to increasing population.

Cities have changed from small, isolated population centers to large, interconnected economic, physical, and environmental features. Urban growth and the concentration of people in urban areas are creating societal problems world-wide. One hundred years ago, approximately 15 percent of the world's population was living in urban areas.

Today, the percentage is nearly 50 percent. In the last 200 years, world population has increased six times, stressing ecological and social systems. Over that same time period, the urban population has increased 100 times, concentrating more people on less land even as the total land devoted to urbanization expands. Yet the temporal and spatial dimensions of the land use changes that shape urbanization are little known, even in the United States.

In the United States, policymakers and the public continue to raise concerns about the effects that unchecked urbanization has on the landscape. In 1998, more than 200 communities across the Nation voted on, and the vast majority adopted, measures to manage urban sprawl. The UDR program provides basic data, predictions, and perspectives to help in forming sound policies for guiding environmentally sustainable growth.

Mapping Land Use Change

Databases developed by the UDR program contain interpretations of urban extent, transportation routes, water features, and other important land uses. Selected regional studies are currently in progress across the Nation. Data source availability for each region, in conjunction with historical significance, determines the time periods that are mapped. Features are interpreted from diverse data sources including historical topographic maps, satellite images, census statistics, and aerial photographs. The resulting temporal database is a spatial record of the pace and extent of the urbanization process.

A temporal database can be visualized as a sequence of maps, such as those shown above and on the next pages, or as computer animations. Sequential maps show urbanization as a static pattern that changes with each time period that is mapped. Animations illustrate the temporal dynamics, revealing patterns and trends that are not possible to discern from tabular data or static maps.

Understanding Land Use Change

The geographic understanding of land use change in urban areas is a key aspect of the UDR program. By analyzing a temporal database for spatial patterns, rates of change, and trends, the UDR program can provide insight into how cities have developed under varying social, economic, and environmental conditions. This analysis requires understanding a region's land use history. Population data, timelines of historical events, and related information are all used to explain the mapped changes. Population data are correlated with the temporal database so that human movement can be tracked and factored into these interpretations.

Population increases suggest economic growth and the availability of jobs in an area, and population declines suggest a decline in livability or economic issues that cause people to leave a region. Timelines of past events and other historical compilations aid in identifying the issues that affected the development of the region.

In addition to gathering statistical and historical information, scientists must have a physiographic understanding of the place and its greater region. Topographic features, climate, and adequate supplies of water and other natural resources can limit or encourage growth and change.

The existence and accessibility of transportation routes have often dictated patterns of urban growth. Urban areas that were established in the 18th and early 19th centuries were usually located along waterways, reflecting dependence on shipping for the transport of goods and people. By the middle of the 19th century, railroads began to connect existing towns and spurred the growth of new urban areas.

The post-World War II era saw not only an increase in the population of most metropolitan areas, but also the emergence of a society dependent on the automobile. The proliferation of the private automobile led to expansive development at the edges of many urban areas. The development of the Interstate Highway system in the 1950's spurred the widespread construction of roads. As road networks expanded and became more complex, urban development followed. As in the past, most recent urban growth has occurred along transportation corridors.

The UDR program provides the data and geographic information necessary to document past land use change. By looking to the past, communities and regions are better informed and equipped to plan and prepare for the future.

Land Use Change Modeling

Historical land use patterns, together with current trends in a region, are used to model future land use. Results from modeling urban growth and land use change can be used by the public, land use planners, and policy makers to anticipate and plan for the future. Land use change models can also generate alternative landscape predictions on the basis of different land use policies and environmental constraints.

These land use change models use simple parameters including present urban extent, major transportation routes, topography, and protected lands. Other factors, such as employment opportunities, land prices, and the millions of personal decisions people make, are not considered in this modeling approach. The primary focus of the modeling effort is to account for physical controls on land use. Acknowledging the uncertainties of models, the USGS uses statistical methods to predict probabilities of urbanization.

Impacts of Land Use Change

Urban Dynamics research in landscape characterization, urban growth models, and geographic understanding provides the data necessary for analyzing the impacts of population growth and land use change. This information can be used to analyze the causes of urban congestion, pollution, and loss of natural resources. Each of these impacts is linked to changes in the extent of urban, agricultural, and forested lands, and (or) transportation systems.

Planners use Urban Dynamics data to evaluate environmental impacts, to delineate urban growth boundaries or service areas, to develop land use zoning plans, and to gauge future infrastructure requirements. Traffic congestion, a common malady of urbanization, is the result of urban growth, increases in population density, and out-dated transportation infrastructure.

By evaluating trends associated with land use change over time, solutions to traffic congestion may be obtainable. Another specific application of UDR data is the correlation of air pollution records with the temporal database to determine if control strategies for reducing pollution have been effective. Many pollution control strategies have been used in the past three decades. Correlation between land use change and pollution helps researchers establish positive or negative trends that indicate whether pollution control strategies have been successful. With this information, policy makers, resource managers, and the public can make appropriate changes for the future.

Hydrologists can use Urban Dynamics data to evaluate new water sources for future urbanization and to analyze water pollution – a problem common to urban areas, industrial sites, and agricultural lands. The amount and degree of water pollution in rivers, lakes, and bays can be predicted on the basis of past and future trends in land use change. A study currently underway in the Patuxent River Basin in Maryland focuses on the sources of water pollution over time. In this study, temporal change maps of urban, agriculture, and forest lands are used to identify and quantify historic trends in sediment and nutrient loads in waters draining into the Chesapeake Bay.

Geologists use data on land use change to evaluate the availability of building materials, such as sand, gravel, and cement. Geologists also use data on existing hazards to correlate with the UDR data to predict the impacts of future natural disasters and the potential damage they may cause. Policy makers can then use these damage or hazard projections to direct future development away from the most at-risk areas. Finally, biologists also use land use change data to compile maps on habitats, species distribution, and land management. Predictions about future urbanization are critical to the protection of ecosystems and the sustainability of communities.

Products

The UDR program provides temporal land use databases, analyses of land use change, and landscape change predictions. Databases for study sites contain digital maps of urban extent, transportation routes, water features, and other significant land uses compatible for use in geographic information systems (GIS). Digital animations are available to help visualize the temporal patterns inherent in the data. A land use change model and documentation are also available. Interpretive papers and maps based on the data and models are published in a variety of formats.

Role of Technologies in Landscape Management

Technologies are always clearly demarcated from the "natural" environment. Whether such technological objects are seen as dangerous and threatening, or as useful tools for the cleaning up of the natural body and the natural landscape thereby improving how these are experienced by human subjects, technologies, as artificial, are almost always seen nature's Other, as that against which the naturalness, non-artificiality and purity of natural environments are defined. In this way, the boundaries between natural forms and environments and those that are technologically and artificially constructed are maintained and reinforced.

Terms such as "the natural environment" and "the built environment", which serve to maintain the boundaries between the natural and the artificial, operate both in popular and academic discourse. For example, throughout much of the history of systematized geographical knowledge, the spaces of physical landscape and the body have both been unproblematically considered as natural. This has had significant practical consequences. In the colonial context, the mapping of the natural landscape of territory to be controlled was crucial to the exercise of power, as was the control of the population. "Natural" differences were seen as the foundation of "cultural" superiority. However, the ways in which "natural" spaces such as the "wilderness" and the body are constructed has been the focus of sustained critical attention in the social sciences. Much of this critique has centered around the ways in which "natural" bodies, and the "natural" environment are discursively constructed and thereby made culturally intelligible.

Reconstructing Bodies

In a seminal work on the place of the body in society, the body is at once the most solid, the most elusive, illusory, concrete, metaphorical, ever present and ever distant thing - a site, an instrument, an environment, a singularity, and a multiplicity. Given this, any attempt to precisely define what "the body" is and map its position in space is a problematic and perhaps foolhardy project. Despite this, an engagement with the forms, experiences, and practices of embodiment is extremely important precisely because the types of bodies referred to when the term embodiment is mobilized may not be restricted merely to "human" bodies.

The work of the French theorist Michel Foucault has provided much of the impetus for the reassertion of the body as an object of study within the humanities and social sciences, largely as result of his genealogical investigations into the production, control, and regulation of bodies and spaces within networks of power.

Particular historically and geographically specific discursive formations constitute regimes of power in that they provide the rules which determine what can be said and how this can be said. This is not to suggest that discourses merely designate and name objects. Rather, discourses may be thought of as composed of practices which actually produce or constitute the objects that they name. This idea has been used to critically interrogate the ways in which discourses constitute particular objects and subjects in particular spaces. Importantly, from such a perspective the exercise of mapping loses its scientific objectivity and comes to be seen as a discursive practice which actively produces the world, a process which renders certain spaces (in)visible and (un)intelligible.

Central to Foucault's work on the body, and inextricably bound up with his conception of power, is the idea of "disciplines" by which he refers those "methods, which made possible the meticulous control of the operations of the body, which assured the constant subjection of its forces and imposed upon them a relation of docility-utility". Organized around an "analytics of space", such disciplines served to individualize "bodies by a location that does not give them a fixed position, but distributes them and circulates them in a network of relations". Disciplines also attempt to control with exact precision the temporal location of the individual body. Thus, "a sort of anatomo-chronological schema of behaviour is defined.

The act is broken down into its elements; the position of the body, limbs, articulations is defined; to each movement are assigned a direction, an aptitude, a duration; their order of succession is prescribed. Time penetrates the body and with it all the meticulous controls of power". In such a "correct use of the body..nothing must remain idle or useless". The relationship between bodies and machines was also defined in terms of a meticulously meshed "body-machine complex".

The body then is the target for a whole range of disciplinary techniques which attempt to regulate its form and control its position. In Discipline and Punish, Foucault argues that carceral spaces such as the prison were key locations for these disciplinary techniques. But the techniques at work in these places were symptomatic of a whole range of disciplinary techniques at work in society, by which bodies where precisely mapped and distributed, which in turn produced docile, obedient, and productive, bodies. These ideas are obviously useful in their explicitly spatial treatment of how particular bodies are disciplined, produced, and regulated.

Significantly, they combine this spatial sensitivity with an appreciation of the ways that disciplines involve the precise mapping of bodies onto machines, in order that the total mobilization of the resources of these human-machinic assemblages may be realized.

For Foucault, the power that is exercised through such disciplinary techniques does not merely "act upon" an individual. Rather, it is through being the object of these disciplinary techniques that the individual comes to know itself. The individual subject is produced and constituted through the action of such disciplinary techniques. According to Foucault, He who is subjected to a field of visibility, and who knows it, assumes responsibility for the constraints of power; he makes them play spontaneously upon himself; he inscribes in himself the principle of his own subjection.

Notions of surveillance and panopticism are important here. Based upon his reading of the workings of Jeremy Bantam's model of the panopticon, Foucault suggests that disciplinary techniques work by internalizing surveillance, the individual then becoming his or her own overseer. Through being engaged in this constant self-policing the individual assumes the responsibility for the maintenance of social order. In his later work on sexuality, Foucault engages more directly with the ways in which the individual subject is produced and comes to know itself by investigating the techniques which individuals practice in order to transform themselves into particular types of persons. In doing this he refers to "technologies of the self" which he says are those practices, which permit individuals to effect by their own means a number of operations on their own bodies and souls, thoughts, conduct, and way of being so as to transform themselves in order to attain a certain state of happiness, purity, wisdom, perfection or immortality.

For Foucault, the multiplicity of technologies of the self which individuals practice upon themselves cannot be considered in isolation from wider technologies of power.

Rather, they must be situated within the broader networks of power that flow, in a capillary-like manner, through societies. From this perspective power is neither merely a macro or micro level phenomena but "is an impersonal set of negotiations between practices, discourses, non discursive events, a mode of management of a multiplicity of relations, a set of technologies linking the most massive cultural movements to the most minute day by day events in interpersonal life". For Foucault then, individual technologies of the self, discursive regimes, and disciplinary techniques are all linked and together contribute to the production and maintenance of what he calls "bio-power" through which the productive potential of individuals as elements of modern industrial complexes is realized.

This liberation of "bio-power" is one aspect of the art of government, or "governmentality", by which Foucault refers to the "right disposition of things, arranged so as to lead to a convenient end". However, the idea of governmentality does not mean that power is "located" in a central authority such as the state. Rather, because power acts at all "levels" of society the "governmentalization" of the economy and society involves the enmeshing of individuals and groups "within the tactics and strategies of a complex form of power whose institutions, procedures, analyses, and techniques loosely manage mass populations and their surroundings in a highly politicized symbolic and material economy".

In this way, individual bodies, the populations that they constitute, and the territories which they inhabit are all worked, arranged, and produced as the target of a range of techniques of governmentality. A crucial aspect of this is the extent to which key metaphors move between the economic and the corporeal, discursively weaving bodies and economic organizations together in a mutual intelligibility. For instance, in the nineteenth century the "human motor" became a metaphor of work and energy that provided nineteenth-century thinkers with a new scientific and cultural framework. Through this metaphor, scientists and social reformers could articulate their passionate materialism, embracing nature, industry, and human activity in a single, overarching concept.

In this way the body came to be seen as a machine requiring maintenance, composed of different parts which, when working, formed a well oiled system. A body conceptualized as a machinic entity needed to be disciplined and trained in order to fit in with the organization of industrial capitalism. The idea of the body as motor, or more accurately as something to be "motorized" and thus brought up to speed with contemporary technological developments continues today. While technological metaphors, whether they be mechanical or informational can give intelligibility to organic bodies the opposite is also true. Various organic discourses are employed in the description of individual economic organizations and economies in general. In much economic discourse for instance, the economy is described using metaphors of the body, the "health" of which needs careful "treatment".

Additionally, particular bodies and the economies within which they exist are constructed as objects within the discourse of development, as a reservoir of productive potential to be brought up to speed with the "developed" world through the application of economic models which, development experts insist, are the best way to guarantee the health of an economy.

In such ways are bodies and machines inserted into larger political, economic and discursive economies. There is therefore, according to Foucault, an "etching of the civilized body by discursive systems" and this "body must be regarded as a site of social, political, cultural, and geographical inscriptions, production or constitution". Foucault's work then, suggests that bodies and embodied subjects are constructed in and through particular spaces by the exercise of power at all "levels" of society.

Bodies and Geography

Foucault's richly suggestive ideas have fed into a growing increase in questions of corporeality across a range of academic disciplines, including geography. Yet, for a long time it is as though the body has acted as "Geography's other, both denied and desired depending on the particular school of geographical thought under consideration". It is not surprising then that within geographical work, bodies (or precisely specified aggregates of bodies) have often been represented as points on a two dimensional map, objects to be enumerated, measured, quantified, and statistically analyzed. In cruder Marxian influenced geographies, the body is that biological space, mapped into the circuits of capital accumulation, from which labor power, and thus surplus value, is extracted.

Some suggests some of the ways that geographers have been guilty of ignoring the body. For instance, she suggests that "time geography tries to ignore the body" because it takes little account of "bodily passion or desire", and thus "represses all reference to a feminized other". Humanistic geographers are seen by Rose as at least attempting to recover the body from its invisibility within geography through their emphasis on the need to "consider differently embodied subjectivities for understanding spaces as places". However, Rose argues that they nevertheless fail to recognize the significance of these bodies as being colored, sexual, and sexed.

Despite this, "even feminist geographers have been guilty of treating the body as Other" in that "by trying to avoid the accusation of biologism they have ignored the possibilities of examining the sexed body in space". Recently though, geographers have engaged with these issues in edited collections such as Body Space, Writing Women and Space, and Mapping the Subject.

In such work there has been an attempt to engage with the ways that the identities of bodies and spaces are intertwined. This relationship can be mapped particularly usefully by employing Butler's ideas about performativity. Butler's discussion of the performativity of bodily identities must be set within the context of her discussion of the materiality of bodies. For Butler, "what constitutes the fixity of the body, its contours, its movements, will be fully material, but materiality will be rethought as the effect of power, as power's most productive effect. Thus the materiality of the body including its 'sex' is, thus, not simply what one has, or a static description of what one is; it will be one of the norms by which the 'one' becomes visible at all, that which qualifies a body for life within the domain of cultural intelligibility". In playing upon the different meanings of the word "matter" Butler refuses to let the category of sex, which is frequently mobilized to reinforce hegemonic heterosexual gender regimes, to stand outside discourse as a "natural" attribute. This does not mean that there is nothing "tangible", "concrete" or "material" that can be touched, felt, worked on, or physically reshaped, but in not being considered pre-, or a-discursive, the "material" construction of the body is always seen as located within and constituted by discursive practices.

According to Butler the identity of bodies is constituted by "performativity" which she understands "not as a singular or deliberate 'act', but, rather, as the reiterative and citational practice by which discourse produces the effects that it names". Thus for Butler, gender has a performative aspect in that it "is the repeated stylization of the body, a set of repeated acts within a highly rigid regulatory framework that congeal over time to produce the appearance of substance, a natural sort of being". It is only in this way that bodies are constructed as coherent, bounded and meaningful identities. In contemporary culture the dominant stylization of the body is one that has a fixed heterosexual gendered identity. Identities other than these, insofar as they transgress the boundaries of this regulatory framework, do not "matter" as much, both in terms of their visibility and acceptability.

These ideas are useful in the sense that they provide an analytical vocabulary to engage with the ways in which the "materiality" of bodies is discursively produced and reproduced. However, Butler's ideas about performativity are not limited to the body. The construction of the spaces that the body "occupies" can also examined in the same way. In a recent discussion of how certain places are produced as adult environments, Valentine "considers the way that the production of space is, like gender, also a performative act, naturalized through repetition". To this end she looks both at repetitive acts, such as media reports and education campaigns, and regulatory regimes, including policing and corporal punishment, which are charged with maintaining this performance. However, this is not to suggest a clear separation between the production of the body and the production of space. Rather, such work lends support to the idea that it is better to think of a mutually constuitive processes in which the discursive practices that give performative force to particular bodies and spaces intertwine.

This engagement with the mutually constitutive relationship between bodies and spaces was in some ways Every such organism is reflected and refracted in the changes that it wreaks in its "milieu" or "environment" - in other words, in its space. Such sentiments are echoed in more recent work. In the context of an examination of how women experience chronic illness, Some suggest that "to differentiate body from environment does injustice to the integrity of any experience".

Similarly, noting that "bodies continually negotiate environments and environments negotiate bodies", Johnston examines how female body builders and their training environments are mutually constitutive, suggesting that "that bodies become constructed and inscribed by the environment". Recognizing this "provides a window through which to examine performative corporeality". These researchers also recognize that engaging with the relationship between bodies and environments challenges existing categories. According to Johnston "conceptualizing bodies as mutually constitutive with the environment radically challenges ontological and epistemological assumptions of Western thought, and Geography in particular".

Reconstructing technologies

The impact of technologies on the organization of space has been a recurrent theme in recent geographical and non-geographical research, the most influential of which has concentrated on the impact of developments in transport and telecommunications, this impact frequently invoked as evidence of epochal political-economic and cultural change. For example, suggests that informational technology has led to the emergence of a "space of flows", referring to flows of information and capital which have become more important than, and have dramatically restructured the geographies (or "geometries") of space as "place". Some argues that the revolution in transport and telecommunications technologies in the latter quarter of the 20th century has led to a situation of "time-space" compression. This annihilation of time and space in order to more efficiently realize profit has undergirded a shift in cultural sensibility, a "postmodern condition". Elsewhere, attention has been focused on the spatial organization of industry as a result of technological change.

There are a number of ways in which these accounts of the mediation of the experiences and reorganization of space by technological developments remain inadequate. The first is the scale 1 at which they operate. There is a tendency to concentrate on the "global" scale, in the process losing sight of microspaces such as the home. Second, while theorists such as Harvey are all too ready to explain shifts in cultural sensibility as a result of technological changes rooted in capitalist organization, they remain somewhat insensitive to the possibility that these technologies themselves are cultural artifacts, that they need to be made culturally intelligible, and that this is a process that occurs in different ways. Third, there is a tendency to attribute too great an ability on the part of technologies, especially information technologies, to effortlessly and efficiently restructure space at will, revealing a willingness to allow a form of technological determinism to creep into analyses of the relation between technology and space.

The space in which such restructuring is assumed to take place often appears as an almost twodimensional Cartesian plane, devoid of any of the complex social, cultural, and indeed natural networks which make the relationship between technologies and space a much messier affair. Indeed, such a proclivity to assume that technologies rapidly and effortlessly effect spatial change is part of a broader tendency to unproblematically accept both the impact and the novelty of "new" technologies and human-technological relations.

Finally, there is little attempt to map the relation between bodies and technologies. Perhaps, wise to consider how transitions in the definitions of space and time through changing social processes are effecting changing conception of the body and consequently of identity, particularities, and where the human body resides in the scale of things, he nevertheless gives little attention to the role of technologies in these processes. Elsewhere, similar opportunities to examine the relationships between bodies and technologies have been missed. For instance, in the book Ground Truth, intended as critical engagement with Geographical Information Systems (GIS), there is little attempt to examine the relationship between bodies and technologies.

Outside the discipline of Geography there has been much engagement with the relationship between bodies and technologies. For example, in the eyes of Kroker and Weinstein the body is becoming "virtualized" and the flesh of the organic body is rapidly deteriorating to the status of some awkward and obsolete corporeal remainder. Given this, they suggest that "the weakened body has become a prosthetic to the media net" and the contemporary "rage against the body results in a flight into virtuality". Within expanding cyberspaces, perhaps virtual bodies do exist, alongside hybridized and virtualized subjectivities. Yet, it is important not to lose sight of the mundane materiality, both of the physical infrastructures that make these virtual realities possible and of the bodies of those who are interfaced with informational technologies, something not adequately captured by more hyperbolic and overstated accounts such as that of Kroker and Weinstein.

Accordingly, it might be more profitable to examine how the contemporary "rage against the body", (which is not so novel in the sense that the inadequacy of the human body for various purposes - flight, industrial production, sporting performance etc. - has always led to attempts to alter its capacities and prosthetically enhance its performance) encourages embodied subjects to enter into environments of self-reconstruction such as those provided by fitness facilities and the manufacturers of home fitness equipment. This would be a necessary recognition that, despite the more enthusiastic claims for the inevitability of virtualization, flesh - whether weakened, strengthened, flexible, or inflexible - still matters.

There is a particular need therefore for methodological perspectives that more adequately handle the relationships between bodies and technologies and how these relationships problematize the boundaries frequently mobilized in descriptions of contemporary embodied environments. The figure of the Cyborg offers one such perspective. The word cyborg is itself a hybrid, formed of a collapsing of the terms cybernetic and organism. "Cybernetic" has its origins in the Greek word kubernetes, meaning "governor", and "organism" in the word organon, meaning "instrument". While ideas about "governing instruments" in the form of cyborg fusions of human and machine have floated about in "hard" science and popular science fiction for quite a while, has been central to the popularizing of the term in academic discourse.

Post-Second World War hybrid entities made of first, ourselves and other organic creatures in our unchosen 'high-technological' guise as information systems, texts, and ergonomically controlled laboring, desiring, and reproducing machines. The second essential ingredient in cyborgs is machines in their guise, also, as communication systems, texts, and self acting, ergonomically designed apparatuses.

Thus, for Haraway, the figure of the cyborg is a boundary creature, material and metaphorical, straddling the boundaries between nature and culture, human subjects and non-human technological objects. Haraway's "Manifesto for Cyborgs" was intended as an ironic yet optimistic fiction, a fiction that would attempt to reclaim some of the ontological territory lost to the world-defining and dominating fictions of "real" and "hard" technoscience. Her work has been crucial in contributing to the problematizing and politicizing of technoscience and its role in the construction and strategic employment of the categories of "nature" and "culture".

By examining the constructedness of, these apparently irreconcilable categories, used to justify what kind of persons "we" are, she opens the door to a range of boundary creatures, monsters that do not fit within dominant liberal ontologies. There is thus a politics behind the creature of the cyborg, a politics that ranges over the spaces of bodies and the scientific knowledges and technologies used to control, construct and regulate them. For Haraway then, categories are not "innocent" - hence her assertion that "grammar is politics by other means".

Haraway's work is perhaps most useful for examining the relationship between bodies and machines, and the category of the cyborg provides a particularly useful analytical fiction with which to examine this relationship. By deploying the category of the cyborg, one can, as Luke notes, "invoke an 'as if clause' in the standard methodological contract allowing us to reread human behavior as if it is cyborg behavior", thereby problematizing the boundaries between the categories of human and machine and nature and culture.

Such boundaries are continually reaffirmed in the advertising images displayed in the United States. To take a mundane, but telling example, artificial breast forms, sold on the basis of offering the wearer the ability to achieve the "natural" feminine bodily look, serve to perpetuate dominant cultural inscriptions of the gendered body . Similarly, sports bras enable the wearer to retain the ideal feminine figure while technologically working out. For instance, Champion, the sports apparel manufacturer, who enthusiastically claim that "only Abs should be flat" offer a sports bra to "put your form in performance".

In contrast, when technologies are used to produce "un-natural" bodies, reactions of disgust and abhorrence are produced. An example of this is the form of the female body builder, which, constructed with the aid of weights and measured resistances is not so intelligible because it upsets and transgresses the traditional masculine/feminine gender dualism. In such ways are technological bodies made (un)intelligible and (un)inhabitable within hegemonic and ontologically purified cultural categories, the meaning of these technologies being produced "by a complex arrangement or articulation of texts, narratives, institutional structures, economic forces, bodily practices, and other material effects".

Haraway invests the figure of the cyborg with radically disruptive and potentially transformative possibilities. However, the heady optimism with which she suggests boundary figures such as the cyborg might disrupt the dominant hegemonic technocultural landscape is probably unwarranted given, that for the most part, it is liberalism and not cyborgs that give "us" our politics. Additionally, Haraway's suggestion that cyborgs have only arisen in the second half of the twentieth century is also dubious because of its failure to attribute sufficient history to the figure of the cyborg. They, or more accurately, "we" are not as novel as we might think. Furthermore, and perhaps more importantly, the methodological fiction of the cyborg may not necessarily be useful for conceptualizing the relation between human-machinic relations at different scales. Indeed, demonstrating an anthropomorphic bias in her analyses of cyborgs may be ignoring other machinic assemblages. If this is the case then cyborgs such as the aforementioned wearer of the sports bra might be situated within and considered constitutive of "humachines", which might be seen as machinic assemblages of power, space, production, energy, reproduction, matter, organization, and information with their own intelligence and agency that constitute the operational settings and sustainable life worlds of cyborg forms.

There is a problematic politics of scale at operation here, in that the mega-machinic is set against the meso-, and also the micro-machinic. If bodies, machines, and environments are mutually constitutive, then mapping the intermediate ground between these and moving between them is not easy, in the same way that moving between the operation of technologies of domination and technologies of the self is not easy.

Reconstructing nvironments

That body of work which has come to be termed Science and Technology Studies (STS) shares with Haraway the goal of critically engaging with the role played by technoscience in contemporary societies. Actor-Network Theory (ANT) has emerged from within STS as an effort to understand how social and technical relations are embodied and perform themselves in the ordering and re-ordering of texts, artifacts, and the "natural world". From the perspective of ANT, materiality is a relational effect, and these relations are not merely those between human actors but also include relations with and between non-human actors. An actor-network then according to Callon et al is an interrelated set of entities that have been successfully translated or enrolled by an actor that is thereby able to borrow their force and speak or act on their behalf or with their support.

Translation here refers to the means by which actor-networks are created and maintained. These means involve (a) the definition of roles, their distribution, and the delineation of a scenario: (b) the strategies in which an actor-world renders itself indispensable to others by creating a geography of obligatory passage points: and (c) the displacement imposed upon others as they are forced to follow the itinerary that has been imposed.

Such processes of translation occur at particular translation centers, defined as, Locations at which translation strategies are evolved, attempts are made to control the diverse elements that make up the actor network, calculations about the return from different strategies are made, [and] which are able to turn themselves into spokesmen for other entities and, in some sense, profit from this asymmetry.

Power, in this context, does not reside anywhere, but rather, in the networks themselves, and the ability of certain centers of translation to shape the strength and composition of these networks. Those centers which are powerful "are not those who 'hold' power but are those able to enroll, convince, and enlist others into networks on terms which allow the initial actors (both human and non-human) to represent the others". These mediators include texts, technologies, and also humans, which together give shape to networks and define the roles played by different actors within these networks.

At this point it becomes clear that such a notion of power is not entirely incompatible with some of the ideas in Foucault's work as discussed above. The "right disposition of things" arranged so as to lead to the most convenient ends can be thought of in terms of attempts on the part of particular centers of translation to construct particular kinds of networks. It then becomes a question of the governmentality of these networks, a governmentality that is nevertheless always unstable, incomplete, and does not take on the form of some overarching totality.

Additionally, like Haraway, ANT makes room for the non-human in ways impossible under the terms of the modern constitution. For Latour, "collectives" are defined by associations between the non-human and the human. What is currently included in the category of the "social", or the "cultural" is, according to Latour, merely one element of our collectives In this way, who or what gets considered as an actor or agent is rethought in terms of actornetworks of nature and culture, human and non-human.

Latour has made a number of clarifications about ANT which are worth including here because they have important implications for questions of spatiality. Put simply, Latour suggests that ANT is a "change of topology", one involving a move from surfaces to filaments. He claims that from the perspective of ANT, societies cannot be described without recognizing them as having a fibrous, thread-like, wiry, stringy, ropy, capillary character that is never captured by the notions of levels, layers, territories, spheres, categories, structures, and systems. What Latour is articulating here is a position that asserts that it is not just networks all the way down, but also all the way up and in all other directions as well. It is also not a matter of networks being created and translated within a passive container, but that the very matter under consideration is all networks. There is no "in-between" from the perspective of ANT. Nothing slips through the filaments that make up actor-networks, except perhaps other networks.

Such topological assertions have profound implications for the way that questions of space and scale are imagined. First, as Latour notes, "the first advantage of thinking in terms of networks is that we get rid of the 'tyranny of distance' or proximity". From the perspective of ANT the network offers a topology which is defined neither in terms of social or "real" space but instead in terms of associations. In this situation "real" proximity does not matter. Rather, what matters is how close and durable are the connections between different actors.

Second, the notion of the network attempts to chart a middle ground between the oppositional scales of macro and micro, global and local . This is because from the perspective of ANT the whole "metaphor of scales..is replaced by a metaphor of connections" in which networks are defined in terms of their length and the intensity of their connections rather than in terms of their size. Thus, one can think of a network as a global entity, in terms of its connections, which is nevertheless entirely local, in the sense that all points in the network are local. It makes little sense from this perspective to counterpose the local and the global, just as it makes little sense to counterpose micro and macro.

Along with jettisoning the oppositional categories of far/close and big/small, Latour also points to the fact that the notions of inside and outside are similarly problematized by the network topology. If one moves from an topology based upon surfaces, in which boundaries exist to separate inside and outside, to one constituted by networks, then one quickly loses sight of these boundaries, because, as Latour suggests, "a network has no outside". However, while Latour seeks to "reshuffle spatial metaphors that have rendered the study of society nature so difficult", this is not the same as asserting that there is nothing such as macro, society, outside, proximity, distance, etc., but rather that these are rethought of in terms of the spatial effects of the work done by actor-networks.

In the process of tracing such networks we quickly lose the ontological reference points which Latour claims are provided by the "modern constitution". Against the terms of this constitution, which struggles to purify the world by categorizing "things" as either subject or object, natural or cultural, human or non-human, Latour argues that the world is constituted by more curious things variously labeled as networks, hybrids, collectives, quasi-objects/ subjects, which exist in a "middle kingdom" between the modern categories of "nature/culture", "subject/object", and "human/non-human". These boundary creatures are "simultaneously real, like nature, narrated, like discourse, and collective, like society". While we "moderns" have struggled to purify, separate, and define different realms of reality through objective scientific analysis, we have been blind to, and have facilitated the proliferation of such hybrids. Despite the rather selective critique of the discipline of geography by Latour, ANT has found its way into geographical work and "network topologies" have been made visible in a number of ways.

Only by differentiating alternative paths and processes in the transformation of nature-society-networks can the complexity of these networks be laid out. The international financial system has also been examined in these terms by Thrift and Leyshon. They identify four overlapping actor-networks - nation-states, the media, organizations of money capitalists, and "machine intelligence" - which form the structures of governance of the international financial system insofar as together they are "able to assemble the agency, power and size needed to develop, produce and distribute money". By doing this they hope to counter the idea that money, and its increasingly global circulation in the form of information, has become completely disembedded from social and cultural networks.

The technological networks that facilitate the increased speed and distance with which money is circulated are only part of broader actor networks and indeed, as Thrift and Leyshon point out, it is the very complexity of the interpretive processes associated with these telecommunication technologies that further embeds them into richly textured socio-cultural contexts.

Bingham also offers another example of the attempt to utilize the insights of the amodern framework of ANT to re-imagine the ways in which materiality is constituted, positing what he suggests is a materialist semiotics as a "means to grant all sorts of things their rightful place in the (co)construction of the world". Such an approach, which is basically a rearticulation of ANT, would, according to Bingham, be concerned with the ways in which "all sorts of bits and pieces - bodies machines and buildings, as well as texts - are associated together in attempts to build order".

These examples confirm Thrift and Olds' suggestion that the "topological presupposition of the network is now in common usage in the social sciences". Thrift and Olds suggest that this presupposition is deployed in 4 ways, (a) in order to facilitate a description of modes of governance, (b) as an analysis of social networks, (c) to analyze the "performative networks of culture", and (d) to examine "the logics of connection and separation of bodies and other things". However, in their own attempt to trace a particular network they neglect to address the last of the ways in which the network topology has been deployed. This omission is symptomatic of a larger deficiency in the ANT perspective, a perspective which has generally failed to engage with questions of the body, embodiment, and corporeality.

A second potential critique of ANT relates to its tendency to offer a totalistic account, which presupposes that the networks being traced can be mapped in their entirety. However, it is only "humanly" possible to begin to "translate" these hybridizations in their local, yet simultaneously global, specificity. The partiality of the ability to map these networks must be constantly recognized and acknowledged, as must the inability of critical observers to remove themselves from the networked environments of which they are part. In this context "collective vision" takes on different meanings, referring not only to the ability of a group of individuals to form coherent sets of goals, but also to the extent to which actor-networks (including those composed in part by geographers) can see the hybridized environments of which they are part. This involves a realization that the ability to "see" these environments is itself a collective vision, a vision not from an abstract omniperspectival "human" viewpoint, but from the networked position(s) of the quasi-object/subject. Armed with a realization of the partiality of collective vision, questions of which "collective" interests promote particular processes of hybridization, and then subsequently purify and deny the existence of these hybridizations under the terms of the modern constitution might become (in)tolerably visible.

Despite these criticisms ANT can contribute to a critical rethinking of what is involved in the construction and constitution of environments. Environments might be provisionally rethought of in terms of networks, and the construction of environments as the governmentality of these networks, a governmentality involving the translation and mobilizing of diverse actors.

Additionally, bodies and machines are not assembled as particular cyborg fusions "within" environments. Rather, environments, bodies and machines are produced together, they are implicated in the construction and constitution of each other, as the length and intensity of the connections of particular networks is increased. This then, is the way that actors are mobilized and translated by particularly powerful centers of translation to create the effect of environments.

Given this, it is necessary here to return once again to Butler, whose idea of performativity, applied to the construction and maintenance of the identity of environments, may now be seen as one part of the processes of translation through which networks of human and non-human, nature and culture, take shape. The discursive construction of the home as an environments of fitness, given performative force by repetitive acts such as those continuously visible on contemporary television screens, in magazines, and in retail outlets, might then be seen as merely one aspect of such hybrid networks, but one which is important in defining the types of humans and non-humans arranged so as to lead to the convenient ends of particular collectives.

Thus, as one element in the larger networks that are simultaneously global and local, the environment of the home might equally be seen as a hybrid, a quasi-object, formed of the network of hybridizations between the "natural" building materials such as wood, stone etc., the gendered "cultural" values ascribed to the space of the home, and technological networks such as electricity, sewage, gas, telephone, Internet, and television. Similarly, and inextricably bound up with the hybrid environment of the home, the body might be seen as a quasi-object formed of the thread woven between the "natural" body, its organs and functions, the cultural values ascribed to and inscribed through these, and the technologies and non-animate objects, such as nutritional supplements, pulse monitors, cathode-ray tubes, and ergonomically designed fitness machines.

3

Urban Population Growth

Through most of history, the human population has lived a rural lifestyle, dependent on agriculture and hunting for survival. In 1800, only 3 percent of the world's population lived in urban areas. By 1900, almost 14 percent were urbanites, although only 12 cities had 1 million or more inhabitants. In 1950, 30 percent of the world's population resided in urban centers. The number of cities with over 1 million people had grown to 83.

The world has experienced unprecedented urban growth in recent decades. In 2000, about 47 percent of the world's population lived in urban areas, about 2.8 billion. There are 411 cities over 1 million. More developed nations are about 76 percent urban, while 40 percent of residents of less developed countries live in urban areas. However, urbanization is occurring rapidly in many less developed countries. It is expected that 60 percent of the world population will be urban by 2030, and that most urban growth will occur in less developed countries.

What is an urban area? An urban area may be defined by the number of residents, the population density, the percent of people not dependent upon agriculture, or the provision of such public utilities and services as electricity and education. Some countries define any place with a population of 2,500 or more as urban; others set a minimum of 20,000. There are no universal standards, and generally each country develops its own set of criteria for distinguishing urban areas. The United States defines urban as a city, town, or village with a minimum population of 2,500 people. The classification of metropolitan includes both urban areas as well as rural areas that are socially and economically integrated with a particular city.

When comparing countries it is often helpful to look beyond the proportion of populations that are rural or urban and instead consider the size of cities. Countries differ markedly in the distribution of their urban population. For example, many urban dwellers in Africa live in cities of fewer than 10,000 residents. In Argentina, 90 percent of the 2000 population was urban, and 38 percent of these people lived in just one city, Buenos Aires. In 2000, 39 percent of the world's urbanites lived in agglomerations of 1 million or more inhabitants, and 15 percent resided in agglomerations of 5 million or more. Only 8 percent of Americans live in cities of 1 million or more.

Migration or Natural Increase

A city grows through natural increase — the excess of births over deaths — and because the in-migration of people from other cities, rural areas, or countries is greater than out-migration. More developed and less developed countries of the world differ not only in the percent living in cities, but also in the way in which urbanization is occurring.

During the 19th and early 20th centuries, urbanization resulted from and contributed to industrialization. New job opportunities in the cities spurred the mass movement of surplus population away from the countryside. At the same time, migrants provided cheap, plentiful labor for the emerging factories. While the proportion increased through rural to urban migration, high death rates in the cities slowed urban growth. Cities were unhealthy places because of crowded living conditions, the prevalence of contagious diseases, and the lack of sanitation. Until the mid-1800s, the number of deaths exceeded births in many large European cities. Migration accounted for as much as 90 percent of city growth during this period.

Urbanization in most less developed countries in the past 50 years contrasts sharply with the experience of the more developed countries. Death rates have fallen faster in urban areas because of greater access to health services. Because birth rates are relatively high in most less developed countries, the rates of natural increase are also quite high in cities. Migration also fuels urban growth in less developed countries as people leave the countryside in search of better jobs.

New York and London are typical of large cities in more developed countries that arose in the 1800s and early 1900s, reached their current size mid-century, and have since experienced slow growth or decline. Cities in some less developed countries, such as Mexico City, grew very rapidly between 1950 and 1980, and are growing more slowly now. Many Asian and African cities, such as Lagos and Bombay, are experiencing very rapid growth now and are projected to continue at this pace.

Megacities

As the population increases, more people will live in large cities. Many people will live in the growing number of cities with over 5 million habitants known as megacities. As the map "Largest urban agglomerations" shows, just eight cities had populations of 5 million or more in 1950, two of them in less developed countries. Megacities numbered 41 in 2000. By 2015, 59 megacities will exist, 48 in less developed countries.

By the turn of the century, cities of 10 million and larger will be more common. In 1950, only one city had more than 10 million inhabitants. By 2015, 23 cities are projected to hold over 10 million people; all but four will be in less developed countries.

Top 10 largest urban agglomerations in 1950, 2000, 2015

1950		*2000*		*2015*	
1. New York, USA	12.3	1. Tokyo, Japan	26.4	1. Tokyo, Japan	26.4
2. London, England	8.7	2. Mexico City, Mexico	18.4	2. Bombay, India	26.1
3. Tokyo, Japan	6.9	3. Bombay, India	18.0	3. Lagos, Nigeria	23.2
4. Paris, France	5.4	4. São Paulo, Brazil	17.8	4. Dhaka, Bangladesh	21.1
5. Moscow, Russia	5.4	5. New York, USA	16.6	5. São Paulo, Brazil	20.4
6. Shanghai, China	5.3	6. Lagos, Nigeria	13.4	6. Karachi, Pakistan	19.2
7. Essen, Germany	5.3	7. Los Angeles, USA	13.1	7. Mexico City, Mexico	19.2
8. Buenos Aires, Argentina	5.0	8. Calcutta, India	12.9	8. New York, USA	17.4

9. Chicago, USA	4.9	9. Shanghai, China	12.9	9. Jakarta, Indonesia	17.3
10. Calcutta, India	4.4	10. Buenos Aires, Argentina	12.6	10. Calcutta, India	17.3

Source: United Nations, World Urbanization Prospects, The 1999 Revision.

Terms

Death rate (or crude death rate): The number of deaths per 1,000 population in a given year.

Less developed countries: Less developed countries include all countries in Africa, Asia (excluding Japan), and Latin America and the Caribbean, and the regions of Melanesia, Micronesia, and Polynesia.

Megacities: A city with a population of 10 million or more residents.

Metropolitan area: A large concentration of population, usually an area with 100,000 or more people. The area typically includes an important city with 50,000 or more inhabitants and the administrative areas bordering the city that are socially and economically integrated with it.

More developed countries: More developed countries include all countries in Europe, North America, Australia, New Zealand, and Japan.

Rate of natural increase: The rate at which a population is increasing (or decreasing) in a given year due to a surplus (or deficit) of births over deaths, expressed as a percentage of the base population.

Urban: Countries differ in the way they classify population as "urban" or "rural." Typically, a community or settlement with a population of 2,000 or more is considered urban. A listing of country definitions is published annually in the United Nations Demographic Yearbook.

Urban agglomeration: Urban agglomerations are areas of 1 million population or more. The concept of agglomeration defines the population contained within the contours of contiguous territory inhabited at urban levels of residential density without regard to administrative boundaries.

Urbanization: Growth in the proportion of a population living in urban areas.

Between 1950 and 2000, the population of the United States increased more than 130 million (87 percent). At the same time, nearly all of the population increase was in urban areas. In 1950, 64 percent of the nation lived in urban areas, while by 2000 the number had risen to 79 percent. Between 1950 and 2000, urban areas experienced a population increase of 126 million, compared to an increase of only five million in rural areas. This urban increase is approximately the same as the population of Japan, but has been housed in an area less than one-half the size. Moreover, the bulk of the increase has been in larger urban areas.

In 2000, 81 million more people lived in urban areas with more than 1,000,000 than in 1950. The increase among urban areas between 50,000 and 999,999 was 46 million. Among smaller urban areas (2,500 to 49,999), there was a decline of 1.2 million. While urban population was increasing 87 percent from 1950 to 2000, urban land area increased 400 percent. Urban population density dropped 54 percent, from 5,300 per square mile to 2,400 per square mile. Most of the decrease occurred between 1950 and 1960, when average population density dropped from 5,300 to 3,100. Since 1980, urban population density has increased somewhat. Urban land areas expanded at a greater rate than the population increase as a result of the following factors:

— Larger lot sizes occupied by single-family houses.

— Larger lot sizes occupied by the newer commercial, industrial and retail structures built to respond to higher demand generated by the increased population.

— Smaller household sizes, which meant that more housing units are required for a given level of population.

From 1950 to 2000, average household size declined 23 percent, from 3.47 to 2.68. The number of households in the nation increased 142 percent, 1.64 times the 87 percent population increase. The nation's urban housing density has, as a result, fallen considerably less than the urban population density. From 1950 to 2000 household density has fallen from 1,500 to 900 per square mile, a decline of 40 percent. Virtually the entire decline occurred between 1950 and 1960. Household density in 2000 is approximately the same as in 1960 and has increased since 1990. Since that time, urban households have increased 126 percent, while urban land area has increased slightly more, at 130 percent.

Nonetheless, population in urban cores dropped substantially faster than household sizes. For example, the city of St. Louis lost 59 percent of its population from 1950 to 2000, the largest population loss for a major city in the world in modern history. Pittsburgh, Cleveland and Detroit lost between 48 percent and 51 percent. Within central cities, even larger population losses occurred. For example, over a longer period, New York's Lower East Side lost 70 percent of its population (from its 1910 peak).

The central city loss trend extends to nearly all municipalities that (1) achieved a peak population of 200,000 or more, (2) have not materially expanded their boundaries and (3) were fully developed at their peak. Among these

23 cities (in 19 urban areas), only San Francisco and Oakland have gained population (less than one percent and three percent respectively). Central city population losses have totalled 5.5 million, while suburban population gains were 29.2 million. Generally, these same trends are masked where cities have been involved in governmental consolidations or pursued annexation.

For example, the population within the 1950 boundaries of Nashville and Indianapolis, which have consolidated with their counties, declined approximately 40 percent from 1950 to 1990. In 1990, the population of Portland and Seattle (each down approximately 10 percent) inside the 1950 boundaries was below that of 1950 as also were the populations of cities involved in sign cant amalgamations, Nashville and Indianapolis (both down approximately 40 percent). Core areas have generally declined in population, with all population growth occurring in areas that would be considered suburban, but for the fact that they had been incorporated into central cities.

International Trends: Virtually the same trends have occurred in other affluent nations. In fact, as measured by the decline in urban population density, suburbanization has been greater elsewhere in the high-income world than in the United States. The historic centers of European cities maintain their "charm" and continue to attract tourists but they are surrounded by sprawling suburbs that contain single-family housing , "strip" commercial developments, "big box" stores and wide freeways.

From 1960 to 1990, urban densities declined 20 percent in the United States, 33 percent in Canada, 30 percent in Western Europe and 32 percent in Australia. Limited data from Japan (Tokyo) indicates a slightly lesser rate, at minus

18 percent. Moreover, international central cities and urban cores have been losing population.

— Like New York, the urban cores of Tokyo and Paris have all lost more than 60 percent of their population since peaking earlier in the 20century.

— Paris provides an example of the manner in which low density suburban development has become the rule rather than the exception in European urban areas. From 1954 to 1999, the Paris urban area (developed or built-up area) has expanded significantly, now covering approximately 1,000 square miles, nearly the size of the state of Rhode Island. The central city ("ville de Paris") covers less than 35 square miles,and has lost more than 700,000 residents since 1954 (nearly equal to the population of Washington, DC and Arlington, VA combined). The central core, containing the most frequently visited tourist sites is barely two square miles.

— All 50 Western European central cities that (1) achieved a peak population of 400,000 or more, (2) have not materially expanded their boundaries and (3) were fully developed at their peak have declined in population. The total population of these cities is 45.9 million, down 10.4 million from the peak of 56.3 million. As in the case of the United States, annexations and consolidations (such as in Antwerp and Leeds) or large tracts of empty land (such as in Oslo and Rome) have tended to mask the same trends by incorporating suburban areas within the boundaries of central cities.

— Land area has expanded substantially even in Western European urban areas (developed or "built up" areas) that have lost population. From 1960 to 1990, the Amsterdam urban area lost 10 percent of its population, while expanding its land area more than 60 percent. The Copenhagen urban area lost 13 percent of its population and expanded its urban area 25 percent.

— Elsewhere in Western Europe, Canada and Australia, like in the United States, urban land area expanded at a greater rate than the population increase, as is indicated in the cases of the Paris, Zurich, Vancouver and Sydney urban areas. Even the Tokyo urban area experienced a substantially greater land expansion rate than population increase.

— Recently released Italian census data indicates that there is little, if any growth large metropolitan areas. From 1991 to 2001, population growth was less than 40,000 in Milan, Naples and Turin combined (areas that total more than 14,000,000 residents). Yet, even in these areas, there was population growth of more than 400,000 in outlying, lower density municipalities, as urban cores have continued to decline. More than 80 percent of this growth has been in municipalities with population densities similar to that of US suburban areas.

— Even in less affluent nations, urban areas are sprawling. Virtually all of Mexico City's growth in the last 20 years has been in the suburbs, while core wards of the city have lost 45 percent of their population since 1960. Between 1981 and 1991, the core wards of Mumbai (Bombay) began losing population. Virtually all growth has been in the suburbs in recent years in Buenos Aires, Seoul, Manila and most of the major cities of Eastern Europe and the former Soviet Union.

Thus, low density suburban development (the development of urban land area at a rate faster than the urban population increase), is occurring around the world, especially in the developed world, where incomes are rising. Like the United States, higher rates of home ownership tend to be exhibited in lower density suburban areas.

For example, the 30 percent of households are homeowners in the central city of Paris, compared to 44 percent in the inner ring suburbs ("Petite Couronne") and 54 percent in the outer ring suburbs ("Grand Couronne"). And, single-family (detached) housing is more typical of the lower density suburbs, as in the United States. For example, more than 55 percent of the housing in the suburbs of Tokyo is detached, and more than 75 percent is detached in the exurbs. This compares to barely 30 percent in the central area. The situation is similar in Osaka-Kobe-Kyoto. The "American Dream" home ownership, the singlefamily house in the suburbs and the car are fast becoming a "Universal Dream".

Incomes: Incomes have risen strongly in the United States. From 1950 to 2000, per capita income rose 175 percent, while income per household increased 141 percent on an inflation-adjusted basis. This higher income has made it possible for more people to own homes, automobiles and experience a higher standard of living. Household income increased in every decade between 1950 and 2000, with a 17.7 percent increase between 1990 and 2000. As was noted above, US incomes remain strongly above those of other developed nations.

4

Urbanisation and Economic Growth

Urbanisation, or the shift of population from rural to urban environments, is typically a transitory process, albeit one that is socially and culturally traumatic. As a country develops it moves from labour-intensive agricultural production to labour being increasingly employed in industry and services. The latter are not land-intensive and are located in cities because of agglomeration economies. Thus urbanisation moves populations from traditional rural environments with informal political and economic institutions to the relative anonymity and more formal institutions of urban settings. That in itself requires institutional development within a country. It spatially separates families, particularly intergenerationally as the young migrate to cities and the old stay behind.

Urbanisation is a spatial transition process. By upper middle income ranges, countries become "fully" urbanised, in the sense that the percent urbanised levels out at 60-90% of the national population living in cities. The actual percent urbanised with full urbanisation varies with geography, the role of modern agriculture in the economy, and national definitions of urban. This idea of a transitory phenomenon is illustrated Figure 1, comparing different regions of the world in 1960 versus 1995.

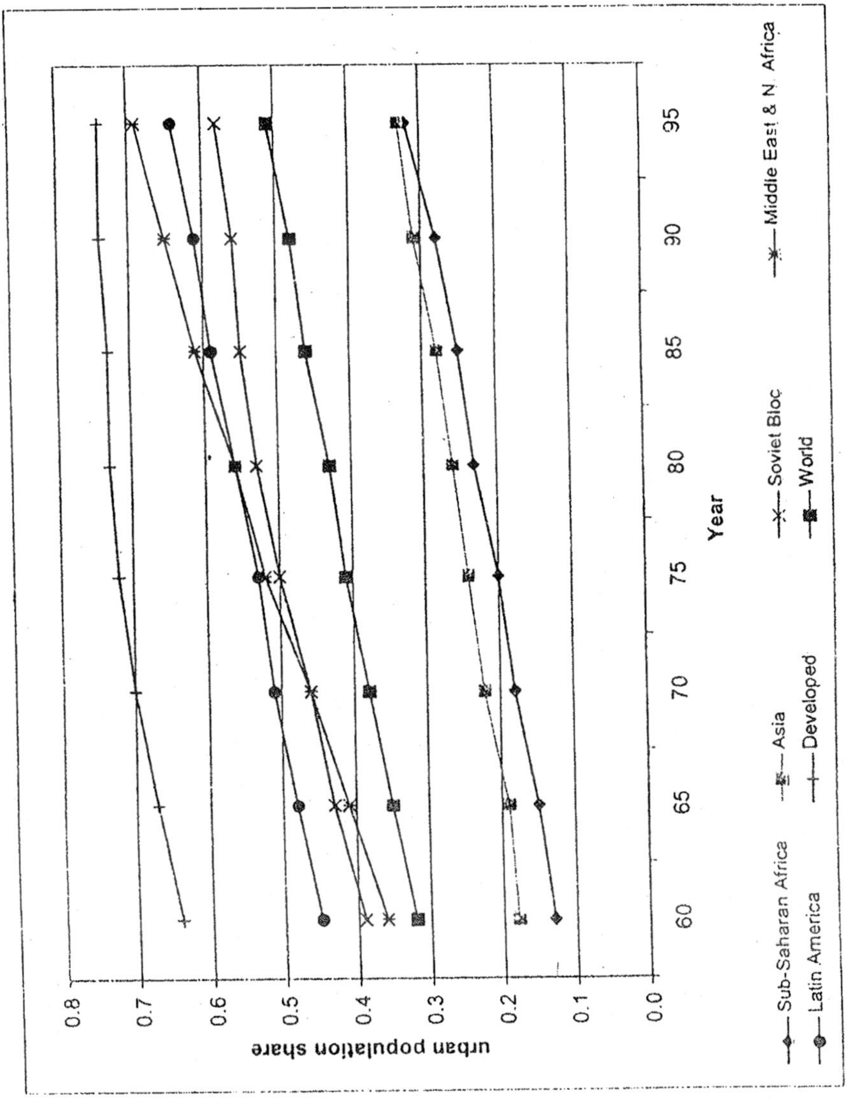

Figure 1. Share of urban population in total population (average over countries within groups)

While urbanisation increased in all regions of the world over those 35 years, among developed countries there is little change since 1975. By 1995 Soviet bloc and Latin American countries had almost converged to developed country urbanisation levels. Only sub-Saharan African and Asian countries still face substantial urbanisation in the future. Although urbanisation is transitory, given the total spatial transformation and accompanying institutional and social transformation involved, as a policy issue urbanisation is very important to developing countries.

Urbanisation is the consequence of changes in national output composition from rural agriculture to urbanised modern manufacturing and service production. As such, Renaud makes the basic point that government policies bias, or influence urbanisation through their effect on national sectoral composition. So policies affecting the terms of trade between agriculture and modern industry or between traditional small town industries and high tech large city industries affect the rural-urban or small-big city allocation of population. Such policies include tariffs, and price controls and subsidies.

The idea that government policies affect urbanisation primarily through their effect on sector composition is a key point of empirical studies of urbanisation by Fay and Opal and Davis and Henderson. These studies show that, indeed, urbanisation which occurs in the early and middle stages of development is determined largely by changes in national economic sector composition and in technology, and government policies tend to affect urbanisation only indirectly through their effect on sector composition.

Urbanisation promotes benefits from agglomeration such as localised information and knowledge spillovers and thus efficient urbanisation promotes economic growth.

Writers such as Gallup, Sacks and Mellinger go further to suggest that urbanisation may "cause' economic growth, rather than just emerge as part of the growth process. The limited evidence so far suggests urbanisation doesn't cause growth per se. Henderson finds no econometric evidence linking the extent of urbanisation to either economic or productivity growth or levels. That is if a country were to enact policies to encourage urbanisation per se, typically that wouldn't improve growth. Finally on urbanisation, there is an informal notion that the transitory urbanisation process follows the same stages as population growth– an S-shaped relationship where urban population growth is slow at low levels of development, then there is a period of rapid acceleration in intermediate stages, followed by a slowing of growth. However the data suggest otherwise at least over the last 35 years.

In 1965, Williamson published an innovative paper based on cross-section analysis of 24 countries in which he argued that national economic development is characterised by an initial phase of internal regional divergence, followed by a phase of later convergence. That is, a few regions initially experience accelerated growth relative to other regions, but later the peripheral regions start to catch up. Barro and Sala-i-Martin present extensive evidence on this for the USA, Western Europe, and Japan, by examining the evolution of inter-regional differences in per capita incomes. While inter-regional out-migration from poorer regions plays a role in catch-up, it may not be critical. For Japan, the authors argue that later convergence of backward regions occurred through improved productivity in backward regions.

The urban version of this divergence-convergence phenomenon looks at urban primacy. Following Ades and Glaeser, conceptually the urban world is collapsed into two regions—the primate city versus the rest of the country, or at least the urban portion thereof. The basic question concerns to what extent urbanisation is concentrated, or confined to one (or a few) major metro areas, relative to being spread more evenly across a variety of cities. Primacy is commonly measured by the ratio of the population of the largest metro area to all urban population in the country.

A more comprehensive measure might use either a spatial Gini or a Hirschman-Herfindal index [HHI] from the industrial organisation literature. Corresponding to Williamson's hypothesis, these papers find an inverted U-shape relationship, where relative urban concentration first increases, peaks, and then declines with economic development. Despite different concentration measures and methods, Wheaton and Shishido examining a HHI using cross-section non-linear OLS and Davis and Henderson examining primacy using panel data methods and IV estimation find that concentration rises, peaks in the $2000-4000 range, and then declines.

Without conditioning on other variables affecting primacy, the inverted *U* . relationship of primacy against income is noisy and only apparent in the raw data in earlier time periods. Lee explores the relationship between changes in urban concentration and industrial transformation for Korea. The idea is that manufacturing is also first very concentrated in primate cities at early stages of development and then decentralises to such an extent that at the other end of economic development it is relatively more concentrated in rural areas, as in the USA today as noted earlier.

Seoul's urban primacy peaked around 1970 and while Seoul's absolute population has continued to grow, its share has declined steadily. At the urban primacy peak in 1970,

Seoul had a dominant share of national manufacturing although the other major metro areas, Pusan and Taegu, also had large shares. During the next 10-15 years, manufacturing suburbanised from Seoul to satellite cities in the rest of Kyonggi province, as well as to satellite cities surrounding Pusan and Taegu. Such suburbanisation of manufacturing has been documented also for Thailand, Colombia, and Indonesia. But the key development following the early 1980's in Korea is the spread of manufacturing from the three major metro areas and their satellites to rural areas and other cities. The share of rural areas and other cities in manufacturing rose from 26% in 1983 to 42% in 1992, in a time period when national manufacturing employment is fairly stagnant and rural areas and other cities actually continue to experience modest absolute population losses. That is, manufacturing deconcentrated both relatively and absolutely to hinterland regions. This deconcentration coincided with economic liberalisation, enormous and widespread investment in inter-regional transport and infrastructure investment, and fiscal decentralisation and is consistent with core-periphery reversal in the new economic geography literature.

Given the urban primacy relationships, the immediate issue is the "so-what" question. How is urban concentration important to growth? For example, is there an optimal degree of urban primacy with each level of development, where significant deviations from this level detract from growth? Conceptually there should be an optimal degree of primacy, where optimal primacy involves a trade-off of the benefits of increasing primacy—enhanced local scale economies contributing to productivity growth—against the costs—more resources diverted away from productive and innovative activities to shoring up the quality of life in congested primate cities.

In the first econometric examination of this so what question, Henderson finds that there is an optimal degree of primacy at each level of development that declines as development proceeds. Optimal primacy is the level that maximises national productivity growth. Initial high relative agglomeration is important at low levels of development when countries have low knowledge accumulation, are importing technology, and have limited capital to invest in widespread hinterland development. However the desirability of high relative agglomeration declines with development. Error bands about optimal primacy numbers are quite tight. Second, large deviations from optimal primacy strongly affect productivity growth. An 33% increase or decrease in primacy from a typical best level of .3 reduces productivity growth by 3% over five years. There is some tendency internationally to excessive primacy, with the usual suspects such as Argentina, Chile, Peru, Thailand, Mexico, and Algeria having extremely high primacy.

There is a considerable literature of government policies and institutions in fostering excessive concentration. In Ades and Glaeser, the basic idea is that national policy makers favour the national capital for reasons of personal gain. For example, direct restraints on trade for hinterland cities such as inability to access capital markets or to get export or import licenses favour firms in the national capital. Policy makers and bureaucrats may gain as shareholders in such firms, or they may gain rents from those seeking licenses or other exemptions to trade restraints.

Indirect trade protection for the primate city can also involve under-investment in hinterland transport and communications infrastructure. Whether as true beliefs or as a justification to cover rent-seeking behaviour, policy makers in different countries often articulate a view that large cities are more productive and thus should be the site for government-owned heavy industry.

Favouritism of a primate city creates a non-level playing field in competition across cities. The favoured city draws in migrants and firms from hinterland areas, creating an extremely congested high cost-of-living metro area. Local city planners can try to resist the migration response to primate city favouritism by, for example, refusing to provide legal housing development for immigrants or to provide basic public services in immigrant neighbourhoods. Hence the development of squatter settlements, bustees, kampongs and so on. But still, favored cities tend to draw in enormous populations.

Is there econometric evidence indicating that politics plays a role in increasing sizes of primate cities? Ades and Glaeser based on cross-section analyses find that if the primate city in a country is the national capital it is 45% larger. If the country is a dictatorship, or at the extreme of non-democracy, the primate city is 40-45% larger. The idea is that representative democracy gives a political voice to the hinterland regions limiting the ability of the capital city to favour itself.

Apart from representative democracy, fiscal decentralisation helps to level the playing field across cities, by giving political autonomy for hinterland cities to compete with the primate city. Davis and Henderson explore these ideas further, examining in a panel context the impact upon primacy of democratisation and fiscal decentralisation from 1960-1995. Examining both democratisation and fiscal decentralisation together, Ades and Glaeser find moving from the extreme of least to most democratic form of government reduces primacy by 8% and from the extreme of most to least centralised government reduces primacy by 5%. Primate cities which are national capitals are 20% larger and primate cities in planned economies with migration restrictions are 18% smaller. Finally they find transport infrastructure investment in hinterlands which opens up international markets to hinterland cities reduces primacy, as the core-periphery models of the new economic geography tend to predict. A one-standard deviation increase in roads per sq. kilometer of national land area or in navigable inland waterways per sq. kilometer each reduce primacy by 10%.

Cities and Its Evolution

Work by Eaton and Eckstein on France and Japan and by Dobkins and Ioannides on the USA, with later work by Black and Henderson and Ioannides and Overman on the USA, establish some basic facts about urban systems and their development in France, Japan, and the USA over the last century or so. Foremost is that there is a wide relative size distribution of cities in large economies that is stable over time. Big and small cities coexist in equal proportions over long periods of time. Second, within that relative size distribution, individual cities are generally growing in population size over time; and what is considered a big versus small city in absolute size changes over time. Third, while there is entry of new cities and rapid growth and relative decline of cities nearer the bottom of the urban hierarchy, at the top city size rankings are remarkably stable over time. Finally, size distributions of cities within countries, at least at the upper tail are well approximated by a Pareto distribution, with Zipf's Law applying in many cases. Establishing these facts raises a variety of issues and different methodological and technical approaches.

The empirical work in Eaton and Eckstein and subsequent work typically looks at the decade by decade development of urban systems. In doing so, there are critical choices researchers must make when assembling data. First is to define geographically what consists of the generic term "city". The usual definition is the "metro area", where large metro areas like Chicago comprise over 100 municipalities, or local political units. The idea in defining metro areas is to cover the entire local labour market and all contiguous manufacturing, service and residential activities radiating out from the core city, until activity peters out into farm land or very low density development. A second choice concerns how to accommodate changes in geographic definitions over time.

Another approach is to take current metro area definitions and follow the same geograpnic areas back in time, focusing on non-agricultural activity. A third problem concerns how to define "consistently" over time the threshold population size at which an agglomeration becomes a metro area, especially since the economic nature, population density, and spatial development of metro areas have changed so much over the last century. Some authors use an absolute cut-off point; some use a relative cutoff point; and others look at a set number of the largest cities. The relative cut-off point approach is attractive because it attempts to hold constant the area of the relative size distribution which is examined over time, as illustrated below. In presenting evidence on the topics to follow, whatever choices researchers make can strongly affect specific results. Nevertheless there are a variety of findings that are consistent across studies.

Evolution of Size Distribution

This section attempts to analyse the evolution of the size distribution of cities, applying techniques utilized by Quah in examining cross-country growth patterns. Cities in each decade are divided by relative size into, say, 5-6 discrete categories, with fixed relative size cut-off points for each cell. A first order Markov process is assumed and a transition matrix calculated. In many cases, stationarity of the matrix over decades can't be rejected, so cell transition probabilities are based on all transitions over time. If M is the transition matrix, i the average rate of entry of new cities in each decade (in a context where in practice there is no exit), Z the (stationary) distribution across cells of entrants (typically concentrated on the lowest cell), and f the steady-state distribution, then

$$f = [I - (1-i)\ M]^{-1}\ iZ \qquad (1)$$

In the data, relative size distributions are remarkably stable over time and steady-state distributions tend to be close to the most recent distributions. In the studies on the USA, Japan, and France, there is no tendency of distributions to collapse and concentrate in one cell, or for all cities to converge to mean size; nor generally is there a tendency for distributions to become bipolar. Distributions are remarkably stable. Much of the world's population in cities over 100,000 are in small-medium size metro areas. 56% are in cities under 2 million, while only 17% are in cities over 8 million. Moreover all these cities only account for 62% of the world's urban population; the rest live in cities smaller than 100,000. So overall 73% of the world's urban population lives in cities under 2 million in population. While the popular press may focus on mega-cities, only a small part of the action is there.

Figure 2 plots the relative size distribution of the approximately 1200 metro areas worldwide over 100,000 in 1960 against the relative size distribution of the approximately 1700 metro areas over 200,000 in 2000.

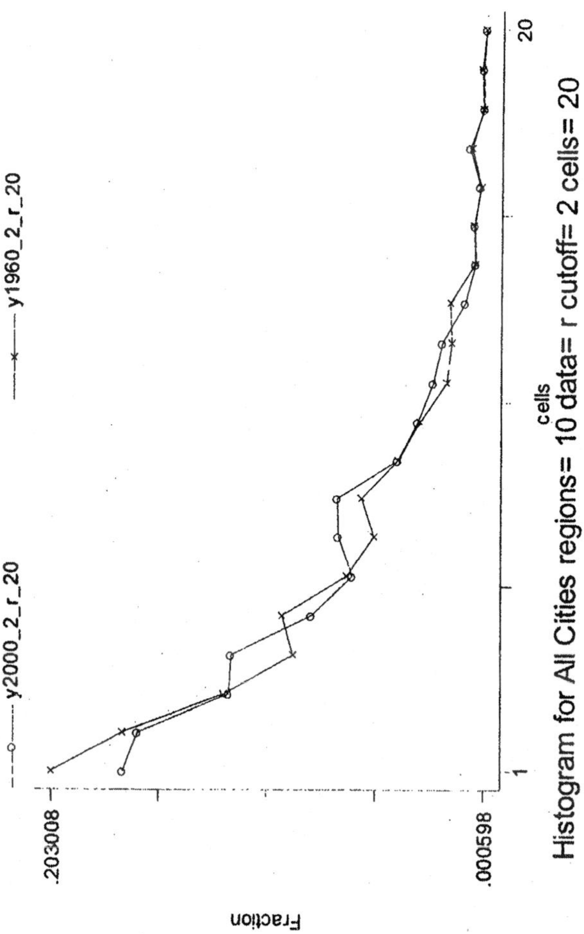

Figure 2a. Relative size distribution of cities for all countries

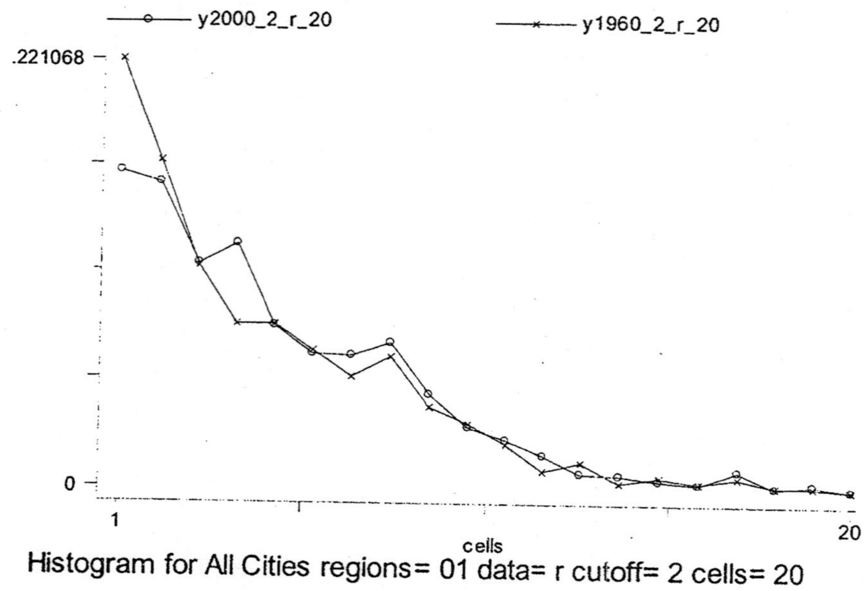

Figure 2b. Relative size distribution of cities in developing and transition countries

Relative sizes are actual sizes divided by the world average size in the corresponding year. The 100, 000 versus 200,000 cut-off points for minimum size are relative ones based on a constant minimum to mean size ratio. Using an absolute cut-off point in this case has little impact on the figure. The figure plots the histogram for 20 cells on a log scale. The 1960 versus 2000 distributions for all cities worldwide (Figure 2a) and for those in developing and transition economies (Figure 2b) almost perfectly overlap. Relative size distributions are stable. Similarly performing transition analysis on world cities for 1960-1970-1980-1990-2000 and calculating the steady state distributions, starting with 5 cells and shares in each of .351, .299, .151, .100, .0991 in 1960, as we move up the urban hierarchy the steady state shares are .324, .299, .138, .122, and .117. Again, this indicates rock stablility of distributions over time.

An alternative way of expressing this is to calculate spatial Gini's. For a spatial Gini rank all cities from smallest to largest on the x -axis and on the y -axis calculate their Lorenz curve — the cumulative share of total sample population. The Gini is the share of the area below the 45° line, between that line and the Lorenz curve. The greater the Gini, the "less equal" the size distribution. The world Gini in 1960 versus 2000 is .59 versus .56 for developed countries, .57 versus .56 for less developed countries, and .52 versus .45 for transition economies.

The research findings reveal that the transition economies have forestalled the growth of mega-cities through explicit and implicit migration restriction. Another finding in examining city size distributions is that, for larger cities, over time there is little change in relative size rankings. In Japan and France, the 39-40 largest cities in 1925 and 1876 respectively all remain in the top 50 in 1985 and 1990 respectively; and, at the top, absolute rankings are unchanged. The USA displays more mobility due to substantial entry of new cities. However, while smaller cities do move up and down in rank, the biggest cities tend to remain big over time. So, for example, cities in the top decile of ranking stay in that decile indefinitely, with newer cities joining that decile as the total number of cities expands. Alternatively viewed, based on the Markov transition process, the mean first passage time for a city to move from the top to bottom cell is thousands of years.

In the world cities data, as in the USA data, the probability in the transition matrix of moving out of the top cell to the next cell is very small: .038 in a decade time frame. Why do big cities stay big? A common answer is physical infrastructure. Large cities have huge historical capital stocks of streets, buildings, sewers, water mains and parks that are cheaply maintained and almost infinitely lived in, that give them a persistent comparative advantage over cities without that built-up stock. A second answer is modelled in Arthur and Rauch where, with localised scale externalities in production, large cities with a particular set of industries have a comparative advantage in attracting new firms, relative to cities with a small representation of those industries. Large cities have an established scale, offering high levels of scale externalities, which smaller cities can only achieve quickly if they are able to co-ordinate mass in-migration of firms into their location, something which may be institutionally difficult to do.

Growth in the Number and Size of Cities

For any steady state size distribution of cities, as urbanisation and growth proceed, both the absolute sizes and numbers of cities have grown historically, as a country's urban population expands through rural-urban migration and overall population growth. City sizes in the USA, Japan, and France over the past century have grown at average annual rates of 1.2 - 1.5%, depending on the country and exact time interval, rates which involve city sizes rising 3.3 - 4.5 fold every century. A small city today which is 250,000 would have been a major center in 1900. In the world city data set, for comparable sets of countries the numbers of metro areas grew by 62% from 1960-2000 using a relative cut-off point. Average sizes grew by about 70%. Using an absolute cut-off point of 100,000, numbers have about doubled and average sizes grown by 36% over 40 years. However, it is clear they have grown in population and numbers on an ongoing basis over the decades.

Glaeser, Scheinkman, and Shleifer in a cross-section city growth framework estimate that controlling for 1960 population, in the USA, cities in 1990 are 7% larger if they had a one-standard deviation higher level of median years of schooling in 1960. Black and Henderson place the issue in a panel context for 1940-1990 for the USA controlling for city fixed effects and examining the impact of percent college educated. They find a one-standard deviation higher level of percent college educated leads to a 20% larger city.

Zipf's Law

In considering the size distribution of cities, especially in a cross-sectional context, there is a large literature on what is termed Zipf's Law. City sizes are postulated to follow a Pareto distribution, where if R is rank from smallest, r, to largest, 1, and n is size

$$R(n) = An^{-a} \tag{2}$$

given the probe $(\tilde{n} > n) = An^{-a}$ and relative rank is $R(n)/r$ or the proportion of cities with size greater than n.

Under Zipf's Law, $a = 1$ or we have the rank size rule where, for every city, rank times size is a constant, A. Putting in log-linear form, empirical work produces a's that vary across countries, samples, and times but many are "close" to one. This empirical regularity has drawn considerable attention and is often used to characterise spatial inequality, using as a first approximation of the true size distribution.

Zipf's Law is just an approximation that does well in some circumstances and not so well in others. If one wants to compare measures of urban concentration across countries, rather than compare estimated a's in eq. (2), a more non-parametric measure such as a Gini might be more reliable. If Zipf's Law holds even approximately, why is that? In an interesting development, Gabaix starts to formalise the underlying stochastic components which might lead to such a relationship, building on Simon. Gabaix shows that if city growth rates obey Gabaix's Law where growth rates are random draws from the same distribution, so growth rates are independent of current size, Zipf's Law emerges as the limiting size distribution. Growth is scale invariant, so the final distribution is; and we have a power law with exponent 1. Gabaix sketches an illustrative model, based on on-going natural amenity shocks facing cities of any size, which leads to Zipf's Law for the size distribution of cities.

While Gibrat's Law is a neat underlying stochastic process, does it hold up empirically? Black and Henderson test whether in the relationship, $\ln n_{it} - \ln n_{it-1} = a + \delta t + \alpha \ln n_{it} + \varepsilon_{it}$, $\alpha = 0$ as hypothesized under the Law. The Law requires ε_{it} to be i.i.d., so simple OLS suffices. Black and Henderson find $\alpha < 0$ under a variety of circumstance and sub-samples, under appropriate statistical criteria, which rejects Gibrat's Law.

Ioannides and Overman examine the issue more thoroughly in a non-parametric fashion, characterising the mean and variance of the distribution from which growth rates are drawn. The mean and variance of growth rates do seem to vary with city size but bootstrapped confidence intervals are fairly wide generally, allowing for the possibility of (almost) equal means.

Geographic Concentration

Geographic concentration refers to the extent to which an industry k is concentrated at a particular location or, more generally concentrated at a few versus many locations nationally. A common measure of concentration of industry k at location i is $l_{ik} = X_{ik}/\Sigma_i X_{ik}$. X_{ik} is location i's employment or output of industry k. Thus l_{ik} is location i's share of, say, national employment in industry k. In contrast to geographic concentration, specialisation refers to how much of a location's total employment is found in industry k, or $s_{ik} = X_{ik}/\Sigma_k X_{ik}$. As Overman, Redding and Venables demonstrate, if we normalise l_{ik} by location i's share of national employment ($s_{ik} \equiv \Sigma_k X_{ik}/\Sigma_k \Sigma_i X_{ik}$) and s_{ik} by industry k's share of national employment ($s_{ik} \equiv \Sigma_i X_{ik}/\Sigma_k \Sigma_i X_{ik}$) we get the same measure—a location quotient,

$$q^k_{ik} = X_{ik} \frac{(\Sigma_k \Sigma_i X_{ik})}{\Sigma_k X_{ik} \Sigma_i X_{ik}} \tag{3}$$

The distribution of q_{ik} across industries, k, compared over time for a city would tell us about how city i's specialisation patterns are changing over time. And the distribution of q_{ik} across locations, i, over time would tell us whether industry k is becoming more or less concentrated over time at different locations. In a practical applications looking at many industries and cities over time or across countries, the issue concerns how to produce summary measures to describe either how overall concentration varies across industries or how one city's specialisation compares with another's. Another issue concerns how to factor in the different forces that cause specialisation or concentration phenomena.

Urban Specialisation

Evidence on countries such as Brazil, U.S.A., Korea, and India indicate that cities are relatively specialised. The traditional urban specialisation literature going back to Bergsman, Greenston and Healy uses cluster analysis to group cities into categories based on similarity of production patterns—correlations (or minimum distances) in the shares of different industries in local employment, s_{ik}. Cluster analysis is an "art form" in the sense that there is no optimal set of clusters, and it is up to the researcher to define how fine or how broad the clusters should be and there are a variety of clustering algorithms.

Using 1990 data for the U.S.A., Black and Henderson group 317 metro areas into 55 clusters, "defining" 55 city types based on patterns of specialisation for 80 2-digit industries. They define textile, primary metals, machinery, electronics, oil and gas, transport equipment, health services, insurance, entertainment, diversified market center, and so on type cities, where anywhere from 5-33% of local employment is typically found in just one industry. They show that production patterns across the types are statistically different and that average cities and educational levels by type differ significantly across many of the types. Specialisation especially among smaller cities tends to be absolute.

At a 3-digit level many cities have absolutely zero employment in a variety of categories. So in the 1992 Census of Manufactures for major industries like computers, electronic components, aircraft, instruments, metal working machinery, special machinery, construction machinery, and refrigeration machinery and equipment, respectively, of 317 metro areas 40%, 17%, 42%, 15%, 77%, 15%, 14% and 24% have absolutely zero employment in these industries.

Kim in looking at the USA examines how patterns of specialisation have changed over time, by comparing for pairs (i, j) of locations $\Sigma_k = s_{ik} - s_{jk}$ and by estimating spatial Gini's for industry concentration. He finds that states are substantially less specialised in 1987 than in 1860, but that localisation, or concentration has increased over time. For Korea, as part of the deconcentration process noted earlier, Henderson, Lee, and Lee find that from 1983 to 1993, city specialisation as measured by a normalised Hirschman-Herfindahl index

$$g_j = \Sigma_k \ (s_{jk} - s_j)^2 \qquad (4)$$

rises in manufacturing, while a provincial level index declines. Cities become more specialised and provinces less so. Clearly the geographic unit of analysis matters, as do the concepts. City specialisation as envisioned in the models presented below is consistent with regional diversity, when large regions are composed of many cities of different types. Henderson for the USA and Lee for Korea show that the g_j index of specialisation in manufacturing declines with metro area size. Smaller cities are much more specialised than larger cities in their manufacturing production. More generally, Kolko demonstrates that larger cities are more service oriented and smaller ones more manufacturing oriented.

For six size categories (over 2.5 million, 1 -2.5 million, ... < .25 million, non-metro counties) Kolko shows that the ratio of manufacturing to business service activity rises from .68 to 2.7 as size declines, where manufacturing and business services account for 35% of local private employment. The other 65% of local employment is in "non-traded" activity whose shares don't vary across cities – consumer services, retail, wholesale, construction, utilities.

Concentration of Industry

In a paper Ellison and Glaeser model the problem using USA data, to determine the extent of clustering of plants within an industry due to either industryspecific natural advantages or spillovers among plants. Plants locate across space so as to maximise profits and profits depend on area specific natural advantage, spillovers, and an i.i.d. drawing from Weibul distribution. The idea is to explain the joint importance of spillovers and natural advantage in geographic concentration. Geographic concentration for industry j is $Gj = \Sigma_i (s_{ji} - x_i)^2$, where s_{ji} is the share of industry j in employment in location i and x_i is location share in total national employment (to standardise for location size). Where $0 \leq \gamma^{na} \leq 1$ represents the importance of natural advantage, where the variance in relative profitability of a location is proportional to γ^{na} and γ^{s} represents the fraction of pairs of firms in an industry between which a spillover exists, under their assumptions, Ellison and Glaeser show that

$$E\left[G_j\right] = (1 - \Sigma_i x_i^2)\,(\gamma_j + (1 - \gamma_j)\,H_j) \qquad (5)$$

$$\gamma \equiv \gamma^{na} + \gamma^{s} - \gamma^{s}\gamma^{na}$$

where H_j is the standard Hirschman-Herfindahl index of plant industrial concentration in industry j. So $E[G_j]$ adjusts γ_j for variations in location size $(1-\Sigma x_i^2)$ and industry concentration H. Using (5) and estimates of G_j, H_j, and $(1-\Sigma x_i^2)$ the empirical part of their paper calculates γ_φ for all 3- or 4-digit manufacturing industries across states and countries. They show for 4-digit industries that $G > (1-\Sigma x_i^2)$ in 446 of 459 industries, where $G \leq (1-\Sigma x_i^2)$ only if $\gamma \leq 0$. That is, almost all industries display some degree of spatial concentration due to either natural advantage or spillovers. Second they argue that 25% of industries are highly concentrated ($\gamma \leq 05$) and 43% are not highly concentrated ($\gamma \leq .02$). In a later article, Ellison and Glaeser argue that, based on econometric results relating location choices to natural advantage measures, 10-20% of γ in eq. (5) is accounted for by natural advantage. The rest is due to intra-industry spillovers, a rather critical finding in urban analysis indicating the importance of understanding the nature of scale externalities.

In an important paper, Duranton and Overman, look at geographic concentration using British data. Rather than model the underlying stochastic process of industrial location under specific assumptions to yield a specific index, Duranton and Overman take a non-parametric approach, where they also focus on how to test statistically whether industries are significantly concentrated. They calculate the distribution of all pair-wise distances between plants in an industry. Distributions shifted to the left have a greater concentration of short pair-wise distances and are more spatially concentrated. The authors have the advantage of knowing "exact" plant locations (basically within a city block or so), rather than having to rely on, say, county locations which in the US can cover vast distances. They develop a framework to test observed industry distributions against the "counterfactual" of what distributions would look like if firms choose locations randomly, given (a) the set of locations in the UK for industrial plants is limited, (b) bilateral distances between all possible points are not independent, and (c) industry sizes or numbers of plants differ. The framework involves repeated sampling for an industry without replacement from the set of national industrial sites with the sample size equal to industry size. Following that procedure, they construct 95% confidence intervals to test if observed distributions depart from randomness.

Compared to Ellison-Glaeser In practical applications their approach captures a nuanced aspect of spatial clustering. For relatively concentrated industries, the Ellison and Glaeser index is typically dominated by the county with the highest share, telling us the extent to which an industry is concentrated in just one place. The Duranton-Overman approach tells us more generally about spatial clustering over the whole country. So in Ellison and Glaeser, an industry which has a high concentration in one county but is otherwise very dispersed across the 3000 USA counties may look more concentrated than an industry which is concentrated in, say 3-4 nearby counties, with little representation elsewhere. But the latter would be well represented in Duranton and Overman.

Cities and Growth

To establish the links between cities, growth, urbanisation, urban concentration and policy, we look at models in which cities are a defined unit, endogenous in number and size. These are systems of cities models which date to Henderson, with a variety of substantial contributors to further development. Here we outline the model in Black and

Henderson which is an endogenous growth model of cities, examining the growth-urban connection.

Systems of cities at a point in time

Consider a large economy composed of two types of cities, where there are many cities of each type and each type is specialised in the production of a specific type of traded good. Here we will see why and when there is specialisation momentarily; the generalisation to many types of goods and cities is straightforward. To simplify the growth story, each firm is composed of a single worker. In a city type 1, in any period, the output of firm *i* in a type 1 city is

$$X_{1i} = D_1 \, (n_1^{\delta_1} h_1^{\psi_1}) \, h_{1i}^{\phi_1}, \; 0 < \delta_1 < \frac{1}{2} \qquad (6)$$

h_{1i} is the human capital of the worker and is his input in the production process. A worker-firm is subject to two local externalities. First is own industry localisation economies, the level of which depends on the total number of worker-firms, n_1, in this representative type 1 city. There is a large literature on microfoundations of localisation economies, with an excellent analysis and review in Duranton and Puga. While the concepts are discussed in Marshall, the formal literature dates to Fujita and Ogawa who model micro-foundations as exogenous information spillovers that enhance productivity but decay with spatial distance between plants. Such spillovers can be made endogenous with the volume of costly "contacts" being a firm choice variable. But the modern literature on micro-foundations as reviewed in Duranton and Puga moves on to try to model why contacts matter, rather than just assuming they matter.

In this section spatial decay is all or nothing – no decay within the city's; 100% across cities. As such in (6), n_1 could represent the total volume of local spillover communications, where δ_1 is the elasticity of firm output with respect to n_1. The restriction $\delta_1 < 1/2$ ensures a unique solution in an economy composed of many type 1 cities. A larger δ_1 results in all X_1 production crowding into one city.

Note the production process ignores land, collapsing the central business district [CBD] to a point. There is a recent literature building upon Fujita and Ogawa where firm density is endogenous in a spatial CDB with information spillover decay. There market equilibrium density is non-optimal because firms in making location decisions don't recognise that choices leading to greater densities would enhance information spillovers. The issue of central city design and zoned density is an important one in the design of cities in developing countries. But this review focuses on other issues.

The second externality in (6) derives from h_1, the average level of human capital in the city, which represents local knowledge spillovers. $h_1^{\psi_1}$ could be thought of as the richness of information spillovers $n_1^{\delta_1}$, so that knowledge enhances (multiplies) local information spillovers, or gives better information. Alternatively it could just represent the level of local technology, which increases as average education increases locally.

Given this simple formulation the wage of worker i in city type 1 is

$$W_{1i} = X_{1i} \tag{7}$$

In an economy of identical individual workers in type 1 cities, individuals will all have the same human capital level (either exogenously in a static context, or endogenously in a growth context). Thus total city output is

$$X_1 = D_1 h_1^{\phi_1+\psi_1} n_1^{1+\delta_1} \tag{8}$$

Equilibrium city sizes

Equations (6) and (8) embody the scale benefits of increases in local employment, where output per worker is an increasing function of local own industry scale. Determinant city sizes arise because of scale diseconomies in city living, including per capita infrastructure costs, pollution, accidents, crime, and commuting costs. In Henderson those are captured in a general cost of housing function, but most urban models consider an explicit internal spatial structure of cities. As noted all production occurs at a point, the CBD. Surrounding the CBD in equilibrium in local land markets is a circle of residents each on a lot of unit size. People commute back and forth at a constant cost per unit (return) distance of τ. That cost can be from working time, or here an out-of-pocket cost paid in units of X_1.

Equilibrium in the land market is characterised by a linear rent gradient, declining from the center to zero at the city edge where rents (in agriculture) are normalised to zero. Standard analysis dating to Mohring gives us expressions for total city commuting and rents, in terms of city population where:

$$1 \text{ total commuting costs} \doteq bn_1^{3/2} \tag{9}$$

$$\text{total land rents} = 1/2\ bn_1^{3/2} \tag{10}$$

Equation (9) is the critical resource costs, where marginal commuting costs are increasing in city population. Rents are income to, potentially, a city developer.

How do cities form and how are sizes determined? We start with a specific mechanism and discuss how it generalises below, and what happens if such a mechanism isn't present. There is an unexhausted supply of identical city sites in the economy, each owned by a land developer in a nationally competitive urban land development market. A developer for an occupied city collects local land rents, specifies city population, and offers any inducements to firms or people to locate in that city, in competition with other cities in order to maximise profits. Population is freely mobile.

The land developer maximises

$$\max_{n_1,\, T_1} \; profit_1 = 1/2\, bn_1^{3/2} - T_1 n_1$$

$$\text{subject to } W_1 + T_1 - 3/2\, bn_1^{\frac{1}{2}} = I_1 \qquad (11)$$

where T_1 is the per firm subsidy. I_1 is the real income per worker available in equilibrium in national labour markets under free mobility, which a single developer takes as given. In the constraint, I_1 equals wages in (7), plus the subsidy, less per worker rents plus commuting costs paid from (9) and (10). Maximising with respect to T_1 and n_1 and imposing perfect competition in national land markets so $profit_1 = 0$ ex post, yields

$$T_1 = 1/2\, bn_1^{\frac{1}{2}} \qquad (12)$$

$$n^{*} = (\delta_1 2b^{-1} D_1)^{2/(1-2\delta_1)} h_1^{2\varepsilon_1} \tag{13}$$

$$\varepsilon_1 \equiv \frac{\phi_1 + \psi_1}{1 - 2\delta_1} \tag{14}$$

This solution has a variety of properties heralded in the urban literature. First it reflects the Henry George Theorem, here the transfer per worker/firm exactly equals the gap ($\delta_1 W_1$) between social and private marginal of labour to the city, and that subsidy which prices externalities is exactly financed out of collected land rents at efficient city size. That is, total land rents cover the cost of subsidies needed to price externalities, as well as the costs of local public goods in a model where good goods are added in. Second the efficient size in (13) is the point where real income, I_1, peaks, as an inverted *U* - shape function of city size, as illustrated in Figure 3.

If $\delta_1 < 1/2$, we can show that I_1 is a single-peaked function of n_1, so n_1^{*} is the unique efficient size. If $\delta_1 > 1/2$ in essence there will only be one type 1 city in the economy, because net scale economies are unbounded. Given n_1^{*} is the size where I_1 peaks, n_1^{*} is a free mobility equilibrium—a worker moving to another city would lower real income in that city and be worse off. Finally city size is increasing in technology improvements: τ declining, δ_1 rising, D_1 rising, or local knowledge accumulation (h_1) rising. By substituting in the constraint in (11), we can define relationships among real income, wages, and human capital. Substituting in first for T_1 and then n_1 we get

$$I_1 = W_1 - bn^{1/2} = (1 - 2\delta)\, W_1 = Q_1 h_1^{\varepsilon_1} \tag{15}$$

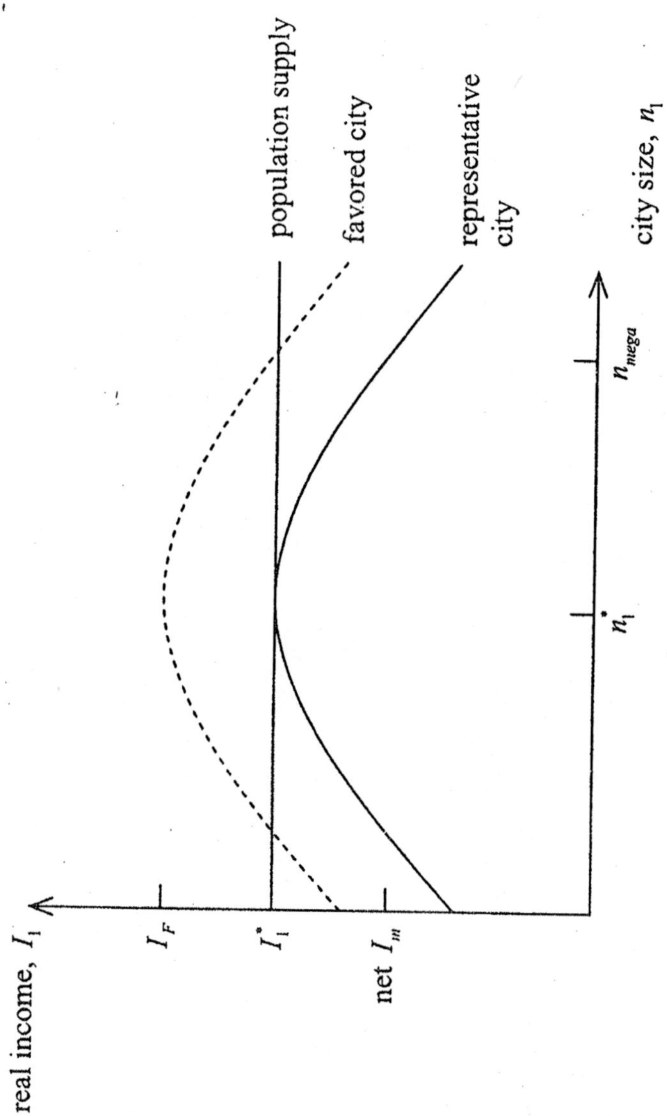

Figure 3a. City sizes: favoured cities

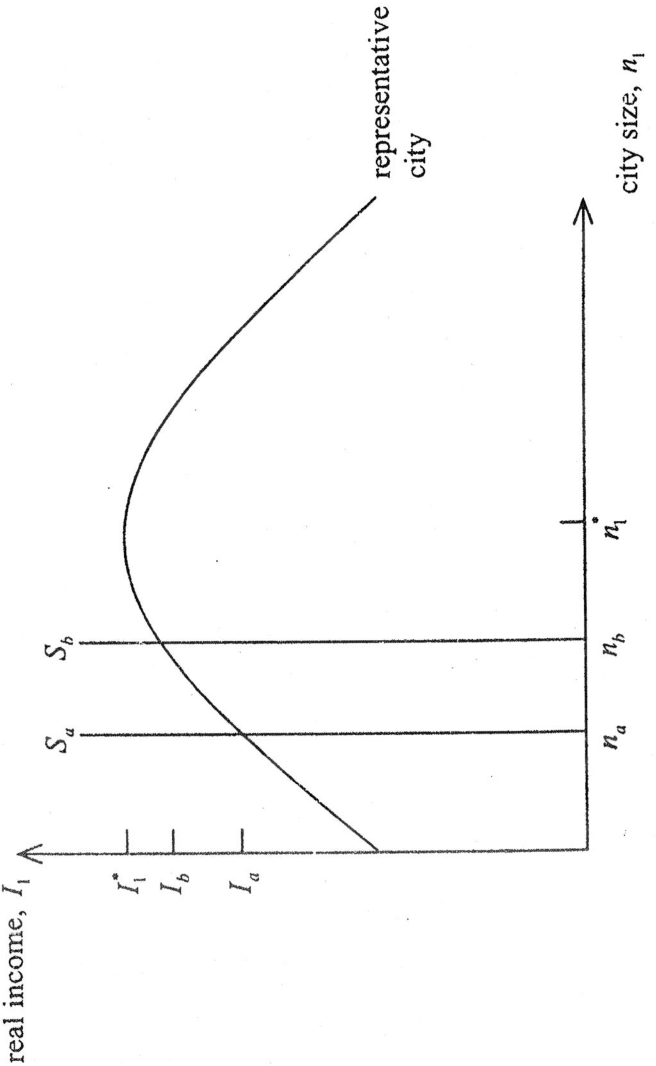

Figure 3a. City Sizes: migration restriction

where Q_1 is a parameter cluster. Note real income is wages deflated by urban living costs; and that real income rises with human capital.

Institutions and city size

Henderson have specified the equilibrium in national land markets, given competitive developers. Helsley and Strange put this in proper context, specifying the city development game, determining how many cities will form and what their sizes (n^*) will be. Henderson and Becker show that the resulting solutions are (1) Pareto efficient, (2) the only coalition proof equilibria in the economy, (3) unique under appropriate parameters, and (4) free mobility ones where the developer specified populations are self-enforcing. They also show that, under appropriate conditions, such outcomes arise (1) in a self-organised economy with no developers where city governments can exclude residents to maximise the welfare of the representative local voter, (2) in a growing economy where developers form new cities and old cities are governed by local governments. Note for developing countries the key ingredients: either national land markets must be competitive with developers free to form new cities or atomistic settlements can arise freely and local autonomous governments can limit their populations as they grow. Absent such institutions, cities only form through "self-organisation".

In the model here with perfect mobility of resources, the result is potentially enormously oversized cities. Nash equilibrium city size in atomistic worker migration decisions lies between efficient size, n^*, and a limit size to the right, n_{max}, where city size is so large with such enormous diseconomies that the population is indifferent between being in a rural settlement of size 1 (the size of a community formed by a defecting migrant) and $n_{max.}$ That is, given an inverted-*U* shape to real income I_1 self organisation has cities at the right of the peak n^*, potentially at n_{max} where $I_1 (n = 1) = I_1 (n = n_{max})$. The problem is one of co-ordination failure.

Consider a large economy with growing population, where, in size, all cities are at or just beyond n^*. Timely formation of the next city to accommodate this population growth requires en mass movement of population from existing cities into a new city of size, n^*. Without co-ordination in the form of developers or city governments, no such en mass movement is possible, so people wait to migrate from existing cities to a new city until existing cities have all grown to n_{max}, where it pays individual migrants to exit to a cities to set up their own tiny "city".

Of course at that "bifurcation point", in equilibrium these milling migrants coalesce into 1 or more new cities of size greater than or equal to n^*, at which point, again, all then existing cities start to grow again with national population growth until they too hit the bifurcation point n_{max}. This dismal process is what faces countries where local autonomy and national markets are poorly functioning, so that there are no market or institutional mechanisms to co-ordinate en mass movements of people.

Other city types

In Black and Henderson, X_1 city type 1 is an input into production of the single final good in the economy, X_2 (from which, hence in a growth context human capital is also "produced"). In many models all outputs of specialised city types are final consumption goods. But here we follow Black and Henderson, without loss of generality. X_2 is produced in type 2 cities where the output for worker/firm j is correspondingly

$$X_{2j} = D_2 \, (n_2^{\delta_2} h_2^{\psi_2}) \, h_{2j}^{\theta_2} \, X_1^{1-\alpha} \qquad (16)$$

As in type 1 cities, per worker output is subject to own industry local scale externalities and to local knowledge spillovers. However now there is an intermediate input, X_{1j}, which is the numeraire good with X_{1j} priced at P in national markets. The analysis of city sizes and formation for type 2 cities proceeds as for city type 1, with corresponding expressions, other than the addition of an expression for P in n_2^* and I_2 and a restriction for an inverted U - shape to I_2 that $\delta_2 < \alpha/2$.

In a static context the model is closed by utilising the national full employment constraint

$$m_1 n_1 + m_2 n_2 = N \qquad (17)$$

where m_1 and m_2 are the numbers of each type of city and N is national population. The second equation (to solve the 3 unknowns P, m_1 and m_2) equates real incomes as in equation (15) across cities ($I_1 = I_2$) where individual workers move across cities to equalise real incomes. Finally there is an equation where national demand equals supply in either the market. That is, the supply, $m_1 X_1$ equals the demand for X_1 as an intermediate input, $m_2 n_2 x_1$ and for producing commuting costs ($m_1 bn_1^{3/2} + m_2 (bn_2^{3/2})$) from eq. (9). In this specific model, the solution yields values of m_1, m_2 and P that are functions of parameters and h_1 and h_2. In a static context of identical workers, one would impose $h = h_1 = h_2$.

In the static context where, labour mobility requires $I_1 = I_2$, in the larger type of city, say type 1, commuting and land rent costs will be higher. Thus, if real incomes are equalised, from (15), $W_1 > W_2$ as a compensating differential for higher living costs. Firms in type 1 cities are willing to pay higher wages because type 1 cities offer them greater scale benefits. Empirical evidence shows as cities move from a small size (say, 50,000) to very large metro areas, the cost-of-living typically doubles, explaining the fact that nominal wages also double.

Policy makers may favour large cities because they view them as "more productive". Indeed for an industry found in smaller towns, it may be that the externalities they face in equations (6) or (16) may be higher in a larger city. However that doesn't mean they locate there. Although externalities may be higher, in order for them to locate there, it must be sufficiently relatively higher to afford the higher wage and land rents, compared to a smaller city. If not, their profit maximising or cost minimising location is the smaller city. Specialisation. This analysis presumes cities specialise in production. That is an equilibrium outcome under a variety of conditions.

In the model described so far, there are no costs of inter-city trade: no costs of shipping X_1 as inputs to X_2 type cities and shipping X_2 back as retail goods in X_1 type cities. All transport costs are internal to the city, given the relative greater importance of commuting costs in modern economies. Given that and given scale economies are internal to the industry, any specialised city (formed by a developer) out-competes any mixed city. The heuristic argument is simple. Consider any mixed city with $\tilde{n}_1$ and $\tilde{n}_2$ workers in industry 1 and 2. Split that city into two specialised cities, one with just $\tilde{n}_1$ people and the other with just $\tilde{n}_2$. Scale economies are undiminished but per worker commuting costs are lower in the specialised cities compared to the old larger mixed cities, so real incomes are higher in each specialised city compared to the old city.

Having own industry, or localisation economies is a sufficient but not necessary condition for specialisation. Industries can instead all have "urbanisation" economies where scale depends on total local employment. However if the degree of urbanisation economies differs across industries then each industry has a different efficient local scale and is better off in a different size specialised city than any mixed city. Mixed cities occur more in situations where each good has localisation economies enhanced by separate spillovers from the other industry or sharing of some common public infrastructure.

A basic problem in these urban models is the lack of nuance on transport costs. Either transport costs of goods across cities is zero (X_1 and X_2) or infinite. A recent innovation is to have generalised transport costs (without a specific geography) where the cost of transporting a unit of X_1 to an X_2 is t_1 and the cost of shipping X_2 back to an X_1 city is t_2, an innovation due to Abdel-Rahman in a model similar to the one used here (one intermediate and one final good) and then generalised by Xiong and Anas and Xiong.

Now whether there are specialised as opposed to diversified cities depends on the level of t_1 and t_2. At appropriate points as t_1 or $t_2$or both rise from zero, X_1 and X_2 will collocate (in developer run cities). More generally with a spectrum of, say, final products, we would expect that some products with low enough t's will always be produced in specialised cities, some high enough t's will be in all cities, and some with middle range t's will be produced in some cities but not others. No one has yet simulated this more complex outcome.

Replicability and national policy

At the national level in a large economy with many cities, at the limit, there are constant returns to scale, or replicability. If national population doubles, the numbers of cities of each type and national output of each good simply doubles, with individual city sizes, relative prices and real incomes unchanged .With two goods and two factors, basic international trade theorems hold. This gives an urban flavour to national policies. For example trade protection policies favouring industry X_1 produced in relatively large size cities over industry X_2 produced in smaller type cities will alter national output composition towards X_1 production and increase the number of large relative to small cities. National urban concentration will rise. Similarly subsidizing an input such as capital for a high tech product, X_1, again, say, produced in a larger type of city will cause the numbers of that type of city to increase, raising urban concentration.

Growth in a System of Cities

Black and Henderson specify a dynastic growth model where dynastic families grow in numbers at rate g over time starting from size 1. If *c* is per person family consumption, the objective function is

$$\int_0^{\infty} \frac{c(t)^{1-\sigma} - 1}{1-\sigma} e^{-(\rho-g)t} dt$$

where ρ (>g) is the discount rate. Dynasties can splinter (as long as they share their capital stock on an equal per capita basis) and the problem can be put in an overlapping generations context with equivalent results, under a Galor and Zeira "joy of giving" bequest motive.

The only capital in the model is human capital and as such there is no market for it. Intra-family behaviour substitutes for a capital market. Specifically families allocate their total stock of human capital (H) and members across cities, where Z proportion of family members go to type 1 cities (taking 1 of the Zh_1e^{gt} of the H with them) and (1–Z). go to type 2 cities (taking (1–Z) Zh_2e^{gt} with them). Additions to the family stock come from the equation of motion where the cost of additions, PH , equals family income ($Zh_1e^{gt} I_1$ + (1-Z)$e^{gt} I_2$) less the value of family consumption of X_2, or Pc e^{gt}. Constraints prohibiting consumption of human capital, non-transferability except to newborns, and non-transferability within families across city types (either directly or indirectly through migration) are non-binding on equilibrium paths.

Families allocate their populations across types of cities, with low human capital types (say h_1) "lending" some of their share ($h = H/e^{gt}$) to high human capital types (say h_2). High human capital types with higher incomes ($I_2 > I_1$ if $h_2 > h_1$) repay low human capital types so $c_1 = c_2 = c$ (governed by the family matriarch). This in itself is an interesting development story, where rural families diversify migration destinations and remittances home are a substantial part of earnings. In Black and Henderson if capital markets operate perfectly for human capital or capital is physical and capital markets operational, one dynastic family could move entirely to, say, type 1 cities and lend some of their human capital to another dynastic family in type 2 cities. With no capital market, each dynastic family must operate as its own informal capital market and spread itself across cities.

In this context Black and Henderson show that, regardless of scale or point in the growth process, h_1/h_2 and I_1/I_2 are fixed ratios, dependent on θ_i eq. (6) and (16). As θ_1/θ_2 (the relative returns to capital) rises, h_1/h_2, I_1/I_2 and also

n_1/n_2 rise. Z and m_1/m_2 are all fixed ratios of parameters θ_1, δ_1 and α under equilibrium growth. Equilibrium and optimal growth differ because the private returns to education in a city, θ_i, differ from the social returns, $\theta_i + \psi_i$. But local governments can't intervene successfully to encourage optimal growth. Why? With free migration and "no slavery", if a city invests to increase its citizens' education, a person can take their human capital and move to another city. This model hazard problem discourages internalisation of education externalities.

Growth Properties

Cities

From eq. (13), equilibrium city size in type 1 cities is a function of the per person human capital level, h_1, in type 1 cities. After solving out the model (for P), the same will be true of type 2 cities. City sizes grow as *h1 and* h_2 grow, where, under equilibrium growth given h_1/h_2 is a fixed ratio, $\dot{h}_1/h_1 = \dot{h}_2/h_2$, where a dot represents a time derivative. Then

$$\frac{\dot{n}_2}{n_2} = \frac{\dot{n}_1}{n_1} = 2\varepsilon_1 \frac{\dot{h}}{h} \tag{18}$$

where $\dot{n}_i/n_i$ is the growth rate of efficient sizes n_i^*. For the number of cities, the issue is whether growth in individual sizes absorbs the national population growth, or more cities are needed. Given

$$\frac{\dot{m}_1}{m_1} = \frac{\dot{m}_2}{m_2} = g - \frac{\dot{n}_i}{n_i} = g - 2\varepsilon_1 \frac{\dot{h}}{h}, \tag{19}$$

the numbers of cities grow if $g > \dot{n}_i/n_i$ Note growth in numbers and sizes of cities is "parallel" by type, so the relative size distribution of cities is constant over time.

Economy

Ruling out explosive or divergent growth, there are two types of growth equilibria. Either the economy converges to a steady state level, or it experiences endogenous steady-state growth. Convergence to a level occurs if $\varepsilon = \varepsilon_1 (1-(\gamma+2\delta_2)) + \varepsilon_2(\gamma+2\delta_2)) < 1$ where ε is a weighted average of the individual city type. In that case at the steady-state, $\bar{h}$, $n_i/n_i = 0$ and $m_i/m_i = g$ or only the numbers but not sizes of cities grow just like in exogenous growth. If $\varepsilon = 1$ then there is steady-state growth, where

$$\bar{\gamma}^h = \dot{h}/h = \frac{A-\rho}{\sigma}$$

where the transversality condition requires $A > \rho$. In that case

$$\dot{n}_i / n_i = 2\varepsilon_1^{\left(\frac{A-\rho}{\sigma}\right)}$$

or cities grow at a constant rate and their numbers also increase if

$$g > 2\varepsilon_1^{\left(\frac{A-\rho}{\sigma}\right)}$$

This "knife-edge" result of whether there is endogenous growth or not dependent on the value of ε is not essential. For example in Rossi-Hansberg and Wright endogenous growth can occur more generally in a context where human capital accumulation involves worker time and the growth rate of human capital is a log-linear function of the fraction of time devoted to human capital accumulation, as opposed to production.

Extensions

There are three major extensions to the basic systems of cities models. First people may differ in terms of inherent productivity or in terms of endowments. Second, while we have discussed the issue of city specialisation versus diversification we haven't developed insights into a more nuanced role of small highly specialised cities versus large diversified metro areas in an economy.

Types of workers

Turning to the first extension, Henderson has physical capital as a factor of production owned by capitalists who needn't reside in cities. Equilibrium city size reflects a market trade-off between the interests of city workers who have an inverted *U*-shape to utility as a function of the size of the city they live in and capitalists whose returns to capital rise indefinitely with city size. There is a political economy story, where capitalists collectively in an economy have an incentive to limit the number of cities, thus forcing larger city sizes.

Helsley and Strange have a matching model between the attributes of entrepreneurs and workers and Henderson and Becker a related two class model. Again the two class model yields a conflict between the city sizes that maximize the welfare of one versus another group, which is resolved in competitive national land development markets. In a different approach Abdel-Rahman and Wang, Abdel-Rahman and later Black look at high and low skill workers who are used in differing proportions in production of different goods.

Black has one traded good produced with just low skill labour and a second traded good produced with high skill workers and inputs of a local non-traded good produced with just low skill workers. High skill workers generate production externalities in the form of knowledge spillovers for all traded goods. In Black, urban specialisation with all high skill workers concentrated in one type of city producing the first type of good is efficient; but a separating equilibrium that would sustain this pattern, where low skill workers and low tech production stay in their own type of city is not always sustainable. Black characterises conditions under which a separating equilibrium will emerge.

It is important to note that there is a much more developed literature on inequality induced by neighbourhood selection, where the characteristics of neighbours affect skill acquisition. That leads to segregation of talented or wealthier families by neighbourhood and can help transmit economic status across generations, promoting inter-generational income inequality.

Metro areas

Simple indices of urban diversity indicate that smaller cities are very specialised and larger cities highly diversified. So the question is what is the role of large metro areas in an economy and their relationship to smaller cities. Henderson and Duranton have a first nature - second nature world, where every city has a first nature economic base and footloose industries cluster in these different first nature cities. In general the largest centers are those attracting the most footloose production to their first nature center.

The Dixit-Stiglitz model opened up an avenue to look at large metro areas as having a base of diversified intermediate service inputs, which generate scale-diversity benefits for local final goods producers. That initial idea was developed in Abdel-Rahman and Fujita and has led to a set of papers focused on the general issue of what activities, under what circumstances are out-sourced.

Theory and empirical evidence suggest that as local market scale increases, final producers will in-house less of their service functions. The resulting increased outsourcing encourages competition and diversity in the local business service market, encouraging further out-sourcing. In terms of incorporating this into the role of metro areas versus smaller cities, Davis has a two-region model, a coastal internationally exporting region and an interior natural resource rich region. There are specialised manufacturing activities which, for production and final sale, require business service activities, summarised as headquarters functions. Headquarters purchase local Dixit-Stiglitz intermediate services such as R&D, marketing, financing, exporting, and so on. Headquarters' activity is in port cities in the coastal region.

The issue is whether manufacturing activities are also in these ports versus in specialised coastal hinterland cities versus in specialised interior cities. Scale economies in manufacturing and headquarters activities are different and independent of each other, so that, based on scale considerations, these activities would be in separate specialised cities. However if the costs of interaction between headquarters and manufacturing functions are extremely high, then both manufacturing and headquarters activities can be found together in coastal port cities. Otherwise they will be in separate types of cities. In that case, manufacturing cities will be in coastal hinterlands if costs of headquarters-manufacturing interaction are high relative to shipping natural resources to the coast. However if natural resource shipping costs are relatively high, then manufacturing cities will be found in the interior.

Duranton and Puga have a very similar model of functional specialisation, without the regional flavour. If there is specialisation, then there are headquarter cities where headquarters outsource local services in diversified large metro areas, while production occurs in specialised manufacturing cities.

In a different paper Duranton and Puga develop an entirely different and stimulating view of large metro areas. In an economy there are m types of workers who have skills each specific to producing one of m products. Specialised cities have one type of worker producing the standardised product for that type of worker subject to localisation economies. Diversified cities have some of all types of workers. Existing firms at any instant die at an exogenously given rate; and, in a steady-state, new firms are their replacement. New firms don't know "their type"—what types of workers they match best with and hence what final product they would be best off producing. To find their type they need to experiment by trying the different technologies. New firms have a choice. They can locate in a diversified city with low localisation economies in any one sector.

In a diversified city they can experiment with a new process each period until they find their ideal process. At that point they relocate to a city specialised in that product, with thus high localisation economies for that product. Alternatively new firms can experiment by moving from specialised city to specialised city with high localisation economies, but face a relocation cost each time. If relocation costs are high, the advantage during their experimental period is to be in a diversified city. This leads to an urban configuration of experimental diversified metro areas and other cities which are specialised in different standardised manufacturing products.

The Duranton and Puga model captures a key role of large diversified metro areas consistent with the data. They are incubators where new products are born and where new firms learn. Once firms have matured then they typically do relocate to more specialised cities. This also captures the product-life cycle for firms in terms of location patterns. Fujita and Ishii document the location patterns of Japanese and Korean electronics plants and headquarters. In a spatial hierarchy mega-cities house headquarters activitiesand experimental activity. Smaller Japanese or Korean towns have specialised, more standardised high tech production processes and low tech activity is off-shore.

Urbanisation and Growth

City sizes grow with improvements in technology but, absent stochastic elements, individual cities grow in parallel, with the relative numbers of different types of cities and the relative size distribution of cities time invariant. Urbanisation involves resources shifting from an agricultural to an urban sector. The dual economy models dating back to Lewis look at sectoral change but are really static models. They focus on the question of urban " bias", or the effect of government policies on the urban-rural divide, and the efficient rural-urban allocation of population at a point in time. These two sector models have an exogenously given "sophisticated" urban sector and a "backward" rural sector. In these models, the marginal product of labour in the urban sector is assumed to exceed that in the rural sector. Arbitrage in terms of labour migration is limited by inefficient labour allocation rules such as farm workers being paid average rather than marginal product or artificially limited absorption in the urban sector. The literature focuses on the effect on migration from the rural to urban sector of policies such as rural-urban terms of trade, migration restrictions, wage subsidies, and the like.

The final and most complex versions of dual sector models are in Kelley and Williamson and Becker, Mills, and Williamson, which are fully dynamic CGE models. They have savings behaviour and capital accumulation, population growth, and multiple economic sectors in the urban and rural regions. Labour markets within sector and across regions are allowed to clear. The models analyse the effects of a wider array of policy instruments, including sector specific trade or capital market policies for housing, industry, services and the like. However the starting point is again an exogenously given initial urban-rural productivity gap, sustained initially by migration costs and exogenous skill acquisition. Ongoing urbanisation is the result of exogenous forces—technological change favouring the urban sector or changes in the terms of trade favouring the urban sector.

As models of urbanisation, these dual economy ones are a critical step but they suffer obvious defects. First how the dual starting point arises is never modelled. Second, and related to the first, there are no forces for agglomeration that would naturally foster industrial concentration in the urban sector. Finally although the models have two sectors there is really little spatial or regional aspect to the problem. There is a new generation of two-sector models, the core-periphery models, which attempt to address some of these defects. The core-periphery models ask under what conditions in a two-region country, industrialisation, or "urbanisation" is spread over both regions versus concentrated in just one region. Industrialisation may occur in both regions or in only one region. One region can become "backward" (under certain assumptions), or, if not backward (lower real incomes) at least relatively depopulated. But these are outcomes solved for in the model. Third the models have some notion of space represented as transport costs of goods between regions. The models are focused on a key developmental issue—the initial development of a core (coastal) region and a periphery (hinterland) region, as technology improves (transport costs fall) from a situation starting with two identical regions. Some work also analyses how under certain conditions, with further technological improvements, there can be reversal.

Unfortunately, to date core-periphery models have been almost exclusively uni-dimensional in focus, asking what happens to core-periphery development as transport costs between regions decline. They are not focused on other forms of technological advance, let alone endogenous technological development. With a few exceptions, Fujita and Thisse and Baldwin, the models are static. But even in these exceptions, there is still the focus on exogenous changes in transport technology.

Compared to the older dual economy literature, generally core-periphery models have no policy considerations of interest to development economists, such as the impact of wage subsidies, rural-urban terms of trade, capital market imperfections. An exception is that some papers have examined the impact on core-periphery structures of reducing barriers to international trade, such as tariff reduction, and papers are starting to explore issues of capital market imperfections. The core-periphery model is an important innovation in bringing back the role of transport costs, largely ignored in urban systems work, to the forefront. The dual economy and core-periphery models are regional models, with limited urban implications. Urban models are focused on the city formation process, where the urban sector is composed of numerous cities, endogenous in number and size. Efficient urbanisation and growth require timely formation of cities. As policy issues the extent of market completeness in the national markets in which cities form, the role of city governments and developers, the role of inter-city competition, and the role of debt finance and taxation are critical.

Urbanisation With Cities

Here we present a simple two sector model of urbanisation with cities, adapting the model following Henderson and Wang. The urban sector is exactly like the X_1 type of city sector earlier with production technology given in (6). The other sector is food produced in the agriculture sector, which we make now the numeraire (since there may initially be no urban sector). As a result, for type 1 cities in the urban sector, equation (7) for wages, equations (9) and (10) for commuting costs and rents, and equation (15) for income are all redefined to be multiplied by the price of X_1, p. The city size equation is the same, invariant to relative prices. Critical here is

$$I_1 = W_1 \ (1-2\delta_1) = pQ_1 h_1^{\varepsilon_1}$$

for Q_1 a parameter cluster.

Agriculture: Rural output per worker is $D_a h_a^{\psi_a} h_a^{\theta_a}$ or $D_a h_a^{\varepsilon_a}$ so rural wages and real income are

$$W_a = D_a h_a^{\varepsilon_a} \qquad \varepsilon_a \equiv \psi_a + \theta_a \tag{20}$$

As such the rural sector is very simple: no commuting costs, no agglomeration economies and no diminishing returns to land. As in the urban sector, productivity is affected by individual human capital accumulation, $h_a^{\theta_a}$, and by sector knowledge spillovers, $h_a^{\psi_a}$.

Preferences and urbanisation: To have sectoral transformation we need to move away from the world of unitary price and income elasticities, so growth between sectors is not parallel. Here we assume preferences have the form

$$V = (x + a^{\gamma})^{\alpha}, \qquad \gamma, \alpha < 1 \tag{21}$$

where a is consumption of agricultural products. In (21) agricultural demand is income inelastic, with a demand function

$$a = \gamma^{\frac{1}{1-\gamma}} \rho^{\frac{1}{1-\gamma}}. \tag{22}$$

Human Capital Market, Migration, Savings

The urbanisation process as a "transitory" phenomenon is not a steady state process. To simplify, following much of the literature, we introduce an explicit market for human capital, as though human capital investments were not embodied. And we assume an exogenous savings rate, s. For the former, now each person in the economy has a human capital level, h, which can be used in production or can be loaned out. The capital market equalises capital returns across sectors so

$$r = p\, \theta_1\, D_1\, h_1^{\theta_1 + \psi_1 - 1}\, n_1^{\delta_1} = \theta_a\, D_a\, h_a^{\theta_a + \psi_a - 1}.$$

Substituting in for n_1 from (13)

$$p = Q_2\, h_a^{\varepsilon_a} h_1^{1-\varepsilon_1} \tag{23}$$

recalling $\varepsilon_a = \psi_a + \theta_a$ and $\varepsilon_1 \equiv (\theta_1 + \psi_1)$. Q_2 is a parameter cluster.

Free migration requires urban incomes defined to be gross human capital returns to equal the same for agriculture, or $I_1 + r(h - h_1) = W_a + r(h - h_a)$. Utilising (15)

$$W_1 - W_a = pbn^{1/2} + r(h_1 - h_a) \tag{24}$$

With free migration equalising real incomes across sectors, urban wages exceed rural wages by cost-of-living differences, and by a factor compensating if human capital requirements in the urban sector exceed those in the rural.

If we substitute in (24) for W_1, W_a, p and r rearrange, we get

$$h_a = h_1 \cdot \frac{\theta_a}{\theta_1}\left(\frac{1-\theta_1-2\delta}{1-\theta_a}\right) \tag{25}$$

A sufficient condition for $h_1 > h > h_a$ or the urban sector to be human capital intensive, is that $\theta_1 > \theta a$, as assumed.

To close the model requires three relationships. First is national full employment of capital and labour so

$$n_a h_a + n_1 m_1 h_1 = hN \tag{26a}$$

$$n_a + m_1 n_1 = N \tag{26b}$$

where m_1, as before, is the number of type 1 cities and N is the national population. The third equation equates the demand for food equal to its supply. But that requires a digression on how human capital is produced and nature of savings.

We assume human capital production in each sector is made from goods from that sector, which is almost like assuming, for a fixed savings rate, a fixed fraction of working time in any sector is needed to produce a unit of human capital. Second, we assume savings at the rate s are from wage income net of rental costs, or from $I_1 - rh_1$, and $W_a - rh_a$, which magnitudes are equalised by migration. Thus in the food market total production $n_a D_a h_a^{\varepsilon_a}$ equals food consumption demand

$$N\ (\rho\gamma)^{\frac{1}{1-\gamma}}$$

plus agricultural savings, or

$$n_a D_a h_a^{\varepsilon_a} = N\ (p\gamma)^{\frac{1}{1-\gamma}} + sn_a\ (W_a - rh_a)$$

Substituting in for r, for p from (22), $D_a h_a^{\varepsilon_a}$ from (20) and for h_a from (25) we get

$$n_a / N = Q_3 h_1^{\frac{\gamma\varepsilon_a - \varepsilon_1}{1-\gamma}} \tag{27}$$

with Q_3 a parameter cluster. We assume $\gamma\varepsilon_a - \varepsilon_1 < 0$, so the social returns to human capital in the urban sector exceed those in the rural sector discounted by γ. With economic growth in human capital, the rural sector diminishes. Note in (27) for there to be an urban sector, h_1 must be large enough so $n_a/N < 1$. Of course h_1 is linked to h through (26a) where with substitutions

$$h_1 \left(1 - Q_4 \, h_1^{\frac{\gamma \varepsilon_a - \varepsilon_1}{1-\gamma}} \right) = h \quad (28)$$

where given $\gamma\varepsilon_a - \varepsilon_1 < 0$, $dh_1/dh > 0$ once there is an urban sector. 4 Q is a parameter cluster.

Urban growth and transformation

Once an urban sector exists, city growth is $\dot{n}_1/n_1 = 2\, \varepsilon_1 \dot{h}_1$, so cities grow with human capital accumulation. The growth in number of cities now depends on the rate of urbanisation, as well. Combining (26a) and (26b), with differentiation:

If we differentiate (27) for $\dot{n}_a/n_a$ and combine this becomes

$$\dot{m}_1/m_1 = g - \dot{n}_1/n_1 + \frac{n_a}{m_1 n_1} \frac{\gamma\varepsilon_a - \varepsilon_1}{1-\gamma} \dot{h}_1/h_1 \quad (29)$$

As before the rate of growth of numbers of cities is increased by national population growth, g , and reduced by growth in individual city sizes. Now it is also enhanced by economic growth which increases relative demand for urban products and draws labor out of agriculture, as captured by the last term in (29).

Economic Growth

Given the savings rule, total human capital increases by

$$\dot{H} = s\left[m_1 n_1 \, (I_1 - rh_1) + n_a \, (W_a - rh_a)\right]$$

Each instant so per person change in capital is $\dot{h}/h = \dot{H}/H - g$. Given $I_1 - rh_1 = W_a - rh_a$, with substitutions we have:

$$\dot{h}/h = sQ_5 h_1^{\varepsilon_a - 1}\left(1\text{-}Q_6 h_1^{\frac{\gamma\varepsilon_a \quad \varepsilon_1}{1-\gamma}}\right)^{-1} - g \tag{30}$$

where $Q_6 < Q_4$, for parameter clusters. In terms of growth, if $\varepsilon_a < 1$ and urbanisation occurs, we have steady state levels given $\dot{h}/h$ declines with increases in h_1, and hence h. If $\varepsilon_a = 1$ we approach steady state growth once h_1 gets large so $n_a N \rightarrow 0$ and the expression in parentheses in (30) approaches 1. However in either case at low levels of development in (27) n_a/N is bounded at 1 where equation (27) defines a critical h_1 and hence h (28), say h_c, below which $n_a/N = 1$. To have steady state levels with urbanisation given we start at $n_a/N = 1$ with $\dot{h}/h = \dot{h}_a/h_a = -g + (1 - \theta_a)\, h_a^{\varepsilon_a - 1}$, requires

$$h_c < (g/(1\text{-}\theta_a))^{\frac{1}{\varepsilon_a - 1}}$$

so we pass the critical h at which urbanisation starts before hitting the potential steady state value of h without urbanisation. Otherwise the economy can be stuck with no urbanisation.

Extensions and Policy Issues

City Sizes

A perpetual debate in particular developing countries is whether certain mega-cities are oversized, squandering national resources that must be allocated to commuting, congestion, and transport in those cities and resulting in low quality of life in the polluted, unsanitary and crowded slums of such cities. In other countries especially former planned economies the debate goes the other way: are cities too small?

The growth connection is straightforward. Either squandered resources in over-sized cities or too small cities with unexploited scale economies mean lower income levels, potentially lower savings, lower capital accumulation and thus lower growth rates. While calculations are tedious, in the steady state growth, where $\gamma' = \dot{h}/h = (A - \rho)/\sigma$, A depends on urban parameters (for example, increasing with human capital returns) and will be lowered if city sizes are inefficient.

Using a simple, partial equilibrium diagram, it is possible to illustrate both issues: the mega-city "problem" and the planned economy problem. The diagrams point to first order effects. For the mega-city problem, suppose there are a, variety of type 1 cities in an economy with free mobility of labor and institutions supporting efficient city formation. In Figure 3a, the representative city has a size n_1^*, where real income as function of city size peaks at I_1^*, tangent to the perfectly elastic national supply curve of labor to the city. Suppose one particular type 1 city is favored relative to the rest. For example it may have special public services compared to other cities financed out of national taxes. Those favours raise the utility, or real income that residents in the favored city potentially receive, shifting up the inverted-U real income curve. That upward shift draws migrants into the city expanding its size to n_{mega}. But at n_{mega}, the net income generated by the city, ignoring its nationally financed favours, is only net I_m. The gap, $I_1^* - I_m$, times the population represents "squandered resources". Of course, such squandering would in general equilibrium affect prices, lowering the height of the population supply curve and the inverted-*U* 's.

A second issue in city formation concerns poor institutions in national land markets and in local governance which limit the number of cities that can form. Suppose that, in villages which might become cities, local governments by institutional restrictions can't expand infrastructure, can't rezone and build on urban fringe land, and can't offer subsidies to incoming firms. And suppose developers can't assemble large tracts of land for development because property rights are ill-defined.

These villages can't grow into cities; nor can entirely new cities form. If the number of cities is bindingly limited, so there are too few cities, all existing cities under free migration are too big. In Figure 3a, suppose we reconsider the figure ignoring the representative city curve and assume all cities have inverted-*U* 's like the favored city. Then, in this reinterpretation of the figure, I_F is the potentially attainable real income in all cities (ignoring general equilibrium effects) if cities could freely form. Given restricted numbers, rather than operating at I_F (with size n_1^*), cities are overcrowded; and in equilibrium they operate at I_1^* (with size n_{mega}), with the same national supply curve of labor as labelled in the figure. The restrictions result in losses related to the gap $I_F - I_1^*$

The planned economy problem is entirely different. Former "planned" economies like China have formal migration restrictions limiting the visas given for rural people to move to cities and limiting migrants access to jobs, housing, medical care and schooling in destination cities to reduce the incentive to migrate. Some former planned economies limited migration through housing provision and land development. If the state provides and allocates all housing assignments, migrants can't move unless housing is provided in the destination.

Countries like China and Russia have very low urban concentration compared to other large countries. Figure 3b captures the essence of the problem. While the representative city has an inverted-*U* where real income is maximised at n_1^*, migration restrictions for cities *a* and *b* restrict sizes to and real incomes to *Ia and* I_b. Au and Henderson estimate these inverted-*U* 's for different types of cities in China in 1997 and find that 30% of cities are significantly undersized – below the lower 95% confidence interval on their equivalent to n_1^*. The productivity losses from being undersized are enormous: 30-50% or more loss in GDP per capita for many cities.

Sequential City Formation and Governance

In a working paper, Henderson and Venables take a new approach to city formation. They assume a context where (1) there is a steady-flow of migrants from rural to urban areas, and (2) urban residence requires a fixed investment in non-malleable, immobile capital (housing, sewers, water mains, etc.). Cities form sequentially without population swings, so migrants all flow first into city 1 until its equilibrium size is reached (abstracting from any on-going technological change), and then all future migrants all go to a second city until its equilibrium size is reached, and so on. This is a very different process than when all resources are mobile: in the usual models in a small economy, when the second city forms, it takes half the population of the first at that instant, and when the third forms it takes one third of the then population of the first two.

Cities grow way past $\dot{n}_1$, shrink back to $\dot{n}_1$, and then grow again, shrink, and on so. With fixed capital, such population swings would mean periods of abandoned housing. With sufficiently high required capital investments all population swings are eliminated in equilibrium. Each new city starts off tiny with no accumulated scale effects and low productivity. It grows steadily absorbing all new rural-urban migrants until its growth interval is complete and it reaches steady state size; then a new city starts off growing from a tiny size.

With sequential city formation without population swings, given discounting of the future, efficient city size requires cities to grow past the equivalent of $\dot{n}_1$ to their steady state size, n_{opt}, at which point real income per worker is declining. Intuitively, growing past $\dot{n}_1$, with declining but still high real income, postpones the formation of a new city with tiny population, no scale effects and very low incomes. The paper then looks at equilibrium city formation in two contexts. First is a situation with no "large agents" in national land markets – no developers and no city governments.

In a model with perfect mobility of resources, city formation with atomistic agents is a disaster due to coordination failure. A new city can only form when old cities are so big that the income levels they offer have fallen to the point where they equal what a person can earn in a city of size one. Having immobile capital presents a commitment device, so individual, sequentially rational builders switch from building in an old city to building in a new one at a "reasonable time".

Real incomes are still equalised across cities through migration. Given big old cities have high nominal incomes and the tiny new one low nominal income, housing rents adjust in old cities to equalise real incomes. Housing rents in old cities change over the growth cycle of a new city, starting very high and then declining. In this context, equilibrium sizes may even be smaller than optimal ones. The deviation from optimum has not to do with coordination failure which is solved despite the absence of "large" agents, but with the present value of externalities from a migrant in an old versus a new city.

With developers or full empowered local governments, externalities are appropriately internalised and city sizes are n_{opt}. However, apart from financing the housing and infrastructure capital, to induce new migrants to move to a new city with its low real income and scale economies in a timely fashion, large agents must subsidize in-migration of worker-firms. To do this they must borrow and, in fact, public debt accumulates over the entire growth interval of a city and only starts to be paid off once it reaches steady state size. Debt ceilings, or limits for cities which are common in many countries curtail subsidies to in-migrants and postpone new city formation. Debt limited cities are too big.

5

Lifestyle in Cities

The changing demographic composition of the population, the desire for an alternative lifestyle to that offered by urban areas and underlying processes of restructuring have resulted in the potential for economic activities to relocate also have a bearing on personal migration.

City Ratings

The calculation of comparison and ratings, increasingly expressed in the form of league tables, is far from new. But, since the 1980s, the rating of cities has reached new heights, with even governments presenting sets of official statistics in the form of league tables and comparative rankings-such as for education and health performance-and employing these ratings in the publicity associated with official statistics, such as recent Regional Trends.

This best-selling publication has been updated several times and reprinted many times, attracting a readership amongst the public as well as professionals concerned with the promotion of cities, with the selling or property in these cities, and with the construction of the city environments which are being assessed. However, the book also appealed to the general public and to companies and organisations who were interested in contemplating business or family moves. The conclusion that Pittsburgh-once seen as the city epitomising the legacy of declining manufacturing industries was the best place to live unsurprisingly challenged public perceptions of the cities of North America and generated considerable and at times legal debates about the merits of the study and the validity of the results and their applications in city promotion.

What marks out the Places Rated Almanac however, is not the actual results, but the fact that it represents the first serious attempt to popularise a statistical ranking of metropolitan areas and to do so on the basis of what has been termed 'quality of life' factors - those elements which define the livability of a place. Earlier research which had also attempted to construct ranks of places in terms of quality of life had been less successful in achieving public acclaim (or notoriety). Smith's and Liu's studies, for example, of the US SMSAs had much greater statistical rigour than the Boyer and Savageau study, but achieved less public impact.

Elsewhere, there has also been a growth in the quality of life indices at a variety of geographical scales which have been generated and have attracted media and public attention. International comparisons have formed the basis of Fortune Magazine's ranking of the world's best cities, whilst a similar title has been applied to Montreal, Seattle and Melbourne from the assessment of livability by the Population Crisis Committee. Indeed, in many of the developed nations, league tables of urban areas have become common. In Britain, not all the studies have focused exclusively on quality of life issues.

Some employ more obvious economic measures-for example, the 'booming town' index with its focus on economic conditions, and the LEAP index of economic activity and potential whilst others, like the Places Rated Almanac, eschew an academic basis and are targeted towards a media and public audience. Amongst these studies there are some which explicitly attempt to measure quality of life. The Northern Lights study marked out a debate in the 1980s about the relative quality of life opportunities in the northern parts of England compared with the southern regions. The research by the quality of life group first at the University of Glasgow and then at Strathclyde University has in many respects become the benchmark of quality of life ratings in Britain. In a series of studies, they have produced league tables of cities, local authority areas and local labour market areas based on an assessment of the extent to which these areas match up to publicly derived lists of attributes of quality of life. Some more popular studies have attempted to replicate the methodology of these studies. Other studies, recognising the growing importance of quality of life ratings, re-imaged themselves on the back of this interest. Reward regional surveys' 'Cost of living index' was relabelled in the early 1990s to become a 'quality of life index', although the basis of the analysis was little changed.

Inevitably, such city ratings attract controversy. First, league tables epitomise the desire for what could be termed a 'reductionist view' of places and their living environments. The representation of the complexity which is urban living by a single value and rank is appealing in an era when politicians, media and public work with simple headlines. But by so doing, such ratings are open to challenge for offering simplicity at the expense of reflecting the multiple facets of a locality.

Secondly, in challenging public perceptions of places, the disparity between people's perceptions of quality of life in a place and the statistical indicators generates scope for debate-or, in more extreme, cases grounds for litigation. Matching its commercial success, Places Rated Almanac, for example, has been criticised on the basis of its conclusions and its methodology, as well as its statistical indicators. Other researchers have attempted to produce new sets of city rankings, having undertaken some variations in method, data or list of comparator locations.

Quality of Life

There is considerable convergence of opinion in the literature that the fundamental context in which cities are currently acting is the heightened mobility of capital. The ability of transnational corporations - and indeed smaller more local organizations - to switch their location of operation around the globe has created a truly global economy. The specific nature of the processes of globalisations and economic restructuring which are operating may continue to be debated, but there is an acceptance that in this context cities are being thrust into new sets of relations to capital; relations in which the relative position of the city is substantially weaker than previously.

The changing nature of the activities being undertaken and their organisation, especially the decline in manufacturing activity and the rise of service sectors, as well as the capacity of capital (and labour) to switch locations has enabled "a new set of local place attributes and new definitions of the accessibility of places to become prominent locational determinants". Associated with the globalising of the economy, cities are becoming more critical agents of economic development. Their greater ability to be flexible and responsive to the changing needs of the markets, technology and culture has provided them with the opportunity to engage with, and respond to, the needs of capital.

Of course, not all locations can respond equally to such forces or opportunities arising from the global changes. The competitiveness of cities reflects not only their current capacity to engage with global capital, but also is a function of their heritage, resulting in a spatially differentiated pattern of competitiveness. The rhetoric of the local is thus embedded within the processes of global accumulation, in what has been described as a fragmented mosaic of uneven development in which competitive places try to secure a lucrative development niche. In this respect, there is scope for quality of life to be a factor which assists in the construction of the niche, and specifically the attraction or retention of fractions of capital which maintain this niche.

Some commentators have tried to operationalise the determinants of this competitiveness. For example,the degree of competitiveness can be viewed as a function of economic determinants (for example, factors of production, location, urban amenities) and strategic determinants (such as governmental effectiveness and institutional flexibility). These approaches offer insights into the elements which shape and constrain the capacity of an area to respond to the external demands of the economy/market in the abstract. Other research focuses on more specific responses, including the interactions between national government policies and local government powers, resources and milieux-what Harvey has termed 'structural coherence' - and organisational responses amongst local institutions and players-as partnerships, regimes-to regulation, especially by the local state.

What is generally accepted is that the task of urban governance has increasingly become the (re)creation of urban conditions sufficiently attractive to lure potential capital into the area. It is within this settingwhat Hall calls the pro-competition zeitgeist of the 1980s and 1990s: the frenetic search for different and novel ways of ensuring that one place can be seen to be more competitive than another-that much of the recent quality of life rankings can be located. The main contribution that quality of life makes in the process of capturing or ensnaring capital lies in the arena of place promotion and marketing, being part of the attempts by cities to forge distinctive images and atmospheres which "act as a lure to both capital and people 'of the right sort'.

The setting of quality of life as part of the competitive environment lies in the changing role of spatiality in contemporary society. Some argues, if capitalists are in fact more sensitive to the differentiated qualities of places across space, then there is scope for those in the elites who control the shaping of these spaces to redesign and reposition them relative to such capital. Thus "the qualities of place stand thereby to be emphasized in the midst of the increasing abstraction of space". This provides the context for interpreting the place promotion and marketing so familiar in the past few decades as a response to the growing fluidity of capital globally.

There are many illustrations of the adoption of quality of life ratings as part of place promotion to attract this capital. For some, quality of life factors have been added to other measures of locational advantage to aid the process of attracting inward investment of global activities.

Livingston, to the east of Edinburgh and rated second in the 1997 British study of quality of life has utilised its rating to assist in this role, with the strategic services section of the local council employing the research findings in the quarterly socioeconomic newsletter. Melbourne, Australia, similarly has readily and happily adopted the title of "the world's most livable city" from the results of the Population Crisis Committee study of 100 of the world's largest metropolitan areas.

Other more marginal places have used the quality of life league tables to raise their profile in the national and international economic arenas. Perth, on the margins of the central industrial and commercial belt of Scotland, for example, made much of its distinction in 1990 as top for quality of life in Britain in trying to persuade, first, the business community that it was indeed at the heart of Scotland and secondly, visitors to the city (tourists and potential residents) that it was a desirable place in which to live. And others, rated highly in terms of quality of life, have employed the ratings to challenge the stereotypical image of being an area of the industrial decline. Teesside's response in the late 1980s to being rated 9th in the UK quality of life research was to utilise the 'independent study' to show how the region was much more attractive than the south-east of Britain—although the misappropriation of Middlesbrough's rating for the whole region of the north-east and London's rating for the south-east was intriguing.

This role for quality of life as part of place promotion and city marketing is far from novel. Burgess' analysis of the place advertising in the UK has noted that throughout the 1970s-prior to the fashionable status of place promotion as a part of the hegemony of selling of place the improvement in the quality of life that would be experienced by those moving formed one of two common themes identified in the advertising literature. The partial and selective nature of the quality of life image being portrayed has been reinforced by Sadler's analysis of the UDC literature of the 1980s and Burgess and Wood's study of the London Docklands literature. The reduction of multifaceted lifestyles and opportunities to a "commodity to be packaged and sold" was reinforced by the appropriated aspects of the local area, culture and economy. The image, as befits much marketing, was selected to be sensitive to the goals of the marketing exercise.

For those places highly rated in the quality of life league tables, such ratings are of course appealing. As Hall notes, the immediate attraction of such lists is not so apparent to those cities, often those associated with industrial decline, which are less highly placed in terms of quality of life. Responses tend to be either dismissive of the basis of the research or merely ignoring them. However, whilst quality of life and league tables produced on the basis of some quality of life assessment have traditionally been equated with the attraction of economic and personal capital, it is evident that for some locations a poor rating in terms of quality of life can be used to attract another type of capital. State expenditure and the redistribution of surpluses through state or national government remains, of tremendous importance. Thus, although there has been a shift away from welfare expenditure by the state towards supporting private-sector involvement in local economies, public-sector expenditure in supporting the quality of life - defined in terms of place-based attributes as noted above - can be significant.

As many commentators have noted the competition ethos has infiltrated the means by which such state financing is distributed, and it is in this competitive setting that poor quality of life ratings/scores can be turned into a positive attribute. Again, most applications of quality of life in this way are not advertised. However, increasingly some forms of capital are employing poor quality of life ratings to act as a lever in obtaining planning permission for new developments 'which will enhance the local quality of life'. And local community groups are also turning to quality of life assessments to ensure that the local state provides targeted investment into the area.

Economic Production

As the research into quality of life and place promotion illustrates, within the setting of competitive cities quality of life has been adopted as one of the array of attributes which can be employed to secure growth and development through the attraction and retention of means of economic production. In the context of global capital arising from the new international divisions of labour and corporate restructuring, there is an assumption that quality of life factors form part of the location requirements of this capital. The implicit notion is that amongst 'the new set of local place attributes' which are being sought by capital is the desire for a high(er) quality of life.

In fact, the evidence for just such a requirement is sketchy. Intuitively, it can be argued that quality of life is likely to be a factor underpinning location, drawing from the fact that many new economic activities are being located in high-amenity areas, in the sun-belt of different countries and away from the older, declining industrial centres and the larger metropolitan areas. As Grayson and Young rightly note, "it is some step from there to say that growth industries seek quality of life locations for their own sake".

It is just as possible to argue from these trends that alternative location factors - communications, office costs and land values, labour force requirements, technological flexibility-are shaping the spatial patterns of new industrial and commercial activity.

Slowly, however, evidence is being compiled to suggest that quality of life can be a significant element in the location decision-making process. Fothergill and Gudgin's study in the UK remains much quoted, with their conclusion that environmental quality is a factor in industrial location. Surveys of industrialists and decision-makers, such as those conducted by Healey and Baker across Europe, provide further evidence. In their study of the largest 500 + companies in the European Union, about 10 per cent include quality of life factors amongst the three most important attributes in their location decisions. Recent relocations in the UK have also been related to quality of life factors. Whilst many are not made public, one recently quoted example was the move of the British Council to Manchester from London. The principal 'push' factor was financial, but the final selection of where to locate was influenced by quality of life and accessibility factors.

In the US, surveys of the late 1980s also concluded that, in industrial location, quality of life issues were a primary consideration in locating a plant or new business. However, as Hart et al., note in their review at the time, the "more recent results may also be limited by their focus on high-technology industries". Their own research, in contrast, was more wide-ranging and based on surveys of 665 Chief Executive Officers in businesses across Oakland County, Michigan. From 37 factors offered in the survey, Hart et al. concluded that "the most important factors to firms' location in the county thus appear to be their proximity to markets and residences, the quality of the local environment, and the area's growth potential". Further, they recognise that quality of life factors, along with other location factors, varied in significance between types of industry defined in terms of level of technology, but that quality of life remained an element in locating production.

Myers' evidence from Austin, Texas, provides a different slant to this issue. His research has shown that quality of life impinges on the economic success of the town, with a favourable quality of life being of importance to the retention of companies by shaping other more traditional locational factors, especially labour. On the one hand, Myer notes that the greater range of options for relocation, nationally and internationally, amongst skilled staff forces local companies to emphasise the local quality of life conditions, whilst on the other, labour costs may be reduced by the converse of the 'disamenity compensation'. Studies elsewhere in North America and in Europe have also pointed to wage differentials reflecting differences in the non-economic and quality of life opportunities on offer locally. Since then, studies have employed the disamenity idea to develop economic equations to derive surrogate quality of life indices.

Indirect evidence also points to the contribution of quality of life elements being of significance in location decision-making. Instead, amongst the 58 factors included in his survey of 450 businesses, a range of elements that elsewhere have been equated with quality of life-cost of living, public transport, security from crime, schools, environmental quality, housing and climate-are in the study.

Personal Migration

The second way that quality of life has been linked to city

competitiveness-through the attraction of capital arising from the spatial division of consumption-has also involved elements of promotion, but in this case the focus on quality of life is targeted towards personal needs and aspirations. Here the focus is on competition for consumer power, arising to quote Harvey because "consumers who do have the money have become much more discriminating", not least about where they reside. For Harvey the gentrification, cultural innovation, consumer attractions and upgrading of the city all represent elements of the response by city authorities to capture such capital. Evidence that quality of life is of significance in shaping the new residential patterns has been gathered in different ways and has built on the earlier notion of 'placeutility' as a measure of the attractiveness or otherwise of an area relative to alternative locations.

First, and negatively, based on past migration patterns and through a comparison of quality of life opportunities outside the urban area with those of the city, research has pointed to the disparity in quality of life on offer. There is little doubt that the late 20th century has seen a rise in the negative, critical accounts of the city. Accounts of individual city development have emphasised the contemporary perceptions of fear and decline-see Soja's narratives on Los Angeles, for example.

The image that is frequently presented and discussed is of cities as desolate, depraved and feared. And to reinforce this negativity, demographic analyses point to the continuing streams of out-migration from the city, at least in relation to the 'Western city'. Many studies have reinforced the point that poor quality of life may be of significance in the out-migration from cities notes in his review of previous research that a major compelling force appears to be selective migration by managers, professionals and more highly qualified workers and their families from cities to smaller towns and villages, largely for quality of life and environmental reasons.

Elsewhere, log-linear analysis of migration patterns across the US that quality of life rather than economic factors holds the key to expllaining out-migration from urban areas; a conclusion which remains contentious. Such analyses point to the growing opportunities and feasibility of people living in non-urban areas and still contributing to economic activities in the city, and the growing desire to achieve a higher quality of life, away from the city.

The dispersal of labour opportunities as employment relocates from the city, the shifts to new work practices-including flexible working hours enabling greater commuting from suburbs and beyond and teleworking from home-and the changing patterns of employment from manufacturing to services have collectively enabled growing proportions of the workforce (and their families) to live in locations separated from the collective workplace or have transformed the home into the workplace.

Secondly, a few surveys have been undertaken of recent migrants to interpret their motivations for moving. In practical terms, it is often difficult to ask migrants to tease out one factor from others, and indeed there may be much negotiation and disagreement between members of a household over the relative importance of any factor. In addition, most evidence that suggests that quality of life issues are significant require recent migrants to analyse, post hoc, their motivations and decisions. Clearly, migrants make decisions to move as a consequence of a range of very different forces; of which quality of life is but one. Thus, quality of life reasons as being of importance to more than

70 per cent of the migrants interviewed; more important than employment opportunities, living costs or family ties. Quality of life and environmental factors also dominated reasons for migration to areas of New South Wales. Some identified retiral reasons (16 per cent), employment reasons (16 per cent) and environmental and aesthetic reasons (41 per cent) to be the primary motivations for migrants moving from Sydney to the coastal areas of the state. Comparable conclusions had previously been drawn from a larger survey conducted by the Department of Environment and Planning for outmigration from Sydney to the region as a whole.

Thirdly, research has focused on the migration into cities. At a general scale, based on an analysis of white male migration in the 1970s in the US, have concluded that quality of life factors linked to life-cycle patterns, are important in explaining the desire of some groups to live in cities. However, most evidence of the significance of quality of life factors in attracting migrants to the city has been in connection with gentrification which, although highly selective in its composition, is common throughout developed nations. Although the theoretical basis of the causes of gentrification remains contentious and arguably gentrification processes are now influencing more than a few, selected groups of the population, most accounts acknowledge that areas being gentrified are places of opportunity matching the quality of life and lifestyle aspirations of those involved.

Conceiving of Quality of Life

In taking the traditional way in which quality of life has been linked to city competitiveness, the above review has illustrated that the relationship between economic and personal location decision-making and quality of life is only partially substantiated by empirical research. Theoretically, such linkages can be expected to exist, but the survey review of the literature indicates the tenuous and problematic relations which have been explicitly shown to operate in motivating either economic capital or personal capital to locate in terms of quality of life. The lack of clarity in this set of relations has, however, not dinted the use of quality of life in place promotional literature.

Secondly, the review has alluded to the way in which quality of life has been defined in this research. It is inevitable that in engaging with global capital, those involved with shaping locations have to respond to the needs of capital. As the assumption is that the interest in quality of life "stems from the face that it is an important location factor" for both economic and personal migration, it is unsurprising that the way that quality of life is conceived should reflect the primary concerns of such influential capital. It is just such a view, that quality of life should be based on a set of attributes of places, which has been employed in the studies reviewed above.

Whilst some studies provide no definition of quality of life, accepting the phrase unproblematically in their study, others offer an insight into their use of the term. Most make explicit reference to the notion of quality of life, listing those attributes included in their assessment and how they conceive of quality of life as an entity. Others, whilst listing characteristics of places, do not analyse quality of life per se but refer to a basket of attributes under this theme. For example, in Michigan does not offer respondents a category entitled 'quality of life'. Instead, the authors themselves group together responses under this heading. Thus, in reaching their conclusion that "the relative importance of criteria appear, to have shifted away from the 'leastcost' factors and toward those associated with area infrastructure, especially aspects of 'quality of life", they include overall quality of the locality, proximity to residence, and long-term growth.

What is evident from Table 1 is that whilst the list of specific elements to be incorporated into a definition of quality of life varies, the focus is consistently on factors such as physical environment, climate, pollution, crime and social facilities linked to education, health. The key point is that in the commodification of the city and the attempts to lure capital, the view of quality of life which has been employed has become narrowly defined.

The view of quality of life embedded in the production of the 'league table' and city rankings, the notions of quality of life used for city promotion and in city marketing, however, reflect a significant shift in interest in the conceptualisation of quality of life. At its core lies the view that quality of life evaluation should focus on the extent to which the necessary conditions for personal satisfaction and happiness-those attributes of the environment which stimulate satisfaction-are achieved.

In this respect, quality of life is being used to relate to the shared environment in which people live. To evaluate this environment, a range of objective social indicators-what could be termed hard indicators describing the environment within which people live and work-are employed to measure the 'reality' of the living environment. This is in sharp contrast to much of the early, and continuing, research conceiving of quality of life at the level of the individual and focused on how personal characteristics and views shape people's quality of life.

Table 1. *Attributes of quality of life: key city ratings*

Research Dimension	*Smith*	*Liu*	*Boyer and Savageau*	*Rogerson et al.*	*Burnley*	*Hart et al.*	*PCC*
	1973	*1976*	*1981*	*1988*	*1988*	*1989*	*1990*
Environment/Pollution	X	X	X	X		X	
Atmosphere/Peace and Quiet				X	X	X	
Climate			X	X	X		
Lifestyle opportunities					X		
Employment				X	X		
Retirement					X		
Housing Costs and Access	X	X	X	X		X	X
Health Care/Public Health	X	X	X	X		X	X
Crime/Public Safety	X		X	X			X
Transport/Traffic flow				X		X	X
Education Provision/Levels	X	X	X	X		X	X
Recreation	X		X				
Economy/Business climate			X	X		X	
Arts/Cultural diversity	X		X	X		X	
State taxes/Development Aid			X				
Commercial space						X	
Proximity to suppliers/market						X	
Food costs/Cost of living			X	X			
Political Involvement	X	X					
Wages				X		X	

Much of the seminal work on quality of life in the 1970s - especially arising from the large social surveys conducted in the US-employed this conception. The associated use of so-called subjective indicators of quality of life was developed around the notion that quality of life expressed the degree of satisfaction or dissatisfaction felt by people with aspects of their lives, or the extent to which pleasure and satisfaction characterised their lives as a whole.

The debate over the relative merits of each approach s a longstanding one and is largely irresolvable. Whilst these two approaches conceive of and assess quality of life differently, they are related and there have been recent calls for attempts to offer an integration of the different conceptualisations.

Figure 1 portrays how these differing approaches can be seen to be related. Studies which focus on the personal aspects of quality of life tend to categorise quality of life either as satisfaction scales or via responses to surveys and interviews on the respondent's own immediate experience and well-being; these studies fall into Type C.

Research which envisages quality of life as relating to places and their characteristics tends to be of two types. Those which select the attributes and characteristics through expert or other non-survey approaches typify Type A studies. The Places Rated Almanac or studies using econometric and revealed preference methods fit this type. If priorities and weightings derived from opinion surveys are included, then some element of the personal characteristics of those involved with quality of life are incorporated and form Type B studies. It is in these two ways that quality of life has been conceived by those involved in city competition.

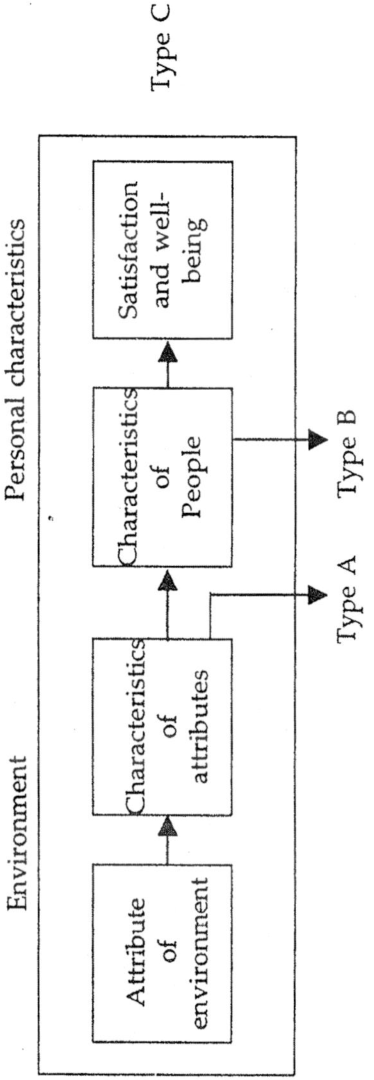

Figure 1. Conceptualising quality of life.

Privileging Capital

The priority attributed to the attraction of capital and associated employment as part of urban growth and development may seem desirable. It rests on the assumption that the well-being of cities can be cast as dependent upon capital investment, and consequently all forms of capture of capital are seen as causes for celebration. The argument expressed is that there will subsequently be a filtering down of financial and other benefits arising from such investment, in the form of higher wages, new jobs, higher house prices and the growth of local tax-base.

In undertaking this, however, the priorities of one group (capital) are elevated above those of others. The recognition of such a privileging is not new. In the context of the politics of economic development, the switch to urban entrepreneurial governance from managerial forms that Harvey expresses is based on a shift across the economy from labour to capital, including the directing of local state finances from welfare provision to the attraction of capital. Whilst such a shift in resources is open to contestation and may result in some dependent populations experiencing greater poverty, it is predicated on the assumption that it will improve the overall standard of living and quality of life of the majority.

Others too have noted that inequality in power in shaping the future of the city arises from the focus on competitiveness for capital as the path to urban growth and development. For example, recognises that in the process of spatial restructuring there is a fundamental distinction between those segments of labour which are shaping the city and those whose voices are being excluded. The frequent examples of how elements of the city's infrastructure and lifestyle have been constructed to meet the demands of capital - as in his argument why developers and financiers support the notion of cultural superstructure to make Los Angeles a world city they have become so integrally involved in the organisation of high culture, not because of old-fashioned philanthropy, but because 'culture' has become an important component of the land development process, as well as a crucial moment in the competition between different elites and regional centres.

The city's image is therefore made to order, tailored to the needs of capital. Mayer makes the connection even more explicit. For her, in the contemporary city there may be a veneer of economic consolidation, but she argues

> it is not a 'pluralism' of lifestyles and consumption patterns which reigns, but rather that the high income consumers' ideas and definitions of the 'good life' have become the influential ones.

The privileging of capital's notion of quality of life has important consequences for the shape of the urban quality of life on offer in the contemporary city. First, and working with quality of life being part of the array of factors shaping urban competitiveness, it is worth noting that alternative ways of conceiving of quality of life can be employed. To date, little emphasis has been given to those studies which consider that quality of life is concerned with life satisfaction and happiness. In the past they have not been favoured in a policy setting because of the lack of insight of prescriptive action which could be taken to improve levels of life satisfaction. In an era of 'image building' and league tables, however, it is surprising that the opportunity to claim that one place's citizens are more satisfied than another's has not been adopted as part of the panoply of marketing techniques. More constructively, perhaps, research by social scientists and others concerned with the measurement of happiness, life satisfaction and well-being has, increasingly being offering important insights into some of the priorities which frame people's well-being and satisfaction with their lives and living environment.

Unlike the studies of people's priorities attached to place attributes, Bowling's research focuses on more personal characteristics. Table 2 portrays the key items men- and tioned in the survey. For some researchers, there remains the perceived constraint that many of the features identified in surveys, such as relationships, religion and politics here, are not immediately amenable to quantification and thus comparative analysis required for the construction of league tables and ratings cannot be easily undertaken. Such methodological difficulties, however, should not be a basis for neglecting the further insights offered by such studies.

Secondly, the actual experience of both the attributes of cities and the overall quality of life associated with urban living has too often been excluded from studies of quality of life. The tendency to employ a view of quality of life which focuses on those features of the urban environment has emphasised characteristics of the environment in terms of availability, accessibility and efficiency of provision-what Rogerson et al. relate to questions of access and manner of delivery. In contrast, as Rogerson et al. argue in viewing the quality of life as being related to the consumption process,

> it is the quality of the experience of consumption which-although often ignored in social research is an important element

and

> patterns of quality of life will potentially be based on the 'them' (having access to crucial life chances provided

through ownership rights to a variety of modes of provision, including private consumption) and the 'us' comprising a minority who lack access via the market to basic consumption.

Table 2.

Items considered most important in people's current lives

Priority	*Item*
1	Relationship with family/relatives
2	Own health
3	Health of someone close
4	Finances/housing/standard of living
5	Relationships with other people
6	Availability of work/able to work
7	Other (inc crime, politics, happiness/well-being)
8	Social life/leisure activities
9	Conditions at work/job satisfaction
10	Education
11	Religion/spiritual life
12	Environment

Whilst some insight into differential quality of life can be evaluated through measures of access and provision, it is only when dimensions of experience are added that the 'city ratings' will be more than advertising hype and meaningful to people. Thirdly, whilst there indeed may be some legitimacy to the claim that the economic and social benefits accruing from the successful capture of capital in the competition for investment and growth will trickle down to all citizens, there can be little doubt that in privileging capital's notions of quality of life other people feel marginalised.

The desires anal opinions of other groups, who are not viewed as significant groups to be targeted in competition for capital, are in danger of being ignored in the discussions of what form of quality of life should be offered in a city. Again let us provide a brief insight. One recent study, using focus groups in Lancashire in Britain to discuss what people consider to be quality of life in the context of sustainability, has illuminated the sense of marginality felt by some urban populations. Arising from the discussions of two of the groups, the research team conclude:

> The two groups who were deeply sceptical about the concept of 'quality of life' were the unemployed and the young men. To the young men on YTS, their life was less about 'quality of life'-a term which conjured up notions of responsibility and a view of the long term-and more about 'quantity of life'-a term they themselves made up to express their desires for immediate gratification . ... Similarly, the unemployed men resented the term, not because they would not like a better 'quality of life', but due to the sheer distance between the sentiments implicit in the term and their own material reality. In effect the term was seen, not as a target, but more as a judgment, a wound, which acted to underline the reality of their own situation.

To these groups, and others like them, the notion of quality of life as considered previously lies therefore outside their daily reality, at best being something to be aspired to, but more likely not relevant to their existence. However, the duality of centrality and marginality constructed by the engagement with the quality of urban life which the above indicates is itself open to question. Whilst undoubtedly in shaping local response to the globalisation processes, primacy is being given to the views of some capital, it does not necessarily follow that other groups need be marginalised. The construction of a vision of the 'liveable city' by residents in Indianapolis offers an important insight into how it is possibleeven within the setting of city competitionfor a more inclusive form of 'liveability' and quality of life to be achieved. In so doing, however, there may require to be space for different conceptualisations of quality of life to be merged together, without losing the attraction of the term to forms of capital and to groups in the local community.

With the evidence pointing to the fact that there are clear links between the attraction of capital and quality of life, it is unsurprising that quality of life has become a part of the promotional tools being employed by city agencies to make their location attractive to different global capital. In so doing, the consequence has been to adopt one definition of quality of life, in terms of place characteristics which are desired by such capital, and thus to disadvantage other groups' views of quality of life. As with many aspects of place promotion and marketing, there are paradoxes within the use of quality of life in this way. Undoubtedly one of the attractions of quality of life in the present phase of capitalism lies in its academic ambiguity.

Encompassing individual and collective elements, public and private roles, and having been used both as a standardised measure of achievement and as a basis for intervention for improvement, it. is unsurprising that capital and the state find quality of life ;ratings so useful. Further, at a time when under globalising tendencies capital is fragmenting into many parts with considerable volatility in the desires and demands of capital-both in terms of production needs and consumption-that quality of life within its relative ubiquity provides an important anchor attached to which those involved in shaping the visions and trajectories of cities can build.

TRANSPORTATION AND COMMUNICATION

One of the many lessons from 9/11 is that terrorism is not just about terror. Terrorism is also an attempt to disrupt the daily lives of non-combatants to achieve political objectives. Physical or virtual networks that are vital to health, safety, comfort, and economic activity are called lifelines. The complete or partial failure of even a limited number of lifelines can have a major impact on economic productivity as well as making peoples' daily lives more difficult and in some cases nearly impossible. This is not just a matter of convenience.

There are members of society with limited resources or other economic, social and demographic constraints, whose very livelihoods depend on reliable functioning of such lifelines. The population explosion of the past two centuries combined with high rates of urbanization means that effective public transit and road networks are indispensable. Increased mobility on a daily or weekly basis or over the course of a lifespan results in an enhanced reliance on communications networks (physical and virtual) in order to conduct daily activities and maintain relations in business, social and family settings. The negative impacts of lifeline disruptions on economies, personal finances, and lives can be so invasive that the terrorists' political ends often are achieved as effectively as through the direct use of force. Transportation and communication lifelines are among the critical networks required for moving material, people and information among locations distributed in geographic space.

The criticality refers to their role as an essential foundation for the relatively plentiful and stable supply of food, consumer goods, and information. To disrupt them produces ripple effects not only in the region where it occurred, but extends outward to the nation and the world. The best example of this was the halting of all commercial air traffic in the U.S. in the few days after 9/11 and its worldwide impact in terms of travel disruptions and economic losses. Since lifelines are so central to the functioning of modern society and yet are so fragile, it is important to understand their vulnerability to planned and unplanned disruptions. Lifeline vulnerability refers to the susceptibility of a system to incidents that cause considerable loss of service.

Understanding lifeline vulnerability can lead to:

1) better protection strategies by identifying particularly vulnerable components of the network (and the benefits and costs of reinforcing those components);
2) improved strategies for recovery from disruptions (by identifying consequences and magnitudes, and effective mitigation strategies); and
3) enhanced support for long-term design and planning and related land-use systems that are less vulnerable.

Indicators of Lifeline Vulnerability

Many approaches have been used to measure lifeline vulnerability but most can be grouped into two major categories: performance based indicators (network reliability and network performance) and user based indicators (accessibility). These are briefly described below.

Network Reliability and Network Performance

Network vulnerability is the susceptibility to disruptions that can cause considerable reductions in network service or the ability to use a particular network link or route at a given time. An important aspect of service is the ability to use a lifeline at a certain place and time. Another aspect of network reliability involves the consequences of disruption, that is, reductions in service. Networks that cannot quickly recover from a disruption with minimal reduction in service are deemed more vulnerable than those whose recovery is faster and with less overall disruption.

Most analyses of network vulnerability use the related concept of reliability or adequate serviceability at a given time. Network reliability theory treats network arcs and nodes as having a random probability of failure. Network reliability also depends on flow and congestion within the network. Since urban transportation networks are increasingly saturated, localized disturbances (such as a traffic accident) can propagate widely through the network causing system-wide delays. There are several ways to estimate reliability, including the probability that an origin-destination pair remains connected by a route after component failures, or that the time required for traveling between the origin-destination pair does not exceed a maximum limit.

Network performance approaches monitor or simulate network flows and evaluate their behavior in response to real or simulated disturbances. They are being used more often now than in the past due to the deployment of intelligent transportation systems for monitoring flows, and the availability of dynamic methods for simulating variable time flows. Network performance measure includes travel time, travel rate (travel time divided by segment length) and delay rate (actual travel rate minus desired travel rate).

Accessibility

Accessibility is a fundamental concept in human geography. Accessibility measures the ability of individuals to participate in activities in space and time, and the use of transportation and communication technologies to achieve this participation. Accessibility is a much broader concept than serviceability and views vulnerability as susceptibility to substantial reductions in space-time autonomy, or the freedom to participate in events distributed in space and time. The concept recognizes that transportation and communication are derived demands and exist not for their own sake but to help people accomplish other activities in space and time. Loss of accessibility greatly impacts abilities to earn a living, access health care, conduct parenting activities, or maintain social relations. For example, survey evidence suggests that time spent driving reduces community involvement and volunteerism.

Network-centric performance-based measures do not capture these potentially widespread and devastating effects of lifeline disruption since they view the network as detached from the context of human activities.

Human Dimensions of Lifeline Disruptions

Time geography is a powerful and sensitive framework for analyzing accessibility in space and time. Two fundamental concepts are the space-time path and the space-time prism. The space-time path traces an individual's movement in geographic space and world time over any time scale (from hours to years). The prism demarcates possible locations for the space-time path during a travel episode given a time "budget" for travel and the maximum travel velocity allowed by the transportation system. Figure 2 illustrates a space-time path and a simple space-time prism (bottom half) where the origin and destination are coincident and with stationary activity time not considered.

The prism geometry is more complex with non-coincident anchoring locations and with stationary activity time. A related concept from activity theory is a space-time pattern. This is an allocation of a limited time budget for certain activities in space and time. Space-time paths, prisms and patterns can be used in two ways to assess lifeline vulnerability: direct losses of space-time autonomy and induced changes in space-time patterns.

Loss of space-time autonomy

The prism can assess directly, the convergence between space and time as a function of transportation network configuration, travel velocities, scheduling constraints, and network congestion. Existing techniques are available for analyzing prisms based on travel in continuous space or within specific transportation networks. These techniques can be extended to lifeline vulnerability analysis by examining changes in the prism before and after a simulated transportation or disruption.

Changes in space-time patterns

A lifeline failure requires fundamental changes in peoples lives. Another strategy for analyzing lifeline vulnerability is measuring changes in the spatial and temporal distribution of activities induced by network disruption. This strategy would analyze changes in space-time paths and patterns at an individual level in response to real or simulated failures. This method would require tracking and recording of the space-time paths before, during and after a planned disruption. The disruption events that drive this

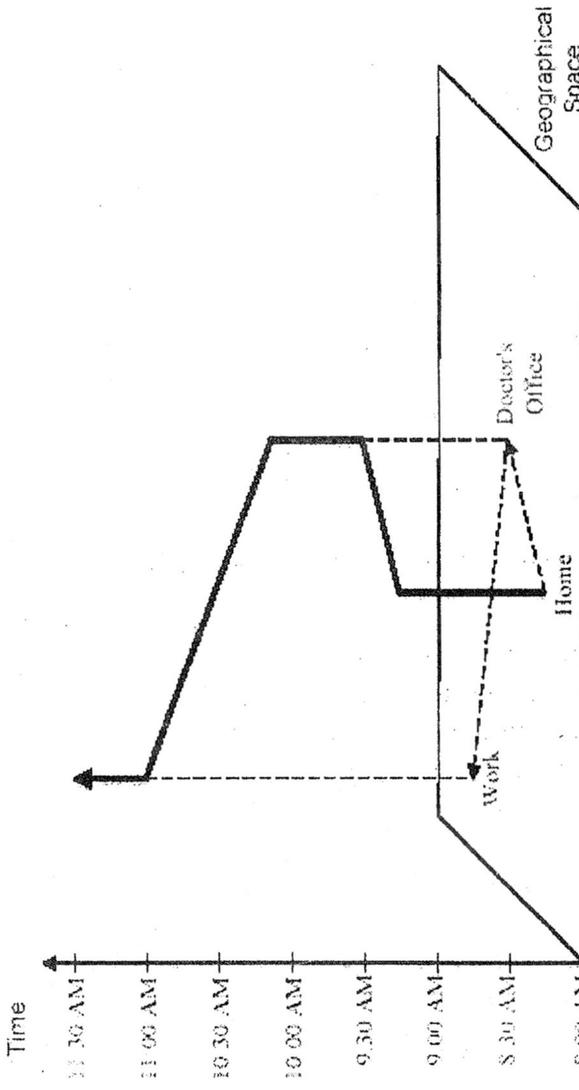

Figure 2:

Space-time paths and prisms; Top half – a space-time path; Bottom half - space-time prism.

type of empirical analysis could be large-scale transportation construction projects such as the "Big Dig" in Boston or the I-15 reconstruction in the Salt Lake Valley.

These large-scale transportation projects produce impacts that approach the scale of major terrorist attacks. Since simulation systems require individual space-time diary data as inputs to infer representative activity paths and patterns, it is important to develop location-aware technologies or intelligent transportation data collection systems to acquire them. There is a wide range of emerging dynamic flow and simulation approaches to linking space-time activity paths and patterns to network performance in order to understand how people will respond and adjust to disruptions. Activity theory also provides guidance on how these adjustments occur.

Time Geography and Information Technology

Accessibility is a concept that is traditionally based on movement in physical space. However, activities are increasingly disconnected from geographic space as a result of the increased use of information technologies (IT). Time geography can be extended to encompass IT-based virtual interaction as well as physical movement. Unlike most accessibility measures, time geography is sensitive to emerging perspectives that view time as the scarce commodity of the information economy and accelerated modern lifestyles. Embedding space-time vulnerability measures within a decision or policy process requires methods for supporting the exploration and comparison of vulnerability scenarios.

A spatial decision support system allows analysts, decision-makers and stakeholders to develop, execute and assess vulnerability scenarios. This requires integrating a space-time prism or activity modeling system with solution exploration and comparison techniques. Geographic Information Systems (GIS) software supports such spatial database management, in addition to spatial-temporal query functions, and geographic visualization tools.

Transportation and communication disruptions immediately following the 9/11 attacks clearly illustrate the dependence of society on transportation and communication lifelines. Lifelines provide convenient opportunities for terrorists to seriously affect economies and lifestyles from the local to the global. In this way, they rank among the nation's most important infrastructure. Analyzing and understanding vulnerability to disruptions in lifelines leads to improved protection, mitigation, and recovery strategies.

Among the techniques used for analyzing lifeline vulnerability, accessibility and time geographic approaches recognize the nature of transportation and communication as derived demands within a broader human activity context. This can allow more sensitive analyses of lifeline disruption on daily lives than methods that examine impacts only on the networks. Spatial decision support and GIS software, as well as digital geo-spatial and human activity data, can make this mode of analysis feasible as well as understandable to policy analysts and decision makers.

9/11 exposed not only our vulnerability to lifeline disruption, but also our lack of knowledge about the relationships between these networks and human activities. There is little fine-grained, scientific knowledge and how critical transportation and communication networks affect daily lives, and the urban dynamics that emerge from the interplay of individual activities in space and time. Gaps in scientific knowledge about the interrelationships between human activities and transportation/communication networks are disturbing since these are also at the heart of transportation science and urban theory.

The relationship between individual activities and connectivity in space and time is also central to policy questions surrounding urban livability and sustainability policy. There are several research and development frontiers where progress will not only advance our understanding of lifeline vulnerability but also help create more livable and sustainable communities that are responsive to peoples' daily lives. Required are new data collection protocols and methods that exploit advances in information technologies and position-aware technologies such as the global positioning system, intelligent transportation systems and location-based services. Also needed are theories and models that have detailed, individual-level linkages between transportation/communication lifelines, the organization of activities in space and time, and the interplay of these activities in creating lifeline demands and urban dynamics. Also required are enhanced versions of the space-time path, prism and other time geographic constructs that can be disconnected from geographic space and referenced within cyberspace. Finally, researchers and developers need to create user-friendly GIS and spatial decision support tools to help emergency managers, transportation planners and other officials to use these advanced, individual-level theories and models in real-world applications.

6

Paradigm Approaches to Environmental Degradation

Environmental Models in Urban Geography

Any aspect of the Earth's environment may be the focus of environmental modelling: a definition can hardly get broader than this. Atmospheric and hydrological processes, land-surface—subsurface processes, biological and ecological systems, natural hazards, ecosystems management issues, are all popular themes. Environmental models cover a full range of geographic scales, from the local to the regional to the global.

Moreover, they cover a wide range of input domains: natural and human, biotic and abiotic, atmospheric, oceanic, terrestrial and socioeconomic. Because the environment is a synthesis of all these domains, environmental models often combine several aspects from one or more of these areas. Thus we have models of the effects of climate change on biota, of fire and forest regeneration, of the interdependence of hydrology and ecosystems, of atmospheric circulation and industrial pollution, of fisheries under the impact of different fishing policies.

There are many reasons why interest in environmental models has greatly increased in the past decade or so. Mounting environmental consciousness in the industrialized regions of the world and an increasing interest among public and private funding agencies to support modelling work related to environmental issues have attracted large numbers of capable researchers. At the same time appropriate techniques, computational resources and especially data of suitable quality and quantity have become widely available, so that the gap between the desirable and the feasible in environmental modelling keeps decreasing. GIS, with its power to integrate diverse databases, undoubtedly played a key role in this development and has become the core technology of environmental modelling research.

While environmental models integrating natural processes have already achieved a certain maturity, those seeking to combine human and natural processes are still in their infancy. It is fair to say that today's frontier in environmental modelling lies at the natural-human interface: this is where some of the most important problems and some of the more interesting research issues are to be found. Researchers and funding agencies alike seem increasingly willing to invest in such cross-disciplinary research, despite the still strong institutional and intellectual barriers separating academic fields. Major examples of integrated human-natural environmental modelling research recently funded by the U. S. National Science Foundation include the two Urban LTER (Long Term Ecological Research) projects at the University of Maryland and the Arizona State University, and some of the projects from the 1998 "Urban Change" competition. Similar efforts are underway in the Netherlands and other European countries.

For 'Good' Environmental Model

Environmental models are developed for research or policy purposes. While the line between the two is a fine one in applied fields, there are certain criteria that make a model more suitable for one or the other purpose. All models must be built on good science, they all need to be based on good data, and they all must deal with good problems. Research models are expected to exhibit a higher degree of scientific rigor and to contribute some original theoretical insights or technical innovation.

In policy models originality is less of an issue (often, the more 'tried and true' a model is, the better!) but transparency, manipulability, and the inclusion of key 'policy variables' are especially important. Clearly, research models can have significant policy implications (as is the case with the global climate models developed in the past decade) just as policy models can make original contributions to the science of environmental modelling.

Nature of Environmental Modelling

Characteristics

Environmental models make up a distinct family different from other classes of models in either the natural or the social sciences. They tend to be data-intensive, cross-disciplinary, dynamic and complex. They often integrate subsystems from several different domains without the support of widely accepted theoretical frameworks to lend credibility to the attempted synthesis. Needing to have explicit spatial as well as temporal dimensions increases their complexity. They depend on data of very variable quality gleaned from a wide variety of sources.

As a result, they face issues of uncertainty and fuzziness to a greater extent than either traditional natural science models, which deal with more homogeneous, usually 'cleaner' data sets, or than social science models, which often aim at producing qualitative rather than strictly quantitative results. Moreover, because of their direct or indirect policy implications, environmental models don't have the right to be wrong!

Facets

Clearly environmental modelling presents special challenges. Distinguishing the wheat from the chaff is not always easy. This is why it is all the more important for model builders to be aware of the different paradigms and approaches that underlie the wide variety of environmental models competing for attention and funding these days. This section outlines a general framework to help put such models in perspective and to help recognize the strengths and weaknesses of each. It is based on Smyth's framework for general geographic modelling adapted to the environmental domain.

According to Smyth it is convenient to think of the modeled world as a microworld defined by an ontology consisting of contents, spatial structure, temporal structure, 'physics' (rules of behavior), and rules of inference or logic. The notion of an artificial world or microworld, borrowed from AI, is useful for reminding us both that models are not the real thing, and that they need to be internally consistent. A closed microworld is autonomous in that the behaviours within it are completely specified through its initial definition without further reference to the external world.

A traditional cellular automaton model is a good example: once the initial conditions, neighbourhood template, and transition rules have been specified, the model will enfold all its possible behavior independently of anything external. Other closed microworlds well known to geographers are the classic models of location and land use proposed by Christaller, von Thuenen and Weber. Similarly, ecologists are well familiar with simple predator-prey models that work out the evolution of interdependent populations within predetermined environments.

Most environmental models however correspond to open microworlds, admitting elements, relationships, causation, and spatio-temporal and logical structure from outside of their ontological specification. More commonly these are referred to as open systems though this terminology is less clear about the fact that it is the model, rather than the part of the world modeled, that is 'open'. Once the ontology of a model has been clarified it must then be expressed in a formal system which will eventually be translated into a computational model and a concrete implementation.

The first things defining the ontology of an environmental model are the entities within it. For example, in an integrated urban-environmental model, the entities may be roads, built-up areas, different categories of land uses, streams, slopes, bodies of water, forests, wildlife populations, and the like. These will most conveniently be modeled as objects though other representations are possible. Entities primarily have an identity on the basis of which their other aspects can be defined. Relevant aspects of entities include: versions (alternative descriptions that may indicate uncertainty as to some properties of an entity: which western boundary of this urban area is the correct one for 1990?); class membership (about which there may be confusion: is that patch pine or spruce forest?);

alternatives regarding the attributes and spatial and temporal descriptions of these entities; and the structures and configurations (e. g. , hierarchies of different kinds) that may relate the different entities in an ontology. Anderson classes of land use/land cover are a well known such hierarchy whereby classes are subdivided into more and more detailed categories ('aggregation hierarchy').

Another kind of hierarchy binds together elements that compose a whole. For example, an ecosystem can be decomposed into its constituent entities (forest, grassland, water bodies, soils, animal and plant species, etc.). What entities will be included in an environmental model will depend to some extent on its intended principal use, i. e. research or policy support. A policy-oriented model must involve entities and attributes of entities that can be manipulated by policy makers ('policy variables'). For example a slope cannot be manipulated but a road network can; the age of a tree stand cannot be manipulated but its acreage can; and so on.

A good policy model will include policy variables that have a significant effect on the behavior of the model. Observing how the microworld is affected by manipulating these variables can give decision makers insights into how to act in the real world. Such requirements for practically 'useful' variables do not apply to models developed primarily for research purposes where description, explanation or prediction are the main goals.

The spatial and temporal structure of geographic models in general has been the subject of considerable research. Several kinds of conceptualizations and frameworks have been proposed for both space and time. Of special interest to the present discussion is the fact that environmental models typically consist of several different modules or subsystems, each based on its own spatial and temporal framework. Problems may arise when these frameworks are very different and perhaps inconsistent with one another in terms of scale, metricity, topological structure, reference frame, and other such properties.

The physics of a microworld are the rules of evolution of entities and of interaction between or among entities that determine what can happen within it: they govern the possible behaviours of a model. These rules may be expressed mathematically, e. g. in the form of differential or difference equations, or computationally, in the form of 'if-then' statements and other such specifications. In a physical model the physics (no quotation marks) are literally based on actual physical theory (e. g. , fluid dynamics, mechanics, electromagnetism, or the theory of chemical interactions) but in most other cases (and models) the term is to be understood metaphorically.

Environmental models often include modules or sub-models backed by the rigor of physical theory but being strongly cross-disciplinary and synthetic, environmental science (and modelling) is by and large a theory-poor domain. This means that a typical environmental model will mix together several kinds of 'physics' (with quotation marks), some based on causal hypotheses (A appears to cause B), some on statistical regularities (A is statistically associated with B), others on empirical rules of thumb (when A, usually B), others still on arbitrary rules of behavior specified by the modeler (if A is the case, then do B). Combining such a variety of partial 'physics' into a whole free of internal contradictions is a delicate task for which few guidelines exist, and which becomes more challenging as the aspects to be brought together are drawn from domains more remote from one another. Thus it is one thing to integrate a sub-model of rainfall with one of runoff to determine flooding potential in an area, and quite another to combine a model of job growth and one of species extinction into a framework for exploring the environmental effects of urban development.

The logic of a microworld completes Smyth's (1998) pentad of a model's ontology. This is what allows new facts to be deduced about a microworld from a given configuration. In the case of mathematical models the logic is indistinguishable from the physics as they are both implicit in the formalisms used. In the case of simulation models however the two are distinct. For example, the logic may include default rules to help decide what will happen in situations where behavior is under-determined (e. g. , in case of a tie), or to help determine which aspects of a microworld must be changed in order to eventually reach a configuration with specific properties. The latter kind of question is particularly pertinent in policy-oriented models where the interest is not just in possible futures but also in desirable ones, and in the means necessary to reach these.

Several formal logics have been developed that in principle can provide rich enough inference mechanisms for environmental simulation models. Most of these are quite complex however and not yet widely used. There will be an increasing need to study the logics of environmental modelling microworlds as more models are developed integrating drastically different kinds of processes (e. g. , socioeconomic and physical). Formal modelling theories such those by Zeigler, Casti can greatly assist the development of logically coherent environmental microworlds, as can the closely related perspective of systems theory.

Smyth's model specification sequence involves, in addition to the choice of an ontology (1), the following steps:

(2), expression of the ontology in a formal system; (3), development of a computational model of the formal system; (4), realization of the computational model in a concrete implementation. Logically however all these aspects remain a necessary part of modelling even if they do not constitute explicit, separate steps.

COMPLEX ENVIRONMENTAL SYSTEMS

System Theory: Philosophy and Key Concepts

In this section the emphasis shifts from the model to the system modeled. This is a subtle change of focus since 'the system' is itself a kind of model: we model an environmental system that is a representation of some part of the real world. The word 'system' goes back to the ancient Greeks and literally means something that hangs (or stands) together. In its modern scientific usage a system is something made up of a set of elements and relations among these elements. This may sound vague but in fact many systems can be defined very precisely by families of differential or difference equations where the variables are the elements and the relations are defined by the mathematical operations on the variables.

More generally the elements of a system are the entities in a microworld's ontology and these are connected to one another through relations of causation, influence, or dependence that together determine the physics of that microworld. Positive and negative feedback, stimulus and response, activation, inhibition, and so on are more specific terms for different kinds of relationships in a system, usually quantifiable. These, along with characterizations of behavior such as self-organization, steady state, instability, oscillation, emergence, and chaos have become an integral part of the system modeler's vocabulary. What is less well known is that these technical terms have strong philosophical underpinnings in the work of Ludwig von Bertalanffy (1968) dating from the 1930's.

Being a theoretical biologist von Bertalanffy was aware of the limitations of the reigning reductionist paradigm (i. e. , the attempt to reduce all scientific explanation to physical laws) in helping describe and explain living things. His General System Theory, composed of system science, system technology, system philosophy, and system epistemology, was proposed as a new way of thinking about, or paradigm for, the kinds of complex phenomena that biologists and other modern scientists in both the natural and the social sciences were studying.

Von Bertalanffy's key insight was that there are laws of systems qua systems, in the abstract, regardless of the domain (economics, engineering, ecology, biology, physics, sociology, and so on) from which particular applications may be drawn. This was a highly ambitious program aiming at unifying all science under the systems paradigm. That integrated environmental modelling is possible at all is evidence of the basic correctness of general system theory's key premise - that systems behave like systems no matter what they are made of.

A number of broad methodological concepts such as systems thinking, the systems approach, the systems perspective, etc. have been derived from principles of General System Theory. Their proponents make fine distinctions between them that need not concern us here. Wilson (1981) following Weaver distinguishes three basic classes of systems. Simple systems have few components and few variables (e. g. , the solar system) and are studied with the traditional methods of classical physics. Systems of disorganized complexity have very large numbers of components and variables but the couplings between them are either weak or random.

Gases are typical examples of such systems which are studied primarily with statistical methods: hence the field of statistical mechanics and theoretical principles such as entropy maximization. The third class is that of systems of organized complexity. These systems too have large numbers of components but there are multiple couplings and interactions among them that need to be considered explicitly.

In these systems, 'the whole is more than the sum of the parts', meaning that their properties cannot be deduced from an understanding of their components. These systems of organized complexity are the ones the systems paradigm is specifically concerned with. Research into complex systems of all sorts has flourished in the second half of the 20th century and has stimulated the interest in the study of environmental systems, which provide some of the most challenging examples of complex systems known.

There are two complementary methodological and theoretical approaches to the study of complex systems. The first is the top down approach, exemplified by systems analysis and systems dynamics. The second is the bottom-up approach, emphasized in complexity theory. Both are directly relevant to environmental modelling and are briefly outlined below.

Environmental phenomena and complex systems

The top-down approach: *decompose and conquer*

More familiar than General System Theory is systems

analysis, one of the many fields under von Bertalanffy's original paradigm. Systems analysis gained prominence after World War II primarily through the spectacular successes of engineering disciplines in building and controlling very complicated systems, from guided missiles to computers. At the same time systems analysis and the closely related field of operations research were being applied to 'soft' fields such as planning, management, and the modelling of human decision making.

The possibility to apply the same basic concepts and methods to natural, engineered and social systems was thus practically established. An excellent though somewhat dated introduction to systems analysis for environmental scientists, addressing both natural and social systems, can be found in Wilson. More abstract but still readable expositions of systems theory and systems analysis are found in Casti and a variety of other sources. The basic principle behind systems analysis is that complex systems or problems can be decomposed into simpler subsystems (or sub-problems), which themselves may be subdivided into even simpler sub-sub-systems, until a level is reached where the component parts may be treated as elementary.

This approach differs substantially from reductionism in that the focus is not on the elementary components but on the relationships among components and assemblies of components at and between the levels of the (de)composition hierarchy. For example, in an ecological model, a spatial-scale decomposition may consider the interactions of individual organisms within patches at one level, and of populations in an ecosystem at another level, the ecosystem being much more than a sum of ecological patches. (By contrast, in a reductionist ontology, the focus would be on aggregation hierarchies that allow properties of entities at one level to be generalized into properties of groups of these entities). Systems analysis may be static, clarifying the internal structure of a complex system, or dynamic, seeking to derive forecasts regarding future system behavior. This latter case is embodied in the paradigm of systems dynamics.

The history of modelling large-scale systems dynamics began in the sixties with the publication of Forrester's series of three, increasingly ambitious simulation models: Industrial Dynamics, Urban Dynamics, and World Dynamics. The latter is one of the earliest integrated environmental models developed, bringing together global population growth, agricultural food production, industrial production, pollution, etc. (however, World Dynamics was not a spatial model). Each of these models consisted of several major coupled subsystems, which in turn included large numbers of linked components. Forrester's models were heavily criticized at the time but made some lasting contributions to complex systems research. Of particular relevance to environmental modelling was the demonstration that complex dynamic models of integrated systems could be built with the same basic techniques and vocabulary used in modelling a variety of physical systems, thus opening the way for the integration of social and natural science modelling. Coupled system models in the tradition of Forrester's are still routinely used. The widely popular modelling platform STELLAâ is a direct implementation of Forrester's approach and several texts are available to teach related methods.

Most systems dynamics models represent phenomena in analogy with complicated hydrological cascading systems, where flows (of matter, energy, animals, people, money...) move between storage compartments within which these quantities are created or transformed. Storage compartments are connected to one another through the flows which are resolved into outputs (quantities flowing out of one compartment) and inputs (quantities flowing into another). Most such models assume an external compartment representing the 'environment' of the model, i. e. the rest of the world within which the system studied is embedded and where some of the flows originate and end ('open' systems). In physical systems the transfer and storage of mass and energy is governed by two groups of physical laws: laws of conservation and laws of transport (also called process and flow laws). The logic is the same for social and ecological systems although there are no corresponding rigorous laws of process or flow for these. Discrepancies in the degree of reliability of physical, biological, and social-science model sub-models of environmental system models constitute one of the challenges of integrated systems modelling.

The bottom-up approach: complexity theory

Mathematically, complex systems are characterized by multiple non- linearities and feedbacks. Physically, these formal properties are associated with active exchanges of matter, energy and information between systems and their environment. These characteristics of complex systems often lead to phenomena such as self-organization, chaos, adaptation, emergence, lock-in, bifurcating trajectories, and other types of surprising and unexpected behaviours unknown to classical science. In the late 20th century a 'new' science of complexity developed around the study of these interesting types of dynamics.

The 'new' science of complexity and its hallmark phenomenon, chaos, produced a long series of articles and books that captured the imagination of scientists and lay people alike. The Santa Fe Institute was founded in 1984 by an interdisciplinary group of high-flying scientists to foster theoretical research into complex systems. The 'complexity theory' paradigm pioneered by the Santa Fe Institute has led to some very elegant mathematical work, to a large volume of interesting publications and to the definition of a new field (artificial life), but has also been criticized as a rather hollow intellectual fad. Just how relevant is complexity theory to environmental modelling?

There is little doubt that the environmental sciences deal with systems that are very complex by any definition. Unpredictable outcomes, major consequences of relatively small disturbances, unanticipated side effects, the fragility of large environmental systems or, conversely, the robustness of others that appear very delicate, all provide empirical evidence of complex systems behavior. Examples of self-organization abound in the natural world: grains of sand forming crescent-shaped dunes; birds flying in triangular formations; surface runoff converging to a few discrete channels. Phillips distinguishes eleven distinct kinds of self-organization that are relevant to landscapes, which may be further aggregated into two broad categories: those that tend to create order and regularity in the landscape, and those that result in greater diversity and differentiation.

On the other hand, outside physics and the laboratory, there are not that many empirical examples of some of the 'sexier' aspects of complex systems behavior (in particular chaos) in environmental systems. For example, the wide fluctuations of animal populations in landscapes were earlier seen as a striking case of chaos in action. But as Zimmer reports, citing a well-known ecologist, "there is no unequivocal evidence for the existence of chaotic dynamics in any natural population". Indeed natural systems are often found to totter 'on the brink on chaos' without quite plunging into it - a sign of Mother Nature's resiliency, if not wisdom, in the face of constant perturbations and assaults.

Very often the interesting dynamics of complex systems are the macro-scale outcomes of simple interactions among micro-level system components. Neural networks are well known examples of complex structures capable of highly organized behavior resulting from the parallel operation of large numbers of interconnected neurons. When the micro-level interactions are restricted to neighbouring elements, the resulting system is intrinsically spatial and under appropriate conditions it will produce spatial organization at the macro-level: molecules in a solution yielding regular patterns on the surface of the liquid, pigment activators and inhibitors creating stripes or dots on animal skins, segregated neighbourhoods unexpectedly arising from simple preferences of individuals for particular levels of racial mix among their immediate neighbours.

Cellular automata (CA) are a well known class of complex systems models that embody that principle, generating macro-scale spatial patterns in a gridded space through the parallel operation of micro-scale rules involving local neighbours. CA models have become increasingly popular with environmental modelers because of their direct compatibility with raster GIS, their ability to make use of detailed spatial data, and their conceptual simplicity, which contrasts with the extreme diversity and complexity of the patterns they are capable of generating. CA models have proven equally suitable for the simulation of physical and social spatial processes, and are thus particularly well suited for integrated environmental modelling.

Agent-based simulation is a more recent development in complexity theory that also involves generating complex macro-scale behavior through modelling micro-scale interactions. 'Agents' are interacting entities that may be sentient (people, animals, organizations...) or non-sentient (any kind of physical or computational objects) and their interactions may or may not be in space. As in CA models (and unlike neural net models) interactions among agents can be based on arbitrarily complex rules. Unlike CA, where the interacting elements are localized cells, interacting agents may be mobile in space, thus providing a straightforward, intuitive way of modelling actually moving organisms or other objects. Applications are already appearing in the environmental modelling domain, such as the simulation of the impacts of visitors on wildland settings by Gimblett et al.,.

Critics of complexity theory point out that the wide variety of surprising behavior exhibited by mathematical and computational complex system models is rarely found in the empirical world. The criticism is primarily directed at the 'bottom up' paradigm which tends to produce especially skittish models, very sensitive to initial conditions and to small variations in the interaction rules. Real-world populations rarely crash and then explode chaotically, local interaction rules are rarely as simple as these models would have it, landscapes don't easily jump from one state of organization to the next, neither natural nor social systems tend to get into runaway positive feedback loops, and 'emergence' seems to be just what the current model cannot explain.

In other words, there is much more stability in the real world than complexity theory would have us think. Some authors contrast 'model complexity' (or 'model chaos') to actual system complexity, and Goldenfeld warns researchers 'not to model bulldozers with quarks'. The issue here is that there is a right level or levels of description for every phenomenon that must be judiciously chosen for the model to work.

This is one of the many lessons that modelers are learning from complexity theory. There are several other lessons: that nature can produce complex structures even in simple situations, and can obey simple principles even in complex situations; that each complex system is different so that similar-looking systems may develop in very different ways. Even though we may never enjoy the intellectual comfort of scientific laws when modelling complex environmental systems, complexity theory has made us more aware of the subtlety, diversity, and interconnectedness of the phenomena we study, and has contributed many powerful concepts, modelling approaches and techniques.

Environmental Modelling and Geocomputation: Modelling 'with' the Computer

Modelling 'without' the computer is inconceivable in the environmental domain these days, except perhaps when developing abstract conceptual models. In many ways the computer has made environmental modelling possible, and not just because of computing in its original, number crunching sense. In this data-dominated age GIS has given modelers the possibility to handle arbitrarily detailed data at any spatial scale and is unquestionably a major driver behind the current blossoming of environmental analysis and modelling.

Statistical, mathematical, graphics and visualization software has complemented the increasingly sophisticated capabilities of commercial GIS, providing additional power to modelers and literally new ways of looking at data. But modelling 'with' the computer means something more than that.

More and more, computer simulation replaces analytic model development as the systems modeled become larger, more integrated and more complex. Step 2 of Smyth's sequence in particular, the formalization of the model's ontology, tends to be merged with step 3, the computational expression of the model. Formal languages such as Haskell and Gofer have been developed that are at the same time algebras and computer languages. Map algebra and image algebra, which are formalisms operating on spatial elements as the variables, have been extended into dynamic spatial modelling languages such as PCRaster.

In addition, graphical, icon-based model construction environments are attracting increasing attention and in simple forms even begin to be available bundled with commercial GIS software. More generally computer visualization has substituted the advanced pattern-recognizing capabilities of the human eye-brain system for much of the deductive work that characterizes traditional scientific analysis. All these developments aim at making environmental modelling easier, more widely available, and more of a collaborative enterprise than it could ever be under the traditional approach.

Just as the logical steps of model building are being compacted and merged, the distinction made in traditional model ontologies between entities, relationships, physics, and logic is becoming less and less sharp with the growing popularity of object-oriented languages and their recent extensions. In this approach objects are defined in terms of the possible and allowable behaviours of the corresponding real-world entities. Object-orientation, with its emphasis on representing quasi-autonomous units within models and submodels, facilitates a bottom-up approach to complex system modelling and especially favours agent-based simulation.

Indeed, object-orientation has been loosely defined as "the software modelling and development disciplines that make it easy to construct complex systems out of individual components". Further developments currently underway in Internet-oriented computer languages are likely to affect modelling practices even further. XML (Extended Markup Language) and its derivatives for example are considered especially well suited for sharing and handling geographic data over the Internet,.opening up the possibility for environmental models that are not just dynamic, but are themselves dynamically evolving with the contributions of modelers 'anywhere, any time'.

Computation is thus taking a life of its own in environmental modelling, increasingly driving rather than just supporting modelling efforts. Some may view this as a regrettable development that threatens to distance environmental modelling from proper scientific practice - except that, of course, similar developments are taking place to a greater or lesser extent in practically all areas of science. Researchers in the spatial sciences are converging around the notion of geocomputation, a novel concept whose definition keeps evolving just as its subject matter does.

Originally no more than a diverse grab-bag of computational techniques, geocomputation eventually came to be identified with GIS practice for some people, but now seems to have acquired an identity of its own as the convergence of computer science, geography, information science, mathematics and statistics. Once its theoretical potential is fully unfolded geocomputation may become synonymous with the computational theory of complex spatiotemporal processes. If that's the case environmental modelling will surely become geocomputation's proudest application field and may benefit immeasurably from a formal convergence of all the relevant technical fields.

URBANISATION AND AIR-POLLUTION

Urbanization is a process of relative growth in a country's urban population accompanied by an even faster increase in the economic, political, and cultural importance of cities relative to rural areas. There is a worldwide trend toward urbanization. In most countries it is a natural consequence and stimulus of economic development based on industrialization and postindustrialization. Thus the level of urbanization, as measured by the share of a country's urban population in its total population, is highest in the most developed, high-income countries and lowest in the least developed, low income countries (Table 2).

At the same time, urbanization is progressing much faster in developing countries than in developed countries (Figure 1). In 1990-95 the average annual growth of the urban population in low-income countries was 3.8 percent and in middle-income countries, 3.1 percent, compared with 0.1 percent in high-income countries. Because the developing world has a larger population, percentages of its population also represent more people. As a result, by 1995 almost three-quarters of the world's 2.5 billion urban residents lived in developing countries. The share of the urban population in the total population of low- and middle-income countries increased from less than 22 percent in 1960 to 39 percent in 1995 and is expected to exceed 50 percent by 2015.

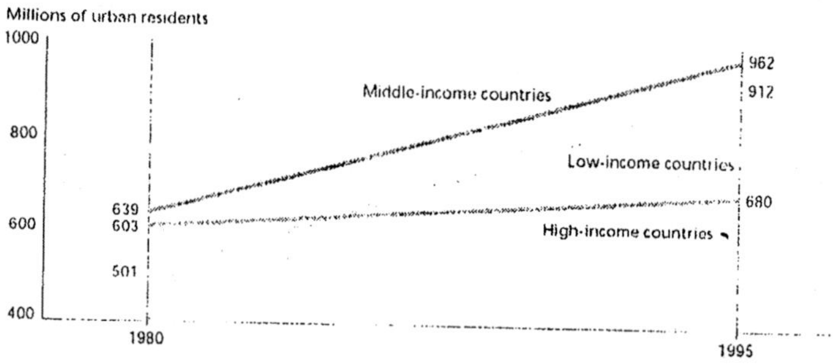

Figure 1. Urban population, 1980 and 1995

A rough indication of the urban contribution to GDP is the combined share of GDP produced in the industry and service sectors relative to agriculture. Judging by this indicator, cities in developing countries are already more economically important than rural, primarily agricultural areas, because more than half of the developing world's GDP originates in cities.

While urbanization is characteristic of nearly all developing countries, levels of urbanization vary quite significantly by region (Figure 2). Most Latin American countries are as urbanized as Europe, with 74 percent of the population living in urban areas. But South Asia, East Asia, and Sub-Saharan Africa remain predominantly rural, though they are urbanizing rapidly.

Most of the world's most populous cities are in developing countries. Many of these cities are in Asian countries with low per capita incomes but big populations, such as China, India, and Indonesia. These cities have high concentrations of poor residents and suffer from social and environmental problems including severe air pollution (Table 1).

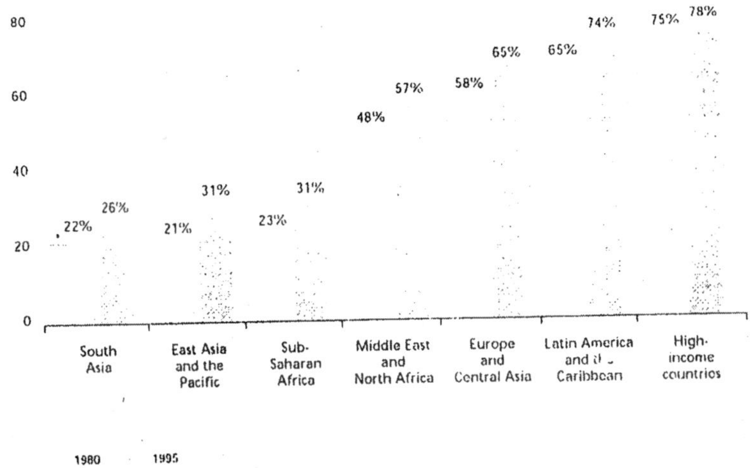

Figure 2. Urban population as a percentage of total population, 1980 and 1995

Table 1. Particulate air pollution in the largest cities, 1995

Country	City	City population (thousands)	SPM (micrograms per m³)
Brazil	Sao Paolo	16,533	86
	Rio de Janeiro	10,187	139
China	Shanghai	13,584	246
	Beijing	11,299	377
	Tianjin	9,415	306
Egypt, Arab Rep.	Cairo	9,690	—
France	Paris	9,523	14
India	Mumbai	15,138	240
	Calcutta	11,923	375

	Delhi	9,948	415
Indonesia	Jakarta	8,621	271
Japan	Tokyo	26,959	49
	Osaka	10,609	43
Korea, Rep.	Seoul	11,609	84
Mexico	Mexico City	16,562	279
Philippines	Manila	9,286	200
Russian Federation	Moscow	9,269	100
Turkey	Istanbul	7,911	—
United Kingdom	London	7,640	—
United States	New York (1987-90)	16,332	61
	Los Angeles	12,410	—

Particulate Air Pollution

Suspended particulate matter is made up of airborne smoke, soot, dust, and liquid droplets from fuel combustion. The amount of suspended particulate matter, usually measured in micrograms per cubic meter of air, is one of the most important indicators of the quality of the air that people breathe. According to the World Health Organization's air quality standards, the concentration of suspended particulates should be less than 90 micrograms per cubic meter. In many cities, however, this number is several times higher. High concentrations of suspended particulates adversely affect human health, provoking a wide range of respiratory diseases and exacerbating heart disease and other conditions. Worldwide, in 1995 the ill health caused by such pollution resulted in at least 500,000 premature deaths and 4-5 million new cases of chronic bronchitis.

Most of the people at risk are urban dwellers in developing countries, especially China and India. In many

Chinese cities air quality is so poor that nationwide, the costs of excess morbidity and mortality for urban residents are estimated at 5 percent of GDP. According to estimates for 18 cities in Central and Eastern Europe, 18,000 premature deaths a year could be prevented and $1.2 billion a year in working time lost to illness could be regained by achieving European Union pollution standards for dust and soot.

The level of air pollution depends on a country's technology and pollution control, particularly in energy production. Using cleaner fossil fuels (such as natural gas and higher-grade coal), burning these fuels more efficiently, and increasing reliance on even cleaner, renewable sources of energy (hydro, solar, geothermal, wind) are some of the best ways to control and reduce air pollution without limiting economic growth.

See Figure 3 for the main sources of electricity in China, Russia, and the United States. Compare these data to the concentrations of suspended particulates in the biggest cities of these three countries as shown in Table 1. Note that coal is considered to be the "dirtiest" of the sources shown, although a lot depends on its quality and methods of combustion.

In many ways nuclear energy is one of the "cleanest" sources of electricity, but safe disposal of nuclear waste and the risks of radioactive pollution in case of a serious accident are of major concern. Sources with the least environmental impact, such as solar energy, are not shown because they account for only a small fraction of generated electricity worldwide.

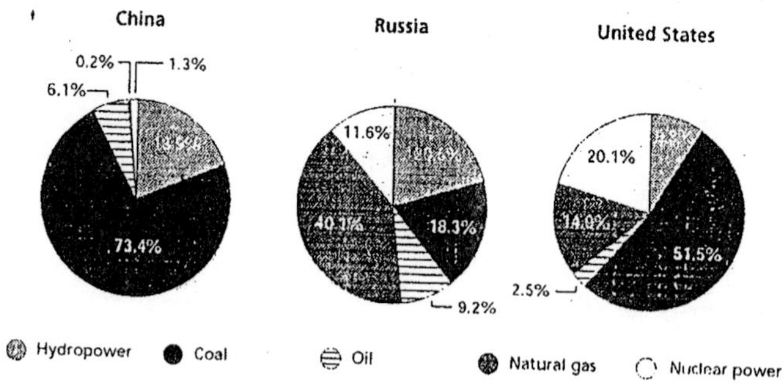

Figure 3. Sources of electricity in selected countries, 1995

Fuel combustion by motor vehicles is another major source of suspended particulate emissions in urban areas. These emissions are particularly detrimental to human health because pollutants are emitted at ground level. Motor vehicles are much more common in developed countries: in 1996 there were 559 of them per 1,000 people in high-income countries compared with just 8 per 1,000 people in low-income countries and 91 in middle-income countries. But motor vehicles in developing countries still cause serious air pollution because they are concentrated in a few large cities, many are in poor mechanical condition, and few emission standards exist.

According to World Bank estimates, demand for gasoline in developing countries tends to grow 1.2-1.9 times faster than GNP per capita. If per capita income growth rates of 6-8 percent a year are typical of industrializing and urbanizing countries, growth rates in motive fuel consumption of 10-15 percent a year are possible. In many transition countries in the late 1980s and early 1990s, the number of cars in use grew rapidly despite the contraction in economic activity and reduced per capita incomes.

In Moscow (Russia) the passenger car fleet grew 10 percent a year during 1984-94 and 17.5 percent a year during 1990-94. Without effective policies to curb motor vehicle emissions, such dynamics can lead to grave health consequences for urban populations.

7

Urban Governance

At the beginning of the 21st century cities are at the front line of the development campaign. Urbanisation offers significant opportunities for post-socialist countries – to increase economic prosperity and to improve the well being of their citizens. Urbanisation is also an important facilitator of sustained economic and social improvement, as well as more democratic governance.

Post-socialist cities have gained political influence since recent political and fiscal decentralisation has shifted power and responsibilities to local governments. In this context, municipal policies affecting urban areas – planning, housing, transportation and delivery of urban services – have major ramifications for the efficient operation of businesses and the social well being of households. Cities in 1990s account for as much as four-fifths of the GDP, they remain the centres of economic growth, finance industry, technological innovation and cultural diversity. But cities also tend to concentrate socially deprived urban population and continue to be a threat to the environment.

Economic Change

The years of economic stress and market volatility have led

to contrasting developments across the region. The transition countries, mainly in Central Europe, have pushed ahead with the more challenging structural and institutional reforms and have been able to maintain macroeconomic stability. The Baltic States still have a more fragile economic environment, problematic corporate governance, and relatively weak financial systems.

Despite the uneven progress in transition and economic performance, growth prospects across the region are encouraging. Recent developments indicate that GDP growth is between 3 – 5.2%, but still below 1989 levels. Poland and Slovenia are a notable exception with economic performance in 2000 exceeding pre-reform conditions. Inflation is under control, but still remains high in the range of 4 – 10%.

Foreign direct investment (FDI), responsible for a third of private capital inflows in 1999, has advanced steadily over the past decade in line with the countries' progress in transition and macroeconomic stabilisation. FDI has provided a major boost to the reform, particularly in the Czech Republic, Estonia and Hungary, where a more liberal and stable environment has attracted strategic investors to enterprise restructuring and technology transfer. Privatisation has made significant progress taking several forms – employee-buy outs, vouchers and competitive bidding. The result is manifested in the growing private sector share of GDP, which accounts for 60 – 80% of GDP in 1998, with Hungary taking the lead.

Fiscal imbalances continue to be a problem in most countries in the region. The Baltics are projected to have a fiscal deficit of 10% of GDP in 2000. Severe pressures on the expenditure side, due to high social security payments and various forms of offbudget support, continue to undermine the fiscal position of central governments.

Managing the process of fiscal transition and spending more efficiently continues to be one of the major challenges in the second phase of transition. Urban economies have responded differently to the changes in macroeconomic conditions. New challenges have emerged due to profound structural changes in the economy in the transition from planning to markets. The pressures of national and international economic forces, and the opening up of previously sheltered markets, have generated rapid adjustment of industries, services and other economic activities.

Economic restructuring has a crucial impact on direction of growth and change, on future specialization in the economic base of cities, their mix of traditional manufacturing industries and advanced services. Empirical evidence suggests that economic diversification, associated with the transition from industrial to service oriented-information based urban economies, has become more prominent and is reflected in the composition of GDP.

CE countries and the Baltic States have experienced a significant growth in the share of service based GDP. Those processes in return bring corresponding changes in the demand for urban resources, land, and infrastructure provision. While the extent of this adjustment is related to macrolevel policies, market integration, technological innovation and the power of international capital, endogenous factors in the urban economy also have a significant role. Land, existing industrial capacity, natural resources, labour, good urban governance also contribute to the competitiveness of cities and their ability to attract new industries and economic activities.

SOCIAL CHANGE

While economic growth prospects in the region have been evaluated positively, the social impact of the transition process presents a major challenge to market reforms. The most significant aspect of social change is associated with labour market adjustment and social differentiation. In response to structural and macroeconomic pressures, labour market adjustment has proceeded through: changing sectoral and regional employment patterns, unemployment fluctuations and wage differentiation.

Industrial employment by large outnumbers agricultural employment with the exception of Poland, where historically agriculture has been particularly vital even during state socialism. Service employment, particularly significant in Hungary and the Czech and Slovak Republics, has experienced significant growth in the second phase of the transition. Furthermore, employment for women is much higher in the service sectors, while industrial employment is still male dominated.

During the transition individual urban areas have experienced a process of differentiated development with some losing and others gaining economic attractiveness. Capital cities and large urban centres have been privileged in that respect attracting a large share of investment in banking, retail and information-based technologies.

In addition to shifts in the occupational structure, labour market restructuring is manifested in unemployment rate fluctuations. Unemployment increased rapidly in most countries at the start of macroeconomic reforms and continues to be excessively high in Bulgaria and the Slovak Republic.

Evidence suggests that unemployment for women is

higher due to employer's discrimination practises, growing burden of domestic responsibilities and changing social pressures.Wages in CE countries tend to be 25 – 30% higher compared to the ones in the Baltic States, but still much bellow the EU average. There is a positive correlation between GDP per capita and wage levels, which indicates a general tendency of income growth in relation to productivity. These broader developments need to be evaluated against the background of rising income inequality, large increases in poverty and growing insecurity across transition economies.

Wages have become more differentiated with a ratio of up to 4 between the lowest and the highest income quintile in the mid-1990s, which is radical social change for these previously egalitarian societies. In the mid-1990s income inequalities, measured by Gini coefficient, tend to be particularly high in the Baltic States and in Poland.

Poverty in the Baltic States is alarmingly high. As much as 46% of the households in Lithuania, 40% in Estonia and 23% in Latvia live bellow the poverty line. The high rate of inequality, particularly in the urban areas, has broad impacts on the social well being, because it reflects the inability of some citizens to participate in society and share in activities leading to improved health and educational attainment. The urban poor are especially vulnerable to economic shocks; they lack access to services, safety nets, and political representation.

Large cities tend to be more expensive, with prohibitive housing costs and transportation constraints, which alternatively create a potential for even greater social problems and inequalities. Cumulative deprivation in these cities often defines urban poverty, with single parent households and elderly women being the most vulnerable social groups. Poverty in post-socialist countries is predominantly an urban problem. Sofia and Tallinn for example have a more intensive concentration of poor people than any other major city in the region. Indeed, the likelihood that a resident of these two cities is poor is only slightly lower than is the likelihood of being poor anywhere in the country. This distribution is far different from the situation in other capital cities, even in countries with lower per capita incomes, where residents in the capital are about half as likely to be poor as are other citizens in the country. This unique distribution of poverty affects local government opportunities and social responsibilities in a profound way.

Redefining Urban Governance

In the context of transition from planning to markets the role of national governments has been redefined to facilitate liberalisation of the economy, to promote economic and social stability, and to ensure distributional equity. This process has included efforts to introduce more local autonomy, citizen participation and rebalancing of public and private sector roles. Local government reforms in the countries of transition have several aspects:

i) decentralisation,

ii) devolution of power, and

iii) privatisation of municipal assets.

The political, fiscal, and administrative decentralisation reflects concerted efforts to make governments more democratic and efficient. However, decentralisation has resulted in excessive fragmentation, particularly in the Czech Republic, Hungary and Slovakia, where majority of local governments are too small to operate basic services independently. Most countries are finding themselves with a very large number of small municipalities without mechanisms to foster necessary co-ordination and economies of scale in management.

Within the framework of institutional reforms national governments have enhanced local autonomy through devolution of power and responsibilities. Local governments have become the principal institutions responsible for urban planning and management. In addition, they have retained the statutory responsibility for the provision and maintenance of technical infrastructure and urban social services. In most cases municipalities have acquired ownership of the fixed assets of water and sewerage companies, district central heating systems and public housing. However, inflation, subsidy restructuring and significant budget cuts have risen the cost of urban services dramatically.

Running schools, hospitals, social care homes and other social facilities has contributed to high local government shares of public expenditure. In this respect, it has placed Hungarian and Polish local governments in the Premier League of European spenders along with the Scandinavian countries. It has also increased the dependency on intergovernmental transfers, since the scale of resources needed far exceeds the potential of any local tax base.Overall, fiscal decentralisation has failed to enhance the ability of local governments to raise resources locally and to have a sustainable tax base. The lack of adequate funding has eroded the quality of urban services and transportation.

Cash constrained local governments have often resorted to privatization of land, buildings and other municipal assets. Privatization of housing has become the flagship of the decade, but has failed to raise the much-needed revenue. Progress has been made in upgrading the region's infrastructure spurred by growing private sector involvement and foreign participation. Although privatization of infrastructure is under way in many countries, mostly though concessions and/or competitive contracting of services, tariff reforms continue to be undermined by weak payments discipline.

Socialist Spatial Legacy

CEE countries are highly urbanised with a share of the urban population as high as 75% in the Czech Republic. Population densities tend to be higher in the Czech Republic and Poland, and as low as 34 people per sq. km in Estonia. Data indicate that urbanization and urban growth have become less pronounced in the 1990s, with an annual growth rates between 0.6 – 1.7%.

Concentration of the population in large urban agglomerations is another characteristic feature of post-socialist cities in the region. Katowice has around 3.4 million inhabitants. Other large metropolitan centres –Warsaw and Budapest – have over 2 million, followed by Sofia, Prague and Lodz with over 1.2 million. The level of concentration is much higher in the Baltic States, where close to 50 % of the urban population lives in the capital cities. Central European urban centres with population over 100,000 accommodate up to 46% of the urban population.

The usually positive correlation between GDP per capita and level of urbanisation is not applicable to the countries under review. Levels of urbanisation are larger in the Baltic States, where income calculated at purchasing power parities is lower compared to CE. The legacy of centrally directed urbanisation, driven by industrial growth under state socialism, has had a much more powerful implications in the Baltics. Correspondingly, countries with high levels of employment in agriculture, such as Poland, have a lower level of urbanisation today, despite higher per capita income. Finally, 'the goulash type of communism' in Hungary with emphasis on existing industrial capacities in small and medium size settlements explains lower urbanisation rates in these countries compared to their much higher income levels.

Post-socialist cities have a distinctive form, which has the following characteristic features:

i) excessively high share of industrial land and

ii) high population densities at the periphery.

For example, industrial land consumes as much as 44% of the built-up area in St. Petersburg and 28% in Crakow, Sofia and Ljubliana.

These outcomes, a direct result of socialist emphasis on industrialization, affect the efficient functioning of the urban systems today. Massive closures of state enterprises and industrial restructuring have left post-socialist cities with huge tracts of land with derelict buildings close to the city centre.

Further, the legacy of the socialist experiments in planning and housing provision has created excessively high densities in the urban periphery compared to the market city. These areas contain a high proportion of system-built housing and some basic social services (schools, medical care, etc.), but lack sufficient retail and employment opportunities. This segregation of land uses contributes to excessively long commuting trips to centres of employment, urban inefficiency and high transportation costs. Mass produced socialist housing in the peripheral housing estates is 'the home' of 50 – 60 percent of the population in large urban centres.

Rapid privatisation of public housing has transferred ownership of those units to former tenants at bellow market prices.The 'nations of home owners' – Hungary, Estonia and Lithuania – have reached levels of home ownership over 90 percent, well above the EU average of 56 percent. On the other hand, Latvia, the Czech Republic and Poland stand out with levels as low as 40 percent.

Urban Transformation

The transition to more advanced, market oriented forms of economic development in post-socialist cities is reflected in series of changes in the urban fabric. Existing industrial zones are in the process of intensification to accommodate the establishment of a large number of new private firms, warehouses and office activities. Continued growth in service sector industries has increased the pressure on areas with good exposure and transportation accessibility. Shifts in technology and communications have established office functions, particularly banking and finance, as a significant com-ponent in the urban economic base of capital cities.

These trends are reflected in dynamic property development of office space and top prices in buoyant office markets (e.g. Budapest, Prague). The retail sector has experienced a dynamic growth particularly associated with the emerging private small businesses. Restructuring of existing retail space according to demand from a diverse retail structure, recycling and redevelopment of unprofitable and underutilized shopping centres tend to be the major trends. Strip retailing has established itself as the largest type of retail activity especially in the inner cities, often with exclusive shops, boutiques and retail spaces that cater for the affluent consumer.

Other forces behind the dynamics of urban change are land reforms, property market differentiation, and fragmentation of investment flows. The impact of these factors should be considered against the background of economic, social and institutional change. Within the new market reality urban development is associated with a wave of investment in land uses offering opportunities for higher return, selective inner city redevelopment by the private sector and gentrification of inner city neighbourhoods. Despite significant demand constraints, private housebuilding has made a remarkable progress towards better quality and diversity of the final product, which is manifested in the improved design characteristics of newly built housing compared to the mass produced dwellings in the socialist housing estates.

Urban Policy Agenda

Urban economies have responded differently to the changes in macroeconomic conditions. New challenges have emerged due to profound structural changes in the economy in the transition from planning to markets. The pressures of national and international economic forces, and the opening up of previously sheltered markets, have generated rapid adjustment of industries, services and other economic activities.

Successes of privatisation and liberalisation of markets need to be expanded to include the more difficult structural and institutional reforms of the next phase of transition. These challenges include governance and economic restructuring, financial sector reforms, infrastructure reform, and fiscal and social sector reforms.Within the urban sector regional and urban inequalities and the slow and uneven progress in tackling the challenges of structural adjustment require a renewed focus on urban economic strategies and a substantial and constructive role of central and local government institutions.

The major trends of decentralisation, democratisation/ devolution of power and privatisation have increased the importance of cities and towns in the process of national development. Despite overall progress towards democratisation, local governments across transition economies are increasingly perceived as crisis managers charged with a lot of responsibilities, but lacking the adequate financial resources to respond to demands for jobs, infrastructure (both new investment, as well as rehabilitation and upgrading of existing systems), finance, and effective governance. Finding alternative strategies to cope with the challenges of urban management is crucial for the economic and social vitality of postsocialist cities.

Comparative analysis of various policy initiatives in post-socialist cities indicates that a variety of sectoral policies have been introduced to overcome the existing urban conflicts: pollution, decay in other parts of the city, lack of adequate provision of transport and social infrastructure, the imbalance of employment opportunities, housing and services, etc. The effect so far has been marginal and the commitment inadequate. Urban reforms have taken a back seat in the overall process of economic and social transition. The environmental problems of urban areas – the "brown" agenda – including pollution of air, land and water, traffic congestion, and noise, have not received sufficient attention.

Urban social problems are mostly related to conflicts over affordability of services, housing shortages and deprivation.These processes, paralleled with immense financial difficulties, economic uncertainty and growing urban poverty, require urgent commitment to the development of appropriate, economically and politically feasible strategy facilitating market efficiency, while taking the most urgent social needs into account. Effective solutions will require addressing these issues through new democratic partnerships and strategic alliances between local governments, private sector agents and communities – all of which are central to the urban development agenda.

Smart Growth and Urban Containment

The dominant strain of current urban and transport planning is "smart growth," which weeks to stop the geographical expansion of urban areas and make them more compact (more dense). Two of the most important strategies for making more urban areas more dense are land rationing, often through urban growth boundaries and other measures that severely limit the amount of land that can be used for development, such as development rationing through impact fees.

A number of economic and environmental rationales have been used to support densification and land rationing. However, not all agree that smart growth has conclusively demonstrated any imperative that justifies its proposed strategies. A group of academics and researchers believe that the "smart growth" movement has not identified any problem of sufficient imperative to justify a number of its strategies, including land rationing. They have drafted a statement of market oriented land use principles, called the Lone Mountain Compact,which asserts:

The most fundamental principle is that, absent a material threat to other individuals or the community, people should be allowed to live and work where and how they like.

Farmland and Open Space: In 2000, more than 400 years after the first European settlement, only 2.6 percent of the nation's land has been subjected to urban development (Figure 1) Moreover, there is no threat to the nation's ability to continue as a prolific agricultural producer.Agricultural productivity has increased substantially over the past 50 years (Figure 2). This means that less land is required for farming, and more than 80 percent of the abandoned agricultural land has been returned to "open space," rather than having been developed. The nation has added open space in an amount equal to the land area of Texas and Oklahoma combined since 1950.

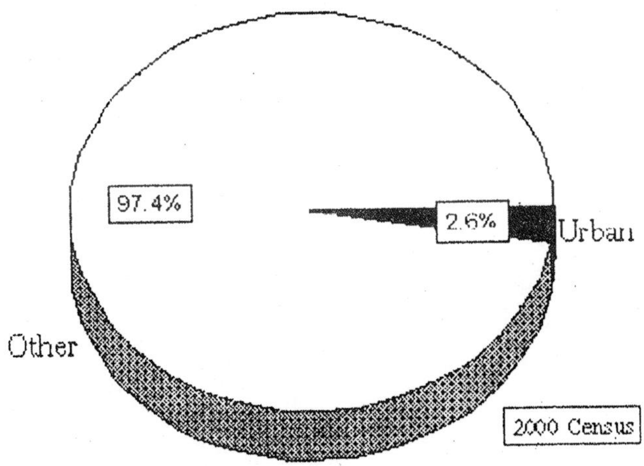

Figure 1.

Traffic Congestion: Traffic congestion increases with density. This can be seen in US Department of Transportation research indicating that traffic (vehicle miles) tends to increase 80 percent for each 100 percent increase in population density (Figure 3). Because more traffic in a confined area means slower traffic, the increase in time spent in traffic is even greater. An analysis of international data makes this even clearer. US urban population densities are considerably lower than elsewhere.

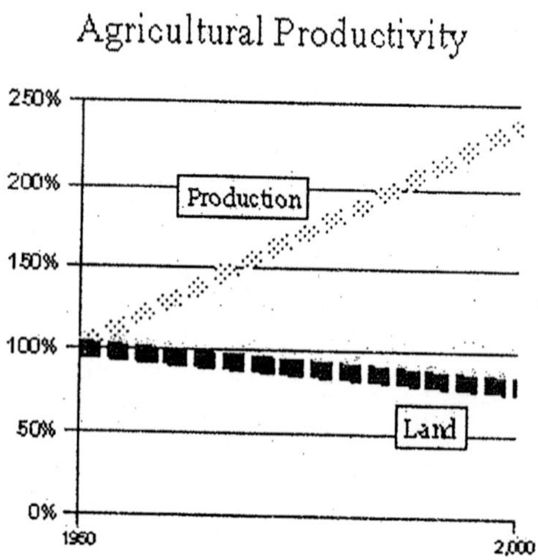

Figure 2.

According the International Public Transport Union Millennium Cities Database,1995 urban population densities exceeded 6,000 in Canada, 14,000 in Western Europe and 29,000 in Asia—compared to under 3,000 in the United States (Figure 4). And, despite the far higher public transit market shares, lower personal vehicle ownership rates, higher fuel costs, higher parking costs and lower incomes outside the United States, traffic congestion is much worse, nearly 30 percent higher in Canada, 100 percent higher in Western Europe and 200 percent higher in the Asian urban areas.

Vehicle miles per square mile are lower in Australia, which has urban population densities somewhat higher than the United States (Figure 5). And, despite the fact that travel times are increasing, US automobile travel is considerably faster than in other nations. US urban travel speeds average 20 percent faster than either Canada or Australia, which have only rudimentary urban freeway systems. US speeds are 60 percent faster than that of European urban areas and nearly double that of Asian areas (Figure 6). This is the result of the higher density of automobiles and traffic and the lower capacity of international roadway systems. As a result, traffic intensity measured in vehicle hours is lowest in the United States.

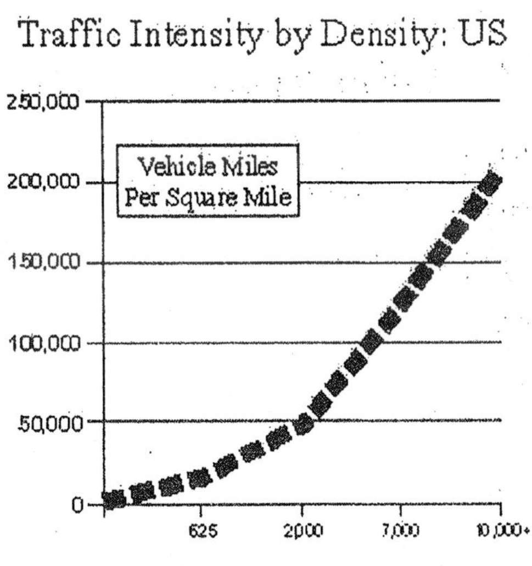

Figure 3.

European rates are more than three times that of the United States, while Asian rates are more than five times that of the United States (Figure 7). Even smaller international urban areas have intense traffic congestion. For example, Geneva, with an urban population of approximately 400,000, has double the vehicle hours per square mile of America's most congested urban area, Los Angeles, with approximately 12,000,000 residents (Figure 8). At least 80 US urban areas are larger than Geneva. Palm Bay-Melbourne, Florida, for example, has approximately the same population as Geneva, but vehicle hours per square mile are estimated at well less than 1/10 that of Geneva.

Still, 73 percent of US workers travel less than 30 minutes to work, and 95 percent travel less than 60 minutes (Figure 9).Further, except in Asia, public transit travel speeds are considerably slower than automobile speeds. As a result, travel times are 80 percent longer on transit in the United States than by automobile and 32 percent longer in Western Europe. Outside Asia, transit tends not to be an attractive alternative for most trips (Figure 10).

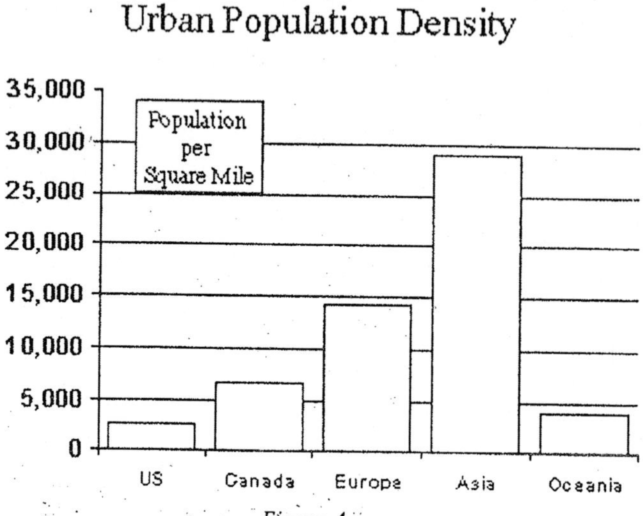

Figure 4.

Air Pollution: It is not a well-known fact, but air pollution has declined markedly in recent decades, largely due to the improvements in vehicle emission technology. From 1970 to 1998, actual pollution reductions were as high as 60 percent, despite a 130 percent increase in driving. As vehicle speeds are slowed by traffic congestion, and vehicles "stop and go" more often, air pollution emissions rise inordinately. This means that the greater traffic congestion associated with higher densities also produces higher levels of air pollution (Figure 11).

"*Jobs-Housing Balance*:" Achieving a better "jobs-housing balance" is one of the principal objectives current urban planning. The assumption is that development patterns in the 20 century created an artificial separation between jobs and residences that has unnecessarily lengthened commute distances and travel times, while intensifying traffic congestion and air pollution. The purpose is to plan urban areas so that jobs are closer to employment. 4 n the United States, the average commuter travels 13 miles to work each day.

International Urban Traffic Intensity

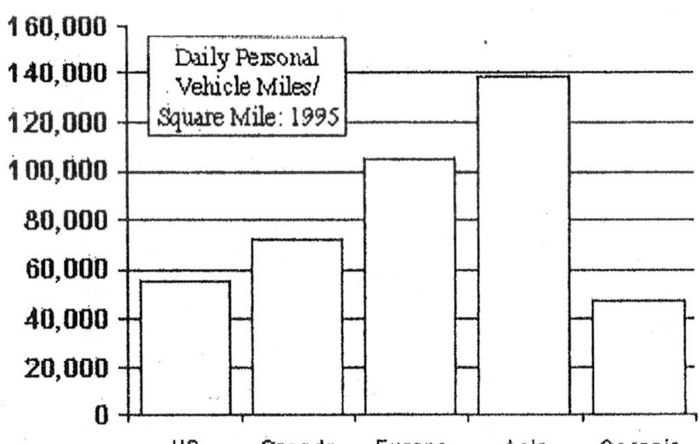

Figure 5.

In a large urban area of average employment density, there is likely to be up 750,000 jobs within a 13 mile radius of a residence. Even in a less dense urban area, there will be more than 100,000 jobs within a 13 mile commuting radius, even if the employee lives near the edge of the urban area. The average commuting distance of 13 miles translates into a commuting area of approximately 530 square miles—an area larger than all but 23 of the nation's urban areas.and more than one-half the size of all but eleven. Within an area this size there is likely to be a balance of jobs and housing.

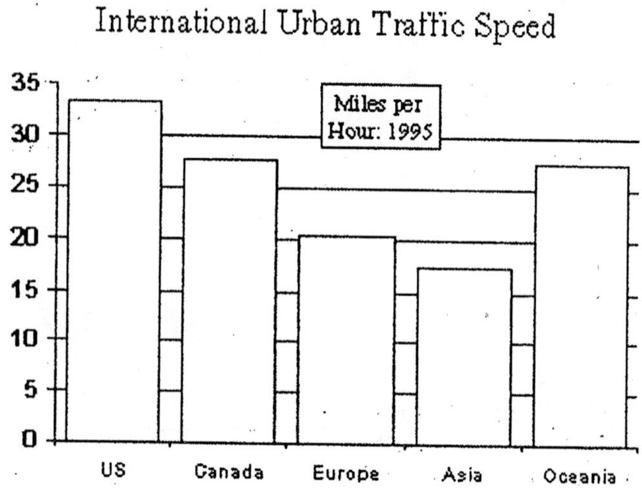

Figure 6.

In Atlanta, perhaps the world's most sprawling urban area, more than 300,000 jobs are within the 13 mile radius. Or, in Los Angeles, wrongly thought by many to be the world's most sprawling urban area (as the most dense in the US or Canada),more than 1,500,000 jobs are within the average 13 mile radius. The situation is no different in Western Europe or Japan. Tokyo-Yokohama commuters travel nearly the same distance to work as in Los Angeles (nearly 11 miles), though it takes nearly twice as long. Outside the Yamanote Loop central business district (the world's largest), there are, on average, more than 2,000,000 jobs within the average commuting radius (not counting the downtown jobs).

In Paris, the number is more than 700,000. People do not travel an average of 13 miles to work because there are no closer jobs. They work farther from home than they need to for a number of reasons. A physician is not likely to be inclined to seek a job at the convenience store-filling station within walking distance of home. Similarly a high-school drop-out is unlikely to be offered a position as a surgeon at the nearby hospital. People often commute from the same household in disparate directions.

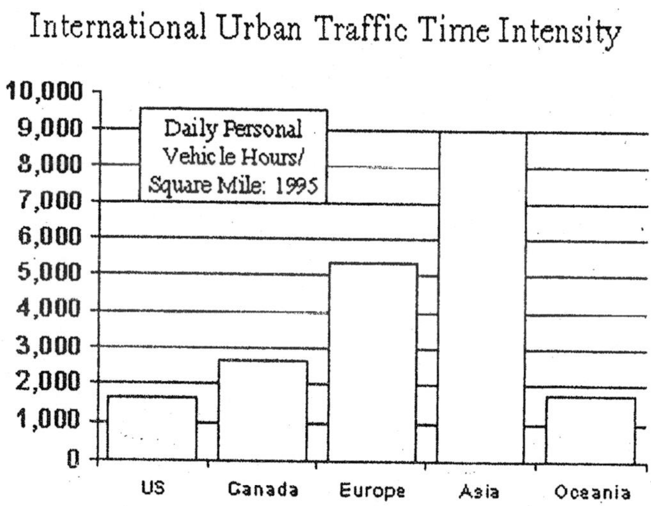

Figure 7.

The job that meets the particular requirements and preferences of the employer and the employee is often not next door. For the jobs-housing balance to work, other balances have to be present as well, such as a jobs-interest balance, a jobs-education balance and a jobs-skills balance. The entire philosophy behind the jobs-housing balance misses an important dynamic—modern metropolitan areas as large labor markets made up of geographically dispersed jobs and workers. These large labor markets are more economically efficient.

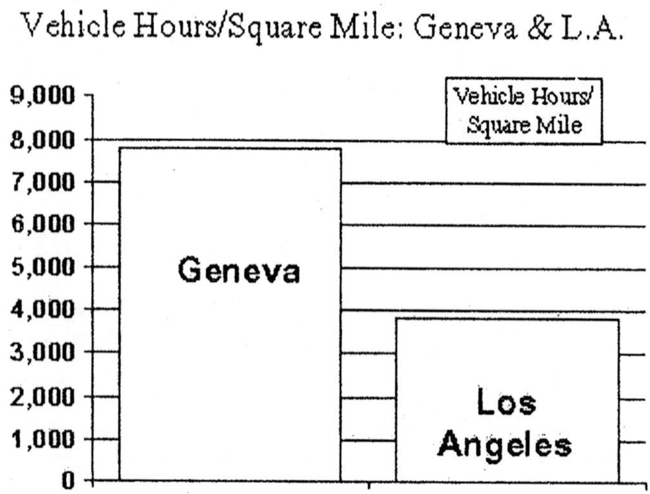

Figure 8.

Data from the latest US Census Bureau American Housing Survey indicates that convenience to employment was the most important reason for neighborhood choice only 22 percent of the time.If the data is weighted to reflect the actual distribution of all owner-occupied and rental housing, the number falls to 18 percent. No planning construct will be successful if 80 percent of the people violate it. The Census Bureau data makes it clear that that people do not regard and optimal geographical jobs-housing balance as very important. Often they are balancing job and housing locations in a manner that obtains them the most agreeable living conditions (according to their preferences) in exchange for a longer commute.

Nonetheless, there are difficulties with the present spatial arrangements. For example, in US urban areas, the less than 10 percent of households without access to cars are disproportionately concentrated in urban cores, while most new job creation is far away in the suburbs. The transit system that could provide mobility for inner city residents to these highly dispersed opportunities simply does not exist and cannot be afforded.

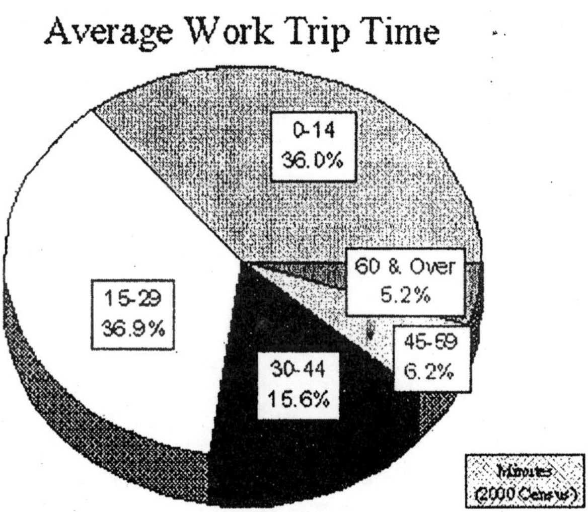

Figure 9.

Consumer Expenditures: US Bureau of Labor Statistics Consumer Spending Survey data indicates that average expenditures are lowest in the lowest density urban areas, and highest in the highest density urban areas (Table 1).

Infill Development: It is suggested that communities with existing infrastructure have the capability of handling additional residential demand. It is presumed that they can assume population growth with smaller increments of infrastructure expansion and smaller staff size additions.

But this is at problematic assumption. Urban infrastructure is often not adequate to handle material increases in population. As is indicated above, traffic congestion and air pollution tend to rise with urban densities. Thus, as more people move into the same area, there will be a need to significantly improve the street and highway system so that the additional traffic can be handled more effectively. Moreover, vehicle operating speeds need to be kept higher and more constant. But, virtually no dense central city is likely to invest in the infrastructure that would be necessary. Streets would have to be widened.

Double-decking of some freeways and major arterial streets would have to occur.Other new freeways would have to be constructed. With respect to transportation, central cities may be politically capable of meeting the demand of higher population only by retarding travel times, increasing congestion and increasing air pollution emissions. In fact, some areas adopting compact city or densification policies, such as Portland, Oregon, have also adopted traffic 6 congestion standards that will allow worse traffic congestion to occur before additional capacity is provided.

Table 1
Consumer Expenditures per Household by Density Category

Density Category	Population per Square Mile	Total	Compared to Least Dense	% Difference
Transportation				
Most Dense	4,500 & Over	$8,714	$1,281	17.2%
Less Sprawl	3,500-4,499	$7,816	$384	5.2%
Less Dense	2,500-3,499	$8,036	$603	8.1%
Least Dense	1,500-2,499	$7,433	$0	0.0%
Housing				
Density Category	Population per Square Mile	Total	Compared to Least Dense	% Difference
Most Dense	4,500 & Over	$13,886	$4,175	43.0%
Less Sprawl	3,500-4,499	$12,042	$2,331	24.0%
Less Dense	2,500-3,499	$11,217	$1,506	15.5%
Least Dense	1,500-2,499	$9,711	$0	0.0%
Food at Home				
Density Category	Population per Square Mile	Total	Compared to Least Dense	% Difference
Most Dense	4,500 & Over	$6,466	$1,276	24.6%
Less Sprawl	3,500-4,499	$5,718	$528	10.2%
Less Dense	2,500-3,499	$5,673	$483	9.3%
Least Dense	1,500-2,499	$5,190	$0	0.0%
Transportatin, Housing and Food at home expenditures combined				
Density Category	Population per Square Mile	Total	Compared to Least Dense	% Difference
Most Dense	4,500 & Over	$29,066	$6,731	30.1%
Less Sprawl	3,500-4,499	$25,576	$3,242	14.5%
Less Dense	2,500-3,499	$24,927	$2,592	11.6%
Least Dense	1,500-2,499	$22,334	$0	0.0%

Calculated from US Department of Labor Bureau of Labor Statistics Consumer Expenditure Survey 1999-2000

There are similar problems with other infrastructure. For example, the Environmental Protection Agency lists more than 700 wastewater systems in the nation that have "combined sewer and storm water" systems.These systems collect sewage and storm water and, under normal conditions, deliver it to wastewater treatment plants. However, heavy rains can cause these systems to overflow into adjacent rivers or other bodies of water. This problem is particularly concentrated in some of the nations older central cities.

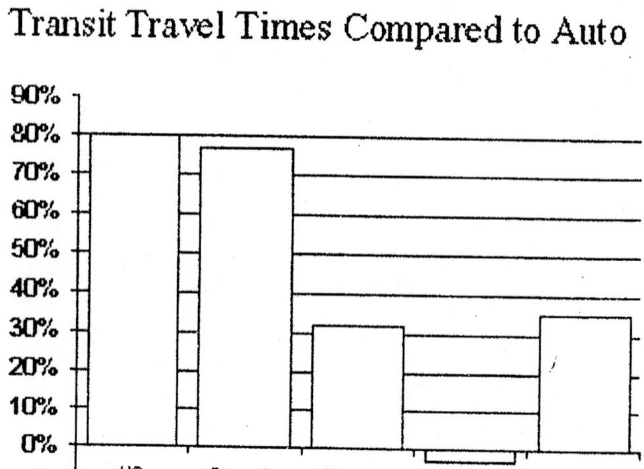

Figure 10.

For example, among the cities that have more than 50 combined overflow outfalls into bodies of water are Chicago, Indianapolis, Louisville, Detroit, New York, Cleveland, Cincinnati, Portland (Oregon), Pittsburgh, Providence, Seattle, Milwaukee and Buffalo. Densification of these cities could exacerbate this problem by increasing the demand on combined systems.

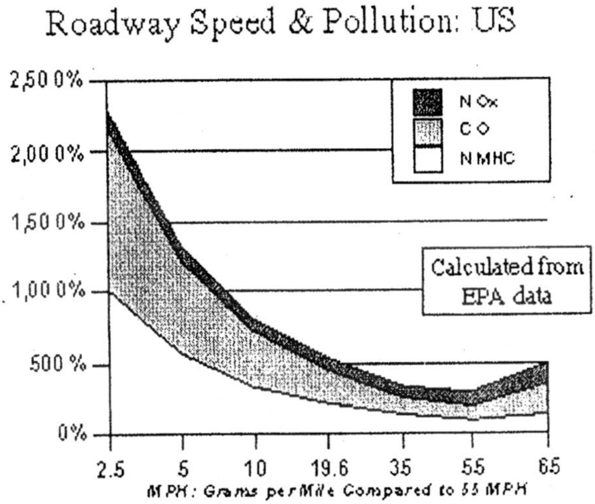

Figure 12.

In other communities, older schools that might have appeared to be theoretically capable of taking additional students have fallen into disrepair, been sold, been torn down or would require significant, expensive retrofits. And, as the analysis above indicates, older more dense communities are associated with higher, not lower public service expenditures. The "economies of scale" that would permit a larger population to be served at a lower per capita operating cost do not result, perhaps because of the political strength of interests that have evolved over a long period of time, such as strong bureaucracies and strong employee organizations that may make the local government less inclined to implement innovative and cost reducing strategies, such as competitive contracting, design/build, labor saving measures or improved management strategies.

Scaling Laws and Measurement

As scaling processes have been analysed in other fields of knowledge, fruitful ideas can be borrowed from various disciplines. Scaling refers to a set of properties associated to a type of complex systems, which exhibit nonlinear relations among attributes of their subsystems, either in their spatial organisation or during their temporal development.

To define an urban entity is a difficult problem, because towns and cities can receive a variety of social meanings. They are usually considered as a permanent grouping of resident population on a small quantity of land, but no universal threshold of population density can be associated to the definition of a town for differentiating urban from rural settlements. Most of the time, urban features are associated to non-agricultural activities, but the urban portfolio has considerably evolved over time with further progress of social division of labour.

The hypothetical purposes or advantages associated to the grouping of population and activities are considered to be of a social character (since proximity permits the maximization of social interaction and therefore, by increasing the probability of encounters, favours the emergence of innovation); economic (since urban agglomeration generate economies of different kinds (scale economies, market economies and sharing of urban infrastructures); or cultural (since symbolic representation and mimetic behaviour may explain why people gather in urban places). Probably all three of these explanations are at least partially valid, and this fact entitles urban settlements to be considered as complex systems! Certainly in the end, a general explanation of urban systems would have to rely on a given social significance and on explicit social processes.

However, the research cannot embrace at once the entire semantic field of urban reality. Observations of regularities in urban systems have tempted some researchers to reduce it to simpler measures, especially of urban size. The size of a town or city is a rather synthetic indicator, which can be correlated with many aspects of city functions and urban life.

Urban growth and the measure of urban size

The most frequently used evaluation of the importance of a town or a city is its number of inhabitants. To determine this may appear as a simple problem of measurement, until it is realised that the resident population has to be counted within a physical geographical object, which is generally expanding over time. If towns and cities were strictly bounded by walls or inside an administrative border, the difficulty of the enumeration procedure would be limited to the usual problems of defining what a "resident" population should include.

But usually, even if a strict delimitation did exist at some point in time, cities have been growing and the new buildings aggregated to the original urban node have spilled over the former walls or the once established administrative boundaries, expanding the urban agglomeration into several communes or counties (in some countries the territorial limits of the authority of municipalities are periodically revised, but this process is not so frequent and never follows exactly the physical expansion). Or, as today in many countries, the new urban buildings are sprawling into the surrounding countryside, functionally depending but no longer contiguously leaning on the original urban core.

For some administrative or political purposes, it may be relevant to identify a town or a city with its official, non-physical limits, and to consider each commune (municipality) as a separate and autonomous entity, even if one is an old centre and the next a contiguous suburb, while for a geographical or systemic study, a better definition is to aggregate within a single urban agglomeration all urban communes (municipalities) which are contiguous and whose urbanisation usually results from the historical growth around an older urban centre. This way of defining an urban agglomeration is recommended by UNO for producing comparable urban statistics. It reflects a concept of a town or a city as a spatially relatively isolated and autonomous entity. That means that a town is spatially organised in a coherent way by a principle of centrality and that it also has a consistency over time, through a relatively continuous aggregative spatial growth process.

On the contrary, an urban commune (municipality) does not correspond to any coherent geographical concept. However, as urban definitions are far from being standardized despite UNO recommendations, too many urban studies are still relying on municipal statistics, because these are almost universally produced, while ignoring that such entities cannot be taken for consistent objects and that they do not offer comparable opportunities for urbanisation.

Of course several other types of urban forms complicate the definition: for instance, two or more urban agglomerations that have grown more or less independently but not far away from each other can merge, creating a conurbation.

Table 2. Rank and population of cities according to three different delimitations

Central urban communes			Agglomerations			Daily urban systems		
Rank	Name	Population	Rank	Name	Population	Rank	Name	Population
1	Paris	2 125 246	1	Paris	9 644 507	1	Paris	11 174 743
2	Marseille	798 430	2	Marseille-Aix	1 349 772	2	Lyon	1 648 216
3	Lyon	445 452	3	Lyon	1 348 832	3	Marseille-Aix	1 516 340
4	Toulouse	390 350	4	Lille	1 000 900	4	Lille	1 143 125
5	Nice	342 738	5	Nice	888 784	5	Toulouse	964 797
6	Nantes	270 251	6	Toulouse	761 090	6	Nice	933 080
7	Strasbourg	264 115	7	Bordeaux	753 931	7	Bordeaux	925 253
8	Montpellier	225 392	8	Nantes	544 932	8	Nantes	711 120
9	Bordeaux	215 363	9	Toulon	519 640	9	Strasbourg	612 104
10	Rennes	206 229	10	Douai-Lens	518 727	10	Toulon	564 823

The spatial continuity of the built-up area admitted for the definition of an agglomeration (usually no more than 200 or sometimes 500 meters between two groups of buildings in a constructible area) has lost its significance with the enlarged range of spatial interaction made possible by the automobile, leading to alternative definitions of urban statistical areas (like the US SMSAs or the more recent French aires urbaines) that rely on a given threshold of labour force commuting to the centre. But not all countries define such more realistic or functional urban entities, and most of the existing urban data bases that can be used for comparative purposes, especially for historical times, rely on the definition of urban agglomeration.

Further arguments may be advocated in favour of adopting the definition of urban agglomeration for comparative purposes: despite urban sprawl, the continuously built-up area still concentrates the major part of urban activities (since more central locations are observed for jobs than for resident population), and there is a rough proportionality between the size of this core and of the daily urban system, which makes the agglomeration rather well representative of the importance of the functional urban area (table 2). Noticeable exceptions are to be found in North America, where the presence of new "edge cities" located far away from an older centre may be blurring the concept of urban agglomeration or even of daily urban system.

Furthermore, we shall see that, when available, the concept of functional urban area may today provide better historical continuity than the traditional concept of urban agglomeration.

Urban size and urban product

If the concept of an urban agglomeration is considered at

the moment as offering the safest and most generally available measure of urban size for international and historical comparisons, the total population of the continuously built-up area (or, more frequently, of the set of administrative local units, e. g. . , communes, within which it is located and within whose limits the population is enumerated) may not always be considered as a measure of the relative importance of the city with respect to all possible bases of comparison. For instance, when comparing towns or cities from developed and developing countries, the same population size may relate to very unequal amounts of urban product and wealth. For example, several orders of magnitude separate the economic size of Lagos or Manillia and Los Angeles, despite their comparable population size.

So, another means of measuring in an objective way the importance of a city would be to estimate its gross local product. This is not easy either, since data of that kind are very rare. Usually, production statistics are collected at the place where headquarters of the firms are located and not at each place where the added value is actually produced personal income cannot be used as a proxy, because such statistics are also very rarely produced at urban level. For measurement purposes, some estimation of urban size in economic terms has been carried out by disaggregating regional gross product. This provides completely different rankings among the world largest cities than those measured by population (table 3).

Table 3. The ten largest world cities after population size and production

City (1)	Population (millions)	City(2)	GDP(billions dollars)
Tokyo	28	Tokyo	854
New York	24	New York	448

Seoul	17	Los Angeles	326
Sao Paulo	17	Osaka	322
Mexico	17	Paris	318
Osaka	15	London	267
Los Angeles	13	Chicago	230
Jakarta	13	San Francisco	171
Mumbay	12	Dusseldorf	108
Manilla	12	Boston	107

After (1) Moriconi-Ebrard, 1993, (2) Prudhomme, 1996

One could imagine comparing cities as economic or ecological systems in terms of their costs of functioning or energetic balance. Once again, there is a lack of statistics about urbanisation costs, and much of the literature in this field has been theoretical rather than empirically founded.

An interesting attempt has been made for comparing cities as ecological systems (MOB programme by UNESCO), but the results were deceptive, mainly because of the difficulty of bounding a city, measuring the in going and outgoing flows, and of estimating in the same units physical consumption and the products of human activities. In summary, then, population statistics remain a solid and universal basis for establishing scaling effects in urban systems, even if they have to be supplemented by other meaningful but partial information.

Scaling in Urban Systems

Scaling laws as observed in natural or social systems are revealed by more or less constant relationships, either linear or non linear, between some attributes of subsystems, which cover usually several orders of magnitude within the system and persist over time. Even according to this very general definition, scaling effects in urban systems may refer to different observed regularities that have to be clarified. They could first refer to the effects of the scale of observation (or, in realist words, to the scale of organisation of urban systems) that lead to define the concept of urban system as including two main levels of aggregation: it may concern the city itself, as well as a set of cities belonging to the same regional or national territory, according to the famous formula by Brian Berry "cities as systems within systems of cities".

But the most frequent and well documented references in urban scaling are about the differences in town and city sizes within a system of cities. They have been summarized in different ways, either by statistical laws like Zipf's rank-size rule, or by central place theory. Less systematic but still strong regularities can be found at the city level between population size, urban surfaces and densities and travelling time, and perhaps this could be connected with observations made at the upper scale of the system of cities regarding the evolution over time of city size and spacing, in the context of an increasing speed of transportation. Finally, the existence of self-similar patterns at different scales, including mainly the reiterated scheme of centres and peripheries in the distribution of nodes and networks, could provide another synthetic view of urban scaling effects.

Zipf's rank-size rule

The same word, "urban settlement", (or ville in French, Stadt in German) is used for designating entities which may vary by several orders in magnitude, a few thousand inhabitants for the smallest up to several tens of millions for the largest. City sizes are not distributed uniformly between these extremes of 10^3 and 10^7, but on the contrary they follow a rather strict statistical law inside a given territory. Zipf had expressed such a regularity as an inverse geometric progression between the population P_i of a city and its rank R_i in a national set of towns and cities, giving an approximate size of one half of the largest city population for the population of the second city and one third for the third one, and so on. This "rank size-rule" formulated as $P_i = P_1 / R_i$ has been generalised as a Pareto-type distribution of the number of cities according to their size, $P_i = K / Ri^{\alpha}$, where the parameter K has a value close to P_1 and α is around 1.

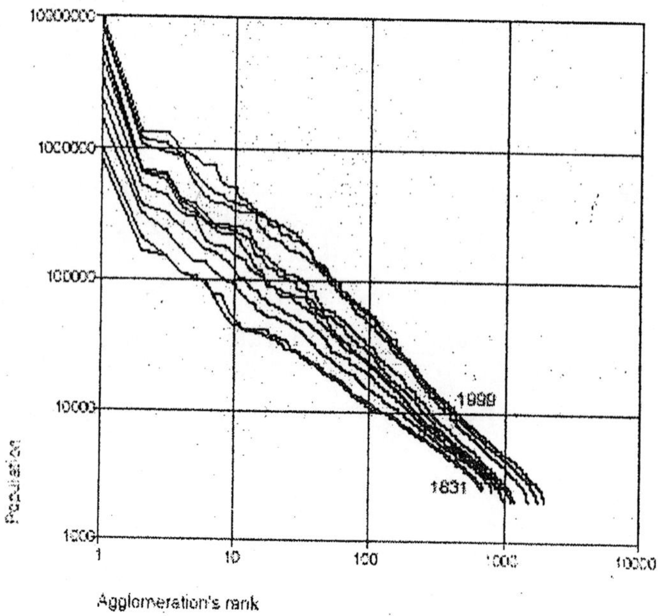

Figure 13. The hierarchical differentiation in urban systems: Rank-size distribution of French agglomerations (1831-1999)

This model has been fitted many times to more or less correctly measured population series of towns and cities (figure 13). When adjusted to the population of the urban agglomerations (towns and cities over 10 000 inhabitants) of each state in the world (including all those having at least 30 urban agglomerations), the estimated values for the parameter α range between 0. 7 and 1. 3. The variation among different countries is rather small: the standard deviation of measured α values is only 0. 138.

The fit of the Pareto model is rather good, even if in many cases better fits can be found to other types of asymmetrical distributions. Usually, when settlements of smaller sizes are included, the lognormal distribution provides better fit than the Pareto mode'. Very often, the upper part of the size distribution, corresponding to the largest urban settlements, does not fit very well to any model: these cases of urban primacy (one to up to eight cities per state whose size exceeds the expected values) were detected a long time ago and seem to be a generality rather than an exception. For two thirds of the world's states, the mean value of the ratio P1/P2 is significantly larger than the one that would correspond to the model.

When this "primacy index" is computed, as the ratio between the population of the largest and second largest city, it is found that in most states of the world it is much larger than the value of two which would correspond to Zipf's rank size rule (for a Pareto distribution with a value of 1. 3 for the parameter α , the expected ratio would be 2. 5) and the mean value for all countries of the world taken together is 5. 2.

Several remarks have to be made, because the literature on Zipf's law is full of ill-founded conclusions, mainly due to small samples of observations and a lack of accuracy in empirical data. It is true that whatever the part of the world and the period of observation, since the 10 000 years when towns first emerged, the model of settlement size distribution has always been reasonably well approximated by a Pareto or lognormal distribution. This has been demonstrated by Fletcher, based on available data on early urban settlements as determined by archaeologists.

During historical times, the inequality in city sizes has been increasing. Empirical evidence from historical data shows a clear evolution from values for the α parameter of around 0. 7 in many countries before the XIXth century, to values significantly higher (at least 0. 9 and often larger than 1) for distributions observed since the middle of XXth century. However, the direction of the most recent evolution is by no means clear: between 1950 and 1990, the value of the α parameter has steadily increased in 19 countries, steadily decreased in 9 others, while it followed no regular evolution in the remaining 21. There is a rather general trend to a diminution of the contrast in city sizes in the more developed countries, but there are exceptions (USA, France, Japan, Russia, Hungary and Greece). The diversity in evolutionary paths is still larger in third-world countries.

Such observations clearly maintain the city sizes distribution within the sphere of attraction of Levy's stable laws, whereas other distributions of inequalities in social systems have evolved towards the attraction domain of the normal law. M. Barbut has demonstrated that the distribution of incomes shifted towards the attractor of the Gaussian model about in the middle of the 1930's in France and about the same time for other developed countries which had undertaken policies of social redistribution. Similarly, the inequalities in the size distribution of firms were reduced by anti-trust regulations.

Over time, there is no indication either of any convergence towards more or less regularity in the shape of the size curve. This contradicts an hypothesis made by Berry and repeated many times since. According to these authors, the existence of a primary city would reflect an earlier state of urbanism, and the size distribution should evolve towards a more regular pattern over time. On the contrary, the persistence of systematic deviations from the Pareto model seems to be the rule, especially in the upper part of the city size distribution. This aspect may be considered as relatively minor in the scaling property of systems of cities, which gives a good fit to power laws for the largest part of the size distributions.

But it may be taken into account by noticing that urban systems never are completely isolated from their environment, and that the larger the cities are, the broader is the range of their relations. Perhaps the largest cities of each country should be considered as being parts of wider territorial systems or networks, which would make their frequently exceptional size more understandable. However, some very large urban systems, as in United States, have very regular size distributions.

In any case, another regularity has to be mentioned. Although it may be rather loose , there is a definite relationship in the magnitude of the size of the largest city of a country (P1) and the total urban population of this country (PT). The proportion of the urban population which is concentrated in the major city varies between 10 and 30%. This proportion tends to be larger in smaller countries than in the large ones. An adjustment of that very much improves the fit is to use the non-linear relationship : $P1 = k\ PT^{0.8}$. This is a direct consequence of the general Pareto shape of all national city size distributions.

Central place theory

Christaller's central place theory succeeded in summarizing a set of interesting regularities related to city size that had been observed long ago. These regularities refer to the correlation between the total population of a city and the number and diversity of urban functions it performs (especially the services offered to the resident population), as well as the total number of consumers it attracts around it, and the spacing between cities of the same hierarchical level. Though it has been tested and rather well verified in a wide variety of territorial and economic environments (even on systems of periodic markets, for instance by Skinner), and is still valid in may respects, central place theory has lost some of its explanatory power with increasing urbanisation, mainly because cities are no longer just central places for surrounding rural populations.

The theory does not take into account the presence of non-service urban activities, even if services to the resident population may still concentrate more than half and often two thirds of a city's labour force. Even though central place theory gives an interesting insight in the explanation of inequalities in city sizes and how they correlate to many aspects or indices of a hierarchy of urban activities, it is difficult to use these relationships to search for scaling laws in urban systems. International comparisons would require that the "levels" that are identified among the cities of one country or regions and the corresponding portfolio of urban activities should be made comparable.

As nomenclatures of urban activities are not defined in the same way in different countries, the statistical shape of the relationship between them and the size of cities has never been investigated systematically in comparative studies. There are also differences in income level, as well

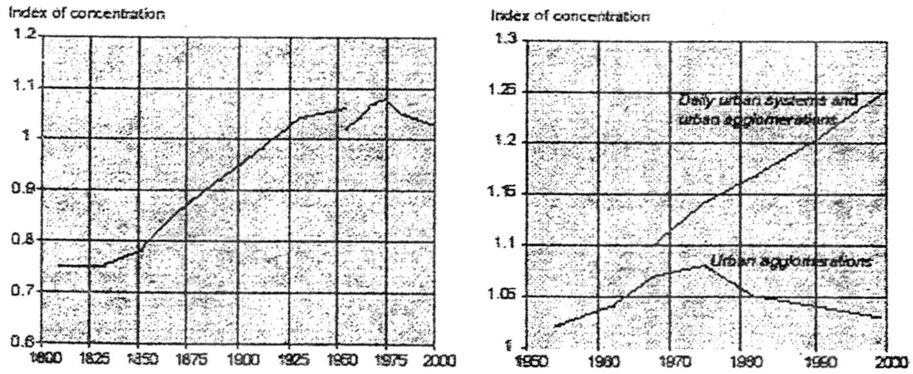

Figure 14. Evolution of urban concentration in France

On the left is plotted the evolution of the absolute value of the slope á in the equation Pi = K/Ri$^{\alpha}$ adjusted to the population of French agglomerations at all census dates from 1831 to 1999. There seem to be a reversal in the historical trend toward stronger hierarchisation, but when urban entities are delimitated according to a more sensible definition (aires urbaines, right side), the continuity of the concentration trend appears.

as cultural differences, that introduce important variations in the ratio between the number of residents of a city and the number of jobs in services supplied to them.

Urban size, spacing and speed of transportation

A simpler theory of urban systems that would include scaling effects comes from considering them as forms of spatial organisation that optimise in some way the space-time budget for daily activities of their inhabitants. At the scale of a single city, the speed of transportation is rather slow, but the concentration of many activities at short distances ensured by the high density allows for a good level of generalised accessibility. Over time, the speed of transportation has slightly increased, from 4km/h to about 16 km/h in the dense central parts of urban cores, until 60 to 80 km/h in the better equipped suburbs.

Zahavi has advanced the hypothesis that where a gain of transportation speed has been possible, it has not been used to reduce transport time; on the contrary, the mean commuting time tends to remain constant (about one hour per day) and commuting distances are increased. This has been roughly confirmed by observations about the recent evolution of commuting times and distances in many countries. As an example, a recent survey estimated that the daily time budget dedicated to transport varies very little from one country to another (among developed countries): from about 55 minutes (as in Hungary and France) to one hour and 24 minutes (in UK) or 1h23 (Belgium), 1h15 (Denmark). Statistics for historical times are more difficult to provide, but most estimates are around one hour per day (for example, this estimate is consistent with observed patterns in the extension of intensively used agricultural land around villages in rural Europe).

If we admit that the time devoted to commuting has remained about constant during historical times, then it is the speed of transportation that explain why the diameter of urban areas has been expanding, mainly first with tramways and railways, then with motorcars, increasing for instance the available surface of a city like Berlin by a factor of 100 between the "city on foot" (2km radius) and the "city by car" (20 km). Meanwhile, the mean urban densities have decreased.

At another spatial scale, it is the length of the intervals between two neighbouring towns or cities that seems to be regulated by the speed of the transport system over long periods of time. As the mean available speed has increased (from less than 20 km/h with horses and coaches to 500 km/h with planes), the number of necessary steps along itineraries has decreased, the weakest towns located in intermediary positions between more important centres has declined, at least in relative terms, and the average spacing between the main urban centres has increased.

This trend is one part of the explanation of the reinforcement of urban hierarchies since the beginning of the nineteenth century and the industrial revolution of the transportation systems (figure 14). As at the same time the general income and production were increasing, enlarging and diversifying the demand for urban services, towns and cities have grown in size and number. Such an increase in the size and number of towns and cities has been especially observed during the period of intense urbanisation from the beginning of the XIXth century in developed countries and from the middle of XXth century in the developing ones.

But as the increase in general wealth of population (or GNP) did not occur at as high a rate as the increase in transportation speed (inducing the apparent shrinking of space), the result is a higher contrast in city size distribution over the past two centuries. More precise measured evidences of this process can be provided.

The regularity of the spacing between towns and cities is not as regular and geometrical as predicted by the hexagonal geometry of classical central place theory. However, when mapped for instance for the whole set of European agglomerations having 10 000 inhabitants or more, the distances between neighbouring towns may reveal very consistent spatial patterns at different geographical scales and levels of the urban system. The resulting pattern shows clearly three main types of urban systems in Europe: a central part with much higher densities (high number of connections), a western part (mainly France and Spain) more contrasted (parts of the territory, as coast lines or main valleys, exhibit concentrations while in other parts the towns are much more apart from each other and there are no connections), and an eastern part with a high regularity in spacing (connections appear in all regions).

Combined with size, these three types would rejoin the typology established by Etienne Juillard who labelled respectively as Rhenish, Parisian and Peripheral such urban networks. But the point is that the general pattern is maintained, if one raises the minimum distance to less than 50 km, and less than 100 km for the subset of agglomerations larger than 100 000 inhabitants. So a simple analysis by a cartographic filtering method illustrates the evidence of the hierarchical and spatial organisation of urban systems that is at the basis of their scaling properties. Obviously history can explain the three different types of spatial patterns, that roughly correspond to distinct political and administrative organisation of the territories (more centralised in France and Spain for centuries, also in United

Kingdom but there the urban system was more disturbed by the industrial revolution; Germany and Italy have been unified much later, that facilitated the persistency of rather large close regional capitals; the regularity of the eastern side may reflect the systematic organisation that was imposed by a late colonisation through settlements from the XIIIth century on...to give only a few clues).

The evolution of the European urban system also demonstrates a high consistency over time, as illustrated by (Bretagnolle et al. , 1998). The effects of increasing demography and income explains the general expansion of the system, in the number of cities and in their size, but hides the structural transformations of the system. Taking into account the relative size of cities, either by computing the share of their population in the total population of the system, or by mapping solutions, put forward the impressive accentuation of city size inequalities, which affects all parts of the system, whatever the region or the hierarchical level under consideration. Space-time contraction due to the speeding-up of transportation means is considered as an important factor responsible for that reorganisation process.

The possible spatial transformations of urban systems have then to be observed, not in a physical space, but in a time (or cost-)-space which is relevant for defining the real possibilities of interaction between cities. Following works by historians, we suggested to introduce in measurements of classical urban population potentials one parameter which accounts for the general and local modifications in the accessibility of cities. The maps of urban population potentials which are produced illustrate in a synthetic way the spatial effects of differential growth in a system of cities. The evolution of the spatial configuration of European urban system shows a regular and slow adaptation of its structure to major changes in energy sources and trade roads.

Fractality and urban systems.

Fractal measures have been applied to urban systems, first at the level of systems of cities, and second, at the level of the internal structure of urban areas, in particular with respect to the the spatial distribution of built-up surfaces.

The urbanised space is actually implemented in a fractal way: it is fragmented, self-similar in the sense that the same patterns, like the dilution from a centre towards a periphery, can be observed at several scales, and hierarchical, including many more small centres than large ones, as well as a many more small narrow roads than very large ones, or many more small urban squares than very large plazas. The same differentiation processes have produced more or less regular gradients in building, population and activities densities around the centres towards peripheries, at local scales as well as at regional or higher scales, according to various degrees of accessibility.

The available measurements that have been computed for a variety of cities throughout the world are not always strictly comparable, since they partly rely on the resolution of the maps that were used for estimating them. Moreover, since urbanism is not the same kind of phenomenon over time, urban structures are probably multifractal; a medieval centre did not have the same factor of dilution of its buildings in surrounding space than does a contemporary suburb. Differences have also been observed between European or Asiatic cities, which tend to have lower values for the fractal dimension of their built-up areas (between 1.4 and 1.8), and Australian or North-American cities, which are closer to homogeneous distributions (dimensions between 1.8 and 2). However, from available measures, it seems that these fractal dimensions of intra-urban structures always have values between 1 and 2. This corresponds to a more or less fragmented occupation of land by the buildings, that remains however consistent and reveals the effect of a principle (coined by concepts like centrality or urban field) that organises the process of urbanisation.

Recent comparisons among European cities built-up areas imply another interesting theoretical interpretation about the concept of urban agglomeration: the spatial limits that are defined for urban agglomerations coincide with the area that is spatially organised according to a fractal law. The external limit of the urban form inside which the buildings are spatially distributed in a fractal way is closer to the geographical limit of the urban agglomeration than of the daily urban system defined after links created by commuting. Moreover, it has been demonstrated that such a limit has moved further away from the centre over time, following the spatial delimitation of the urban agglomeration.

The spatial expansion of cities then consists in the progressive integration of urban built-up space into a fractal structure. A new and more universal definition of cities could perhaps be suggested, as portions of geographical space where the habitat obeys an ordering principle that is a fractal law.

Whereas most often the spatial distribution of built up areas or population in rural space does not differ significantly from homogeneity, the analyses of the interurban distribution of buildings or population have shown fractal dimensions which are usually below 1. This could be attributed to another way of occupying space, more diluted, for less frequent relations, as mentioned above in a space-time interpretation of urban systems.

Such observations confirm our conception of two distinct levels in the spatial organisation of urban systems: 1) the intra-urban level, or the "urban field", including as a functional organising principle the accessibility to the centre (not exceeding 30 minutes time in radius, and inducing variations in density levels which may reach a 100 or 200 order of magnitude and in land prices per sq meter which may rise to 30 times between the centre and the periphery), proceeding over time from a peripheral spatial expansion as well as from variations in the intensity of land use; 2) the interurban level, or the system of cities, where the size and spacing of towns and cities are organised according to a hierarchical access to services, resulting from a competitive process for capturing and accumulating resources. (especially from innovation), inducing a spatially distributed process of growth on very long periods of time, but with heterogeneities leading to a differentiation in city sizes which usually can reach a factor of 1000 within a single country.

We suggest using the term "hierarchical organisation" to describe the existence of two distinct levels in urban systems (the levels of the city and of the system of cities), whereas we reserve the term "hierarchical differentiation" to refer to the macroscopic property of urban systems that leads to a Pareto distribution of city sizes.

On Autonomy And Control

When looking for social or spatial processes that could explain why the configuration of , and sometimes their urban systems exhibits rather regular scaling phenomena, it is very difficult to assess where the control of such regularities could come from. Several hypotheses can be made, and one has to be chosen in accordance with the way the scaling effects will be modelled. We shall discuss here only a few.

Do scaling laws result from random growth processes?

Urban systems involve large numbers (of settlements, and persons) regularities have been conceived to be a consequence of general statistical effects or stochastic processes. For instance, a static explanation of the rank-size rule has been suggested by describing cities as the aggregation of a variety of activities. As each of these industries follow Pareto laws of distribution (for the size of firms), and since a sum of Pareto laws is still a Pareto law, this could explain the shape and regularity of the distribution of city size. Of course this leaves the problem of how to account for the Pareto distribution of firms within an industry. And it does not explain how cities come to concentrate variable amounts of firms and activities.

Moreover, the growth process of firms is not at all the same as the one for cities. Firms can merge or divide, they also can collapse, many are created or die during a short period of time. If we leave aside the rare cases of cities merging (forming conurbations) and of cities dying (this seems to happen very rarely during modern historical times) cities are growing or declining in their population from natural increase, or by migrations. They can grow more or less rapidly, and towns entering the system usually are former villages which overcome the threshold of urban definition.

Better solutions than static explanations can be found by looking at the urban growth process. In the literature two contradictory affirmations are found when justifying the existence of a scaling law like Zipf's distribution by the growth rules of the system. As it has been demonstrated that a random process like the "law of proportional effect" could explain the lognormal distribution, the stochasticity of such effects could be at first sight admitted, and sometimes is claimed. Simple application of "the law of large numbers"? According to Halloy, "possibly the primal feature of complex systems is greed (or more euphemistically, resource attraction) and competition as its secondary outcome.

It is this resource attraction and competition which in turns determines the primary interactions between agents, as well as the adaptive nature agents changing rules to outcompete others". But a deeper insight into the growth generating process and in the way it is distributed among cities would lead to a less simple explanation. Which social processes can maintain urban growth dP as an average proportion of the initial size of a city and why should the growth rates (dP/P) be randomly distributed at each short time interval, as observed by Robson for British towns as well as the French ones?

When observing carefully how cities transform over long periods of time, it can be shown that the urban changes (new techniques, but also new economic activities, professions, physical infrastructures, as well as fashions, cultural practices and so on) are adopted in each very quickly, compared to the general speed of change. But cities are adapting to the changes (that they contribute to create as well) by small discontinuous adjustments: the deviations from the mean change are generally not found in the same cities at two successive time intervals. On the whole, urban qualitative changes (and corresponding quantitative growth) diffuse themselves rapidly within the entire urban

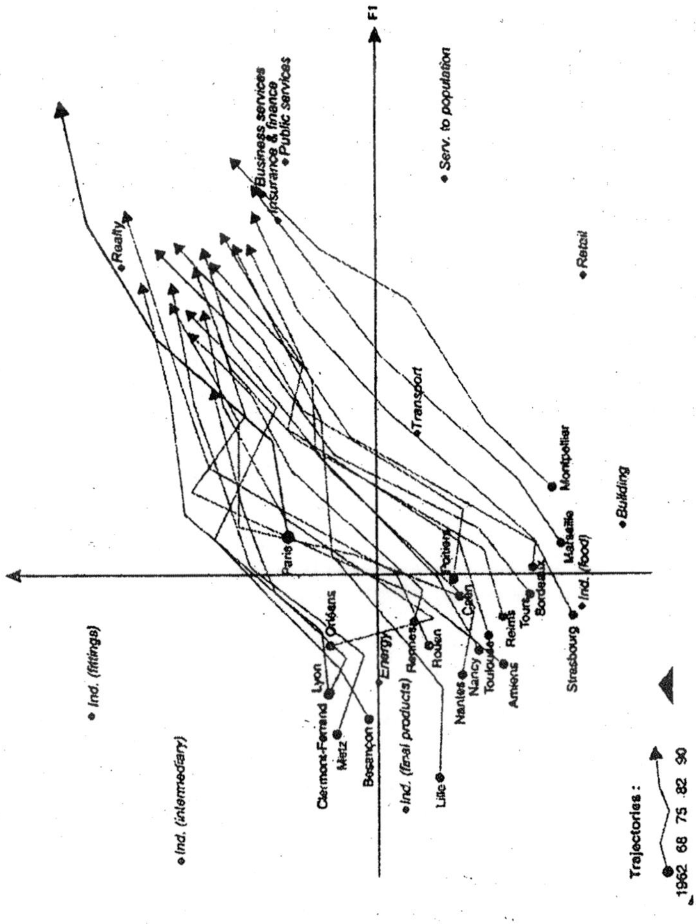

Figure 15. Co-evolution of economic profiles of French agglomerations (1962-1999).

system and therefore do not alter the initial structure of the system; the relative situations (in terms of size or economic specialisation for instance) remain the same. This can be illustrated by the evolution of the position of cities projected on a graph defined by a multivariate analysis of their economic profiles at different dates (figure 15).

This is made possible because every town or city within the system is "trying" to do the same as its neighbour. Or, put in another way, they are in competition for the same thing (to attract population and activities, to capture investment or the benefits of innovations). In some sense, they "behave" as if they were "greedy". So even behind a process that could apparently be reproduced by a purely stochastic model, there may be a substantive explanation in social terms.

Are scaling laws the product of any optimisation principle?

Cities are neither firms nor simple institutions. They don't have any general aim or function to fulfil and, even if subsets of interested actors or some specialised institutions can be identified for representing an activity sector or a partial group of citizens, there is no responsible omnipotent body for supporting the general city development in all its dimensions. This could have been the case in historical time for instance in Europe when cities were governed by a prince or a bishop having full authority over the population and territory. Actually such cities should be considered as "states" and in fact are identified as "city-states" by historians. Their rivalries and the events in their development could be related to well identified "actors" who took decisions according to their representation of what their city should become.

On the contrary we have shown, when discussing the difficulty of providing reliable urban statistics, the usual mismatch between consistent physical or functional urban entities and the administrative limits on which they are built. Today the real political power that controls a city's development has been delegated to upper levels of governance of territories or economic institutions and is no longer unified at the scale of a single city.

At another scale, namely systems of towns and cities, there is neither any decisional body that would take decisions for keeping the size of cities within the general model of city sizes. Of course towns and cities are connected by a multitude of links corresponding to a variety of social networks. A few networks can be identified that would be interested in lobbying for the sake of cities that belong to them. But no single institution, nor even a few competing ones, can be taken for being directly responsible for the persistence of the general model of city size distribution. As mentioned above, if cities keep relatively constant shares in general economic, demographic and cultural or technical developments, it is probably by a deconcentrated process of many decisions taken at a micro level (to invest in such activity, to migrate to a city, to adopt such innovation...), that drives the transformation of each town or city, in an incremental way, towards the general direction of change.

The economic theory could provide explanations by demonstrating that this structure of the urban system corresponds to an optimisation. However, the urban economic theory mainly conceive cities as places where agglomeration economies can be produced for attracting firms. City size is theorised as resulting from the compromise between agglomeration economies and congestion costs (both quantities are very rarely empirically measured or estimated). Usually such a theory leads to the conception of an optimal city size. The economic models which try to produce as an output a rank size distribution remain theoretical and have not been empirically tested.

Economic theory cannot yet explain why there should be a Zipf's law, and it is highly significant that in their last book on spatial and urban economy, Fujita, Krugman and Venables devote a whole chapter to that question, entitled: "an empirical digression: the size of cities"! They quote a suggestion by Krugman to develop an analogue between cities and river networks, forgetting to recall that such an analogy was already suggested by Chorley and Haggett in their book on geographical models in 1967.

Moreover, Krugman suggests that the "percolation theory" of physics could be used for modelling urban hierarchies as the result of a diffusion process. However, it is well known that diffusion processes in urban systems are very often "hierarchical", in the sense that the adoption of innovation "jumps" from a large city to a very distant large one before going to the closest and that it cannot be simulated by a passive and contiguous diffusion process.

Alternative approaches for models of urban growth

Playing with power laws and trying to generate them from agent based models or multi-agents systems that define rules of interaction at a mico-level is not specific to the urban sciences. A large variety of examples can be found, from stock market and wealth distribution in a population , to the size of firms in a nation state or length of words in languages. However, hypothesis and results should not simply be transferred from one discipline to the others, because the selection of relevant variables and processes is very specific, if one wants to represent even in a simplified way the empirical knowledge associated with each field.

S. E. Page proposes an agent-based model for simulating the emergence of cities, from very simple assumptions about agent's location behaviour, depending on a preference for agglomeration and an average distance to other agents. However, in this model an agent's utility is defined that refers to the distribution of agents on the lattice, it is not very plausible that real agents could attain such an information. Axtell and Florida provide a more detailed microeconomic multi-agent model of endogeneous firm formation, allowing agents to move between firms and between clusters of firms (then assimilated to cities).

Under the hypothesis of increasing returns from clustering at the level of the firm, they simulate a size distribution with constant returns (average growth rate) at the aggregate level. A stationary macro-structure is generated from a non equilibrium microeconomics. However appealing because it conciliates two apparently contradictory but observed processes (search for increasing returns at the individual level, no decisive increasing returns at the aggregate level), this model has not yet reached the stage of validation from empirical observations.

Anderson et al. use an algorithm building « scale-free » networks. This corresponds to a class of growing networks whose node degrees are power law distributed. In their model, the nodes of the network represent pieces of land which become over time more and more connected by edges representing exchanges of goods and services (actually the result of this trade is simulated by a trade benefit or financial investment directed from one node to another). The model proceeds by adding new links between already developed nodes, with a probability which is proportional to the relative size of the node in the total of nodes, and by selecting new nodes. The mean probability of developing existing nodes is significantly higher than the one attached to the development of new nodes. Spatial rules are added for specifying this selection process, according to hypothesis about a distance-decay interaction model.

The model is calibrated in order to fit an impressive empirical data set about land values in Sweden (almost 3 million observations). The paper demonstrates the ability of the model to reproduce the global statistical distribution (frequency of land squares with according to land price) and its main parameter (Pareto exponent of 2. 1). The authors assume a linear relationship between the value per unit of urban land and the size of urban population, so their model could be used as a starting point for fitting population data as well.

The paper is not clear bout the scale of application of the model: whereas referring at first to Zipf's law, which is a model of the interurban distribution of city sizes, it represent "systems of specialised trading activities" that "can be resolved to any resolution down to individual transactions", whereas the explanation of the model in "an urban economy context" seems to refer mainly to intra-urban land values formation (for instance, looking at different processes at the perimeter of urban areas and predicting the emergence of urban sub-centres). In any case, the model predicts a single and unified statistical distribution of land values at a country scale, making no distinction between the intra-urban gradient of land prices and the interurban distribution of land values. The model produces only a sharp break between rural and urban land values.

To be coherent with the existing state of knowledge, the authors should have tested the variations of land prices inside the nodes (between centres and peripheries) as well as between the aggregated nodes. It could happen that the rather high level of inequalities they find between land prices is more linked with intra-urban inequalities than to interurban. Actually, when I looked at the average housing, offices and land prices per urban area in France, I discovered that prices are surprisingly similar from one city to the next (low variance) and the correlation with city size (as measured by population figures) is rather low for the entire distribution (even if a very large city like Paris has the highest prices in the country). Meanwhile, the inequalities between the prices per hectare inside the same city may reach a factor 10 and more, at the block level.

The simulation by network building is however an interesting way of specifying a growth process in an urban system. Models of distributed growth are at the basis of the generation of power law distributions. This was shown as early as 1922 by Willis and Yule in a deterministic model explaining the linear relation between the logarithms of the numbers of genus and species; such a model was applied for cities by Steindl who demonstrated again in 1965 that two hypothesis are sufficient for generating a rank-size distribution: all towns and cities have the same growth rate, and there is a constant ratio over time between this urban population growth rate and the rate of appearance of new towns in the urban system.

Before that, other authors willing to take into account the numerous fluctuations of observed urban growth rates between cities and over time had invented stochastic processes including similar principles: H. Simon, transposing a model first elaborated by Yule, shows how a Pareto-like distribution, which is characteristic of contagious processes, can be generated if the probability for a migrant to reach a city of size i is proportional to the total number of people already living in cities of size i and if the individual probability of migrating to a new town remains constant over time; R. Gibrat demonstrates that the "law of proportional effect" as a stochastic model is sufficient for explaining the emergence of a lognormal distribution of city sizes.

Our first SIMPOP model generates rank-size distribution from a multi-agents system simulating a spatially competitive urban growth. We made the spatial process of urban growth more explicit by including the centre-periphery effects in a less detailed but more powerful simulation model. In these models, we did not look at the intra-urban distribution of population, obviously for reasons of limitation of computer memory capacities, but also because we think that intra-urban and inter-urban distributions have different forms, which may be explained by different morphogenetic processes. Anderson and his colleagues may be right in considering the urban land values as a scale-free distribution for a whole country, but they seem to neglect an essential feature of such a distribution, its multi-fractality.

As observed in the case of spatial distributions of population or of built-up areas, there are at least two different gradients, one inside intra-urban aggregates and the other for inter-urban nodes. We would like to develop a theory that generates both, if possible within a single model. The urban space has not the same properties within and between cities. The land use is somehow more intense inside cities, generating a better accessibility to a larger diversity of activities, together with a high level of mobility, but the transportation speed for connecting intra-urban places is rather slow. The space between cities is more diluted, accessibility and frequency of use are lower, but the speed of connection is much higher.

The solution could be to include a model of growth with similar characteristics as the already existing models that can generate skewed distribution of size aggregates, but at two different scales according to the intensity of activities allowed by speed of transportation, and with evolving speed and range over historical time. The fractal dimension of the generated aggregates could be used for validation of the model.

The outcome of a constrained evolutionary process?

Rather than conceiving, as economists do, that at any time there is an optimisation, or an equilibrium, our observations would lead us to consider that urban systems do evolve far from equilibrium. The general structure of urban systems, including scaling effects, could be the result of social evolutionary processes : as in biological sciences, one can identify effects of mutation, competition, cooperation and selection, but in this case the evolution is also partly driven by a cognitive activity of inventing technical and social artefacts.

Improvement of accessibility to more and more sophisticated activities, in order to reduce life uncertainties (ecological and social), could be considered as the main constraint operating on the evolution of the system, at both scales of analysis. But the action of this organising principle on the spatial structure of the urban systems is almost always indirect : especially at the level of the system of cities, there is no conscious will neither no responsible institution for organising and adapting the system to ensure this increasing power of accessibility. The global structure and its more or less continuous adaptation are emerging from the interurban competition.

In such an interpretation, the accessibility constraint would be the systemic ordering principle of the spatial structure of urban systems. It could be a kind of collective "rationale", distinct from the actual individual intentions of urban actors, which could be, on the whole, to make a better living by adding value to the urban "heritage" (global value of urban estates, production capital of firms, human capital of resident population, development potential of activities and urban capacities, symbolic value inducing urban attractivity, and so on). This very general aim (?), at the level of urban actors, produces, when aggregated, the apparent "greediness" at the level of each city, which explain their competitive incremental adaptation to change and the process of creation and capture of innovation that characterises their interactive dynamics within the systems of cities. It is this historical competitive process which explains the persistence of a continuum of towns and city sizes, representative of individual stories of towns which succeeded or failed to adapt at each step of the evolution. The city size (and the correlated variety and complexity of the activity portfolio and social and cultural sophistication) is the cumulated product of such an history.

The largest metropolises usually have very long stories of successful adaptation. For instance, Paris and London in Europe, even if they were state capitals, have both benefited from the industrial revolution of the XIXth century - probably because they also were since a long time the largest city in their country, and then the more likely to be open to any kind of innovation. The industrial revolution can be seen as a major perturbation for the European urban system because specialised cities, sometimes very large, as Birmingham, or Manchester, or cities of the Ruhr area, were boosted from a status of small towns to the upper ranks of the urban hierarchy.

The industrial revolution had another important effect by reinforcing the inequalities in city size all over Europe (mainly through the effects of rapid transportation means).

But despite this, it has to be recalled that the urban hierarchy in Europe was not totally upset by the industrial revolution: the correlation between the rank of cities in the middle of eighteen century, before it started, and their rank in 1950, long after its end, is very high (coefficient around 0. 8!). The capacity of this system of cities to absorb big shocks was already attested in XVth century by its recovery, making it similar both in cities' size and ranking, one century after the Black Death had divided the population by a factor two.

This is another indication of the number and strength of the links that have for centuries tightly knotted the network of European towns and cities, making their co-evolution a fully competitive process much before the continent was equipped with direct and rapid transport connexions between all of them. The major transformation that happened between the XVIth and XVII century, transferring the core of the system from the Mediterranean coast to the Nordsea was a very slow process. The development of functionally specialised cities is usually linked with different economic cycles which have favoured the growth of particular places : before the industrial revolution, there are references to similar "generations" of cities, that were once driven by textile industry, trade with the colonies, or since the end of nineteenth century by mass tourism. A recent version of this specialisation process would occur for instance in the cities of high tech, or finance activities.

However successful during the boom of the specialising activities, such places may have difficulties to continue their further adaptation to new cycles of products, or ways of producing, unless they continuously invent new kinds of innovation. Some of them may share the destiny of the smallest towns, that were once successful but not for long -but that can become again adapted to some innovation and are susceptible to grow again, even if the probability that they would ever challenge the largest metropolis is very small.

At least three time scales have then to be considered for describing the main processes of this evolution of urban systems : the short time process of innovation and competition, as it may be seen at the actor level, the mean time -usually a few decades- process of specialisation as related to economic cycles at the level of each town and city, and the long time process of the emergence and slow transformation of the urban hierarchy - in general, several centuries- at the level of the whole system of cities.

8

Urbanisation and Socio-economic Restructuring

The decline of traditional mass production during the 1970s and 1980s has led to a profound restructuring of the economic sphere of society. Highly capitalized units and centralized production structures have entered a long-lasting crisis everywhere in the world, and the advanced capitalist countries have endured serious problems of deindustrialization. Large plants, which formerly served to maximize economies of scale and reduce production costs, have become too rigid to respond to new consumer demands.

The immediate response to these problems has been changes aimed at optimizing production and decentralizing and "flexibilizing" production decisions. These restructuring efforts, firms have become capable of manufacturing high-quality products, while keeping costs low and enabling, at the same time, the reinforcement of links between manufacturers and consumers. The shift from mass production methods to flexible ones and the increasing integration and globalization of the world economy have not only altered economies, but have also transformed prevailing social, political, and territorial patterns.

As a result, a more flexible model of spatial organization that challenges long-established disparities seems to be emerging. In this new spatial configuration, service activities are likely to play a much greater role in economic growth and the significance of subnational entities is likely to increase, to the detriment of nation-states.

Many studies have sought to confirm the appearance of new post-Fordist landscapes and new patterns in the spatial distribution of wealth. Most empirical research on the topic, however, has been restricted to case studies focusing on growth poles and industrial districts in formerly lagging areas.

European countries provides us with a space that has been clearly affected by the decay of mass production and the rise of flexible methods; it is also the part of the world where the greatest advances toward economic, social, and political integration have been achieved. Fordism engendered a territorial system based on the accumulation of capital and labor in urban agglomerations—the "development poles"—with satellite industrial spaces strategically placed in natural resource or energy sites and along the great communication axes.

Labor and capital tended to concentrate in large industrial plants and production units in core regions, in order to take advantage of internal and external economies and economies of scale and scope. The German Ruhr, Wallonia, and the South Yorkshire and Manchester areas in Great Britain represent paradigmatic examples of this type of spatial organization. The decline in manufacturing increasingly threatened the great industrial regions created around large industrial complexes. Challenges were both external and internal. As Storper and Scott point out, "Internally, market saturation and thorough-going spatial decentralization in response to worker militancy were creating high levels of unemployment and productivity slowdowns in the core.

Externally the competition from Japan and the newly industrializing countries was cutting dramatically into domestic markets in North America and Western Europe. The net result was intensified industrial restructuring and rationalization in the core lead into more plant closure, more decentralization, and greater unemployment." These processes led to "new industrial foci" in areas where "the social conditions built up in Fordist industrial regions could be avoided or were not present".

A major tenet of the literature on the spatial consequences of post-Fordism is that socioeconomic restructuring has produced new spatial cleavages. According to Castells, decision, information, and financial "growth-promoting" service centers tend to become concentrated in core areas, whereas production units and research and development complexes tend to be dispersed to intermediate and peripheral regions, mainly in previously nonindustrialized areas. Routine activities and "Taylorist" unskilled manual tasks are uprooted from central locations to "offshore" placements in the search for low production costs and weak labor organization.

This viewpoint holds that the new territorial pattern is dichotomous. On the one hand, capital and information are becoming increasingly concentrated in core service-oriented regions. In addition, global networks link international banks and trade services into a worldwide network of international financial nuclei. As a consequence, "ownership is more and more international and global, divorced from national definitions".

In recent years, we have seen a shift from a predominantly sectoral and urban model to a more supple one, apparently less constrained by former hierarchical bonds with neighboring cities, but still heavily reliant on and integrated with economic circuits and world networks. As a result, core countries have experienced in the last two decades a steady decay in urbanization rates and a corresponding increase in industrial and service workplaces in rural areas.

Some rural areas, furthermore, have experienced a growth in employment and income, whereas the pace of deindustrialization has been accelerated in former centers of mass production like the Ruhr, the North and North-West of England, the Scottish Strathclyde, Wallonia, or the Nord-Pas-de-Calais region. In sum, the restructuring literature has outlined major spatial trends related to deindustrialization and the establishment of flexible production methods: the appearance of new development poles in formerly lagging areas and the distortion of the traditional clear-cut division between centers and peripheries.

These trends reduce the influence of national borders in spatial patterning of development. The room for maneuver left to national entities is shrinking rapidly as the integration of the world economy continues to erode national "sovereignty." Subnational entities, such as regions or local communities, are acquiring more relevance in articulating space, to the detriment of nation-states. In spite of efforts to maintain national control, the integration of the world economy leads to a blurring of state borders and a revision of the role of the nation-state.

National economic actors and stock exchanges "can no longer expect to monopolize trading in the shares of companies in their country or region, nor can trading be confined to specific cities or exchanges". The power of the nation-state is being challenged on two fronts: On the one hand, economic and political integration in areas such as the EC is inducing important transfers of power to supranational bodies like the European Council or the European Commission; on the other hand, the increased concentration of economic activity in regional clusters, together with the revival (in some cases) and the creation (in others) of regional political movements and parties, is helping to propel the relevance of the regional dimension in the EC.

Therefore, according to Krugman, "as Europe becomes a unified market, with free movement of capital and labor, it will make less and less sense to think of the relations between its component nations in terms of the standard paradigm of international trade. Instead the issues will be those of regional economics". Regions arise as the spatial post-Fordist unit par excellence. They are regarded as a unique environment for economic competition and the return to more liberal market structures, closely identified with flexible production methods.

Changes in Territorial Structure

Explanations of changes in territorial structure are twofold. Several authors have stressed the internationalization of capital and the fact that the growing integration of economic circuits has led to greater economic interdependency. This interdependence has contributed to the appearance of new developing areas and to a reduction in the gap between advanced and lagging regions. Areas hitherto isolated from what was considered the advanced economy have been fully incorporated in world capitalist circuits. This catch-up effect has been observed on an international scale; the Pacific Rim, once peripheral to the development of the world economy, is becoming a key area in the evolution of the new modes of production.

But it is on a subnational level, within the developed world, where phenomena such as the ascension of the "sunbelts" or the development of the "Third Italy" are attracting most attention. A second set of explanations focuses on deindustrialization, the rise of service and high-technology industries, and the development of new technologies and systems of management as potential causes of the changes in the spatial pattern.

Improved technological systems have allowed a rapid response to the major challenges affecting the old industrial order. In fact, technology is often considered the ultimate means of surmounting the problems related to decreasing productivity growth rates, to the lags and high costs in passing from innovation to manufacturing, and, above all, as the most effective way to elude the rigidity of mass production.

As O'Brien notes, "the impact of technology on the method and speed of communications and calculation, gives the ... markets a wholly new dimension". Technology has enabled the routinization of a large number of service activities and has eased the process of decentralization of traditional manufacturing activities to suburban locations or distant regions.

Information technology has been studied as key to spatial change. As Stöhr underlines, transfers of information, innovation, and entrepreneurial initiative from outside of as well as within the local community are key to the development of a particular space. In sum, explanations of territorial pattern have tended to emphasize the dynamics of transformation. Advances in technology, improvements in communication, and the development of market structures are frequently cited in interpretations of the new spatial dynamic. This fact might have induced the overemphasis on innovation and dynamic elements in the restructuring process and produced the widespread impression that a new and distinctive post-Fordist spatial configuration was emerging.

From that perspective, the increasing mobility of traditional locational factors and the removal of resource bottlenecks are fostering growth in areas where development was almost precluded during the Fordist era of mass production. Innovation and technology are frequently seen as allowing growth to occur almost anywhere, since the factors that activate development have become extremely mobile in recent years and know no national or legal borders. Taken to its limit, this argument implies that "location no longer matters".

The economic restructuring is reducing the sway of local conditions in growth and is increasingly randomizing growth patterns is highly disputable. Traditional locational constraints are gradually losing relevance, but this does not imply that "location no longer matters" to growth. Restructuring means precisely that locational factors and constraints that used to be relatively unnoticed or ignored have come to the fore.

Social circumstances, in particular, have attracted little attention in empirical cross-sectional research, which has focused largely on economic indicators and on dynamism, while neglecting persistent forces and start-off conditions. Existing social conditions may play an.essential role in an area's receptivity to and assimilation of foreign trends and processes. The successful adoption of novel technologies, techniques, and information relies heavily not only on the capacity of a few individuals or companies to invent new procedures and to compile massive amounts of information, but also on the capacity of any space to supersede old production structures and to respond rapidly to challenges.

The current level of development of a nation, a region, or a locality is the outcome of how different production systems, social and political regimes, and cultures have been successively combined in space. Several authors have stressed the importance of start-off conditions for the assimilation of imported innovations and thus in the growth and development capacities of certain territories.

Regions in peripheral countries (except Greece), regardless of their initial level of development in the EC, experienced much higher growth rates than regions in core countries such as Belgium, the Netherlands, Germany, or France. Furthermore, whereas peripheral countries shared a distinct growth pattern, regions in core countries had fairly similar growth rates throughout the period. The results of preliminary regressions conducted with this dependent variable confirmed the strong dominance of the state effect, in contrast to what the literature on post-Fordism tends to consider a fundamentally regional phenomenon.

Regional data in these regressions were purposely introduced in national order, so that scores in the Durbin-Watson test could be considered significant. Durbin-Watson results were extremely low in all models. These types of autocorrelated errors constitute a typical example of spatial autocorrelation, through which "in regional cross-section data, a random shock affecting economic activity in one region may cause economic activity in an adjacent region to change because of close economic ties between the regions".

The pattern of residuals shows that values for regions tend to follow clear national patterns. An obvious explanation is that progressive specialization, incentives to invest, and government intervention through an active regional policy pay off. Notable catch-up effects are found. The evidence supports the postulates of equilibrium theories, which argue for the long-term convergence of development levels among nations. The catch-up hypothesis cannot be defended, however, when development levels within nations are scrutinized. The catch-up hypothesis would predict that within peripheral countries lagging regions would grow at a greater pace than advanced ones.

Both in Italy and Spain it was mainly the richest regions that grew the most quickly. In the case of Italy, the only three regions that had higher GDP per capita than the average of the EC in 1980 grew more than the average of the nation. In Spain, growth was mainly concentrated in the richest regions, such as Madrid, Catalonia, or the Balearic Islands. The results suggest that the nation is still a solid unit of analysis when studying spatial restructuring.

Although the importance of national borders for growth patterns might be diminishing, the pace of change is significantly slower than that suggested by the literature on economic restructuring. Social factors and the defense of sovereignty act as strong obstacles to change in spatial structures. The most salient point is that ignoring either the national or the regional dimension may strongly distort any conclusions emerging from the analysis of growth trends. Therefore, the growth rate used as the dependent variable in the following analyses will account for distortions created by the national dimension: annual regional growth rates are divided by a national coefficient, which represents the relationship between national growth rates and the EC's average growth. This method allows us to avoid misinterpretations provoked by very high growth rates in Italy, Spain, and Portugal, which otherwise would have led to the consideration of social and economic conditions in those three countries as the stimulus for regional growth.

The Social and Economic Dimensions

The causes of the changing pattern in the distribution of GDP, social and economic independent variables, representing the dialogue between innovation and tradition, as well as the start-off conditions have been introduced into the equation. The general model (Model 1) takes the following form:

$$y = \alpha + \underline{\beta}_1\underline{G} + \underline{\beta}_2\Delta_s\underline{G} + \underline{\delta}_1\underline{E} + \underline{\delta}_2\Delta_s\underline{E} + \varepsilon \tag{1}$$

where

y is the mean annual rate of growth of GDP between 1980 and 1989,

G is the start-off share of each of the main socioeconomic sectors (agriculture, industry, and services) in GDP,

ΔsG is the mean annual rate of growth of the share of each sector in GDP between 1980 and 1989,

E represents the start-off employment levels in each sector, and

ΔsE is the mean annual rate of growth of the share of employment in each sector between 1980 and 1989.

The model represents how static social and economic variables (G and E) combine with change over time (ΔsG and ΔsE) in space in order to generate growth. Value added and level of employment in each sector to depict two of the main social spheres. The proportion of gross value added at market prices portrays the original situation and the evolution of economic sectors, whereas data on employment reflects the social distribution of labor.

In any period of time, and especially in transition periods from one productive system to another, changes in the economic sphere are likely to occur more quickly than are social changes. The initial situation or start-off conditions are identified by a collection of static.variables, the percentage of gross value added (GVA) and employment in each of the main socioeconomic sectors in 1980. On the other hand, the actual outcome of the dialogue between innovation and tradition in the economic and social spheres of society is represented by a group of dynamic variables: the annual variation rates in value added and employment between 1980 and 1989.

Two important questions to be addressed prior to analyzing the factors that stimulate growth is (1) whether start-off conditions play a greater role than dynamic trends in generating growth and (2) whether persistent social conditions dampen transformation from a Fordist spatial model to one of flexible production. These questions can be answered with the use of econometric encompassing tests, which provide an adequate means for discriminating between competing non-nested social and economic, static and dynamic models.

This econometric testing allows us to differentiate among competing models. Rival hypotheses are dealt with symmetrically in order to select the model expected to perform best (the encompassing model) with regard to a particular loss function. The rationale behind each test is "to derive from one model an explanation or prediction of certain aspects of a contending model and contrast that with the result actually obtained by that rival model". There are four possible outcomes in encompassing tests:

(1) both models are accepted;

(2) Model 1 is accepted and Model 2 is rejected;

(3) Model 2 is accepted and Model 1 is rejected;

(4) both models are rejected.

At this point, general model divided (Model 1) into four different submodels (Models 2 to 5) and apply encompassing testing to the competing models in order to determine if any of the sets of variables included in Model 1 is able to explain by itself growth trends in Europe in the 1980s.

Start-off Conditions and Growth

Using encompassing tests, there are two non-nested models. In both models regional growth is regressed against sets of variables. The first one (Model 2) includes the share of GVA in each sector as a percentage of GDP in 1980 and the second (Model 3) the share of employment in each of the three main sectors in the same year.

The encompassing tests show that, from a statistical point of view, none of the models provides a valid explanation for growth rates in the EC in the 1980s; that is to say, none of the models analyzed "encompasses" the other. At a level of significance of 5 percent, the values of the tests clearly demonstrate that both models are rejected, since the numerical results obtained exceed the critical values of the different encompassing tests.

Dynamic Trends and Growth

In the second encompassing test annual rates of regional growth are regressed on two sets of dynamic variables. The first one (Model 4) consists of the mean annual rate of growth of the share of sectoral participation in GDP during the 1980s, while the second one (Model 5) includes the mean annual rate of growth of the share of employment in each of the three main sectors for the same period of time.

The results of this test are very similar to that of the previous one. Once more, the numerical results of the encompassing analysis exceed the critical values for each test and lead us to reject the hypothesis that one model "encompasses" the other. Therefore, the results confirm that the annual rates of growth in neither the share of employment nor in the share of sectoral GVA participation to GDP act as exclusive explanatory variables of growth. The encompassing test results clearly contest the idea of the supremacy of economic structural models over social structural explanations of development and growth.

All four economic and social, static and dynamic models were rejected, and none was judged better than the others. Such evidence supports the contention that regional economic growth is not just the result of the interaction of a limited number of economic factors, but the consequence of a complicated and multifaceted process in which social, political, and cultural elements—along with economic factors—play significant roles. When capital and labor tend to move freely, traditional economic locational factors are no longer able to explain on their own how and why economic activity flourishes in certain areas and not in others.

On the other hand, sociostructural variables alone also do not suffice to interpret a burst of regional growth in a particular territory. What elements are responsible for triggering growth? What circumstances concentrate growth in certain areas and not in others? The results of the encompassing tests encourage us to think about explaining regional growth in terms of both economic and social structural aspects such as productivity per employee in each sector. We also need to take account of static and dynamic dimensions of growth. The capacity of one region to grow faster than others may depend more on the initial conditions that predispose it to develop at a faster pace than neighboring areas than on the actual economic and social processes occurring in a determined territory over a certain period of time.

The final portion of the analysis is a cross-sectional study of socioeconomic structure, the social (employment) and economic (GVA) dimensions, as well as the combination of both.variables (labor productivity), in their static and dynamic forms. My goal is to identify the sectoral variables that have affected the development of growth rates most strongly during the last decade and to see if a new territorial pattern is emerging.

SOCIOECONOMIC RESTRUCTURING AND REGIONAL GROWTH

If traditional economic locational factors do not explain economic activity and growth in the EC sufficiently, what structural factors have promoted regional growth in the EC in the last decade? All twelve variables used in the encompassing tests are included in the final analysis. They capture start-off conditions and rates of growth in the share of employment and start-off conditions and rates of growth in the share of GVA. Data in this set describe the productivity of labor (P) across different sectors in 1980, in its static dimension, and the rates of growth of sectorial productivity during the 1980s, from a dynamic point of view. The final model (Model 6) is

$$y = \alpha + \underline{\beta}_1\underline{G} + \underline{\beta}_2\Delta_s\underline{G} + \underline{\delta}_1E + \underline{\delta}_2\Delta_sE + \underline{\gamma}_1\underline{P} + \underline{\gamma}_2\Delta_s\underline{P} + \varepsilon \quad (2)$$

where $\underline{P}$ is the initial labor productivity in each of the three main socioeconomic sectors, and $\Delta s\underline{P}$ is the mean annual rate of growth of labor productivity in GDP of each sector between 1980 and 1989.

Regression Analysis

Several preliminary regressions were executed with all

variables. In order to obtain the final empirical model, *t*-tests and a joint *F* test were performed on the coefficients of the redundant variables. At a 95 percent level of significance, an empirical model was accepted as a valid simplification of the general theoretical model. The empirical model is

$$y = a + \Delta E1x + \Delta E3x + P1x + P2x + \Delta P2x + \Delta P3x + e \qquad (3)$$

Significant variables selected in the empirical model represent fairly well the distribution of variables in the theoretical model. Both variables indicating the start-off conditions as well as those representing processes are included. Employment and productivity variables also appear in the model. There is only one significant absence: none of the six variables containing sectoral GVA as a share of GDP emerged as significant.

Such an outcome could not be expected a priori, since it is normally regarded as logical that GVA, as an endogenous component of GDP and thus of its rate of growth, may have a more solid effect on regional development than completely exogenous factors, as is the case of employment. Nevertheless, this fact serves to reinforce the idea of the influence of social or socially related factors in economic growth in a post-Fordist society.

The outcomes of the regression of annual regional growth rates during the 1980s on the six variables included in the empirical model. This model reveals a close relationship between labor productivity trends and regional growth rates. Nonetheless, dynamic labor productivity variables are more strongly related to growth than static ones. As the regression shows, the initial conditions of labor productivity in agriculture and industry, in spite of high levels of significance, do not have a decisive positive or negative influence on growth rates.

Increases in labor productivity in industry and services during the 1980s do have positive or negative impacts on growth. Any increase in the productivity of the tertiary sector is negatively related to growth, while labor productivity increases in industry result in increasing development rates. This is fundamentally due to the fact that the regions that have experienced a moderate rise in productivity in the tertiary sector are the peripheral regions of Spain, Portugal, and the Italian Mezzogiorno, where this increase is mainly concentrated in small wholesale and retail and administrative services.

Productivity in other types of services more closely associated with post-Fordist restructuring, such as financial services and services to industries, changes little throughout the period. On the other hand, the regions with the highest increase in industrial productivity tend to be formerly intermediate regions that had the initial socioeconomic conditions necessary to attract flexible production plants.

The model clearly suggests that large increases in employment in agriculture and in the service sector during the 1980s curb the possibilities of regional economic growth. Results in the service sector are extremely significant. There is a strong negative correlation between employment in the tertiary sector and regional development. he whole model raises interesting questions about the real role played by the emerging service economy in a restructuring society and about the prominence of service activities as the new motor of growth.

The service sector has experienced the largest expansion in Western Europe during the 1980s. Nevertheless, this expansion in employment has not been matched by a similar development of growth rates during the 1980s. It is true that some types of services (e.g., services to industries) trigger an increase in productivity and thus encourage growth.

And it is also true that some of the regions with the highest growth rates have developed a strong, dynamic, high-quality service sector. This is the case of Baden-Württemberg, Bavaria, Hessen, Lombardy, and Tuscany, all regions that at the beginning of the decade already possessed strong service sectors.

Nevertheless, these regions constitute the exception, not the rule. The service sector has boomed in areas that had small tertiary economies at the beginning of the 1980s. Regions undergoing strong industrial decline (such as Wallonia, Saarland, the Basque Country, or Asturias) and, in particular, old agricultural regions like Galicia, Cantabria or both Castiles in Spain; Burgundy in France; Abruzzi, Basilicata, Molise, Calabria and Sicily in Italy; and Centro, Alentejo, and Algarve in Portugal constitute the new expanding tertiary spaces.

In those areas, economic restructuring has meant the emergence of a new, poorly paid, and precarious service economy where labor productivity increases are negligible. In those relatively lagging regions, the service sector has absorbed workers escaping from industrial decline and the crisis in agriculture. It is a very different "tertiarization" from the one occurring in core areas, where, to a certain extent, highly educated and dynamic individuals enter a productive tertiary sector. In lagging areas, a precarious service economy has become a substitute for unemployment: a sort of social policy, financed through budgetary solidarity, whose goal is to avoid social and political unrest.

In addition, the results demonstrate that industry still plays a significant role in regional economic growth, although development is by no means fostered in traditional mass production regions, as it was in the 1970s (start-off conditions in industrial productivity have a slight negative association with growth). Old Fordist areas, such as Wallonia, Nord-Pas-de-Calais, Lorraine, Liguria, Yorkshire, and the North and North-West of England are among the regions with the lowest growth rates during the 1980s.

Growth has occurred in those regions that have managed to transform their old industrial fabric into a flexible production structure in a shorter period of time than the traditional Fordist areas. This has been achieved mainly in core and capital regions, like the South-East of England, Brussels, Bremen, Île de France, or Lazio, where financial and informational concentration meet with highly skilled and highly qualified labor. Some other intermediate regions, such as Scotland, the Limousin, Languedoc-Roussillon, and Veneto, have accomplished this step with relative success.

Current Economic Geography

Ash Amin and Nigel Thrift presented a gloomy picture of current economic geography. From their point of view, economic geography is seriously ill and needs urgent treatment. Among the many ailments that affect economic geography several can be highlighted: it fails to attract and recruit students and staff; the subject is perceived as "narrowly specialised, increasingly focused on industrial districts, learning regions, clusters, and the like"; and, above all, it is unexciting and "fails to fire the imagination".

Strong drugs are thus needed in order "to revive economic geography as an imaginative, relevant, and socially useful subject". However, according to Amin and Thrift, these drugs cannot be the traditional 'mainstream' economic pills; the patient has become immune to them and they may not cure the infection. Instead we should look for remedies in the form of what they consider to be more imaginative approaches to the discipline and of alliances with "new areas of economic study" such as evolutionary political economy, economic sociology, feminist economics, parts of environmental economics, cultures of economies and so on. Only in this way will we be capable of deconstructing and constructing economic discourses and of understanding the micro-practices in firms.

That economic geography regards itself as being in crisis is nothing new. Economic geography has never been a mainstream subject and lacks the numbers of practitioners which could endow the discipline with the kind of confidence that Amin and Thrift identify in other sciences and, especially, in economics [where, by the way, confidence does not mean lack of introspection. Economic geographers have been constantly asking themselves questions about the nature, the aims and the scope of the discipline.

Ian Gordon in his comments to an earlier version of the paper suggested two possibilities: a) anorexia (a post-Marxist, post-modernist, fashion conscious flight from talking about the boring old economy, leading simply to less economic geography, in the sense of work on the productive economy); and b) inadequate engagement with evidence (equally true of the 'new economic geography') and particularly with attempts to link theory logically to important empirical outcomes dominating paradigms. Amin's and Thrift's intervention represents another welcome step in this process. However, when introspection becomes endemic, apprehension turns into hypochondria.

And in the case of economic geography there may be no need for that. Indeed, if we take a look at economic geography now in comparison to economic geography a few decades ago or in comparison to other sub-disciplines within geography, the picture may not be as bleak as Amin and Thrift describe. It may even be stronger both from a recruitment and a scientific point of view. From a recruitment perspective, joint degrees in geography with economics are thriving. Masters degrees in economic geography are also healthy and attracting increasing numbers of students from outside geography.

The recruitment problems Amin and Thrift refer to tend to happen at MPhil/PhD level. But it is questionable whether this recruitment shortage has anything to do with any global failure of economic geography to 'fire the imagination', as Amin and Thrift claim. It is more likely to be linked to the more mundane and rather parochial conditions of the British labour market, where any decent graduate in economic geography with good quantitative skills can expect to earn a starting salary not much different from that of many university professors.

Other geography graduates have, unfortunately, lesser chances of being offered similar starting salaries. In a certain weird sense economic geography fares better than much larger and more established disciplines such as economics or mathematics where the problems of MPhil/ PhD recruitment are dire. Yet, no one - at least within those disciplines - is suggesting that the reason for such shortage is that the subjects they deal with are 'unexciting'.

From a scientific perspective, the claim that economic geography is in crisis can also be questioned. In contrast to when the discipline was dominated first by the neo-positivist and later by the Marxist paradigm, the panorama is now much more complex. It is true that post-modern approaches prevail, although this may be a fundamentally British phenomenon. However, the range and variety of approaches, methods and topics currently covered by the discipline is huge.

Unless the different groups within economic geography become too narrowly focused and insular, such variety can only benefit the discipline and encourage the dialogue with other disciplines. Another factor which is contributing to the good health of economic geography is the increasing interest of other social sciences in spatial phenomena. Economic sociologists and mainstream economists, among others, are crossing the interdisciplinary boundaries and using geographers' analytical tools in their research; and some geographers are increasingly applying analytical tools borrowed from sociologists, economists and econometricians to geographical problems.

Although this phenomenon is not completely new, it is now happening to a greater extent than ever before. Of special interest is the case of the so-called 'new economic geographers'. For the first time in a long period there is a group of prestigious mainstream economists who, after having developed an interest in the analysis of the spatial agglomeration of economic activity, are not only happy to call what they do geography, but in some cases are even willing to move to geography departments, despite having similar opportunities in departments of economics.

The result is that there is now more scope than ever for collaboration and dialogue across disciplines. Although it may still not be happening at the level some geographers would like to see, there are already encouraging signs: the increasing popularity of regional studies and regional science (at least outside Britain) conferences have made them an ideal ground for cross-fertilization. Multidisciplinary regional studies and regional science journals, as well as the new *Journal of Economic Geography* - which has attracted some of the most reputed economic geographers from geography and economics to its editorial board - are or may prove to be important vehicles for this interdisciplinary dialogue.

Although there are some reasons for concern, economic geography is in relatively good shape. But let us assume for a moment that I have made the wrong diagnosis and Amin and Thrift got the symptoms right. That economic geography is not a malade imaginaire as could be deduced from the previous section, but seriously ill; that it has really become 'narrowly specialised', 'unexciting' and 'fails to fire the imagination'.

Although there are a few geographers who still read 'mainstream' economics, the fact is that the bulk of the discipline is completely detached from 'mainstream' economics. The few geography journals concerned with formal modelling - especially Geographical Analysis - have almost been deserted by geographers and colonised by economists and, above all, engineers.

Over the last decade large sections of economic geography have been dominated by what has become known as the 'cultural turn'. The ascent of this approach has had notable benefits. Significant progress has been made in many areas of economic geography and the understanding of some economic phenomena is certainly better than it was a decade ago. Yet, despite all this exciting contribution by what are mainstream economic geographers, Amin and Thrift argue that the discipline is in crisis.

It is 'narrowly specialised', 'unexciting' and 'fails to fire the imagination'; it 'bores' existing students and 'fails' to attract new ones. If this is the case, the focus of the infection cannot be 'mainstream' economics but only a 'cultural turn' disorder. And this affection may be provoking a serious case of macrocephaly in the discipline. Despite the many claims of dealing with the 'real world' (and what is the 'real world' anyway?), if there is one thing that has characterised many 'mainstream' economic geography journals in recent years it is an excess of theory, too little empirical evidence, and empirical evidence too selectively drawn and narrowly analysed.

Ironically a criticism that geographers have levelled at economic journals. These 'mainstream' economic geographers have been so busy deconstructing and constructing discourses, that they have forgotten about building an empirical and analytical body around this theoretical corpus. Several geographers have already raised the alarm. Markusen and Martin have cogently shown that despite the current theoretical emphasis by some 'mainstream' geographers, the discipline is besieged by problems such as fuzzy conceptualisation, lack of methodological rigour, lack of clarity and a tendency to favour description to the detriment of analysis.

Perrons and Martin have expressed their concern about the disappearance of maps from economic geography articles. And it is not just maps. Tables and graphs are also almost absent from some of the top economic geography journals. When empirical evidence is used, it is often limited to a series of cases studies which are repeated almost ad nauseam and based on a limited amount of often anecdotal information. The fact that a large section within the discipline may be focusing on the trees without seeing the forest may also explain why economic geography has had so little impact on policy making.

It is clear that if there is a crisis, its sources are internal rather than external. However, instead of making economic geography swallow the bitter pill of internal scrutiny, Amin and Thrift prefer to look for the symptoms elsewhere and prescribe greater doses of 'cultural turn'. This is a strange remedy, since it hopes to cure the patient by overdose. More construction and deconstruction and more alliances with 'alternative' economics would only reinforce the crisis.

The 'cultural turn' in economic geography has contributed to the expansion of the limits of our discipline, but is has been found wanting in explaining in a comprehensive way what growth, development and inequality are all about beyond a few case studies. Perhaps it is time to stop and think about constructing a solid empirical corpus around the new theoretical developments in the discipline. Geographers need to consolidate what has been achieved by expanding the number of cases and conducting cases in a more systematic way and, why not, by trying to use quantitative methods to test some of the new theories developed in recent years.

This is a task that economic geography cannot achieve alone. It needs, as Amin and Thrift claim, allies. But not just evolutionary political economy, economic sociology, feminist economics, cultures of economies and other disciplines that Amin and Thrift favour. Mainstream economics, quantitative sociology, political science, and other sciences and theories may also have a significant role to play in helping us understand the basic questions in economic geography. Otherwise, just more of what has been the dominating trend in the discipline in Britain over the last fifteen years risks killing economic geography by a 'cultural turn' overdose.

Bibliography

Beatley, Timothy. *Green Urbanism : Learning from European Cities*. Washington. D.C. 2000.

Blake, Nelson M. *Water for the Cities: A History of the Urban Water Supply Problem in the United States*. Syracuse. NY: 1956.

Chant, Colin, and David Goodman. (eds). *Pre-Industrial Cities and Technology. (Cities and Technology)*. London. 2000. NR

Frey, Hildebrand W. *Designing the City: Towards a More Sustainable Urban Form*. 1999.

Ginsburg, Norton. *The Urban Transition: Reflections on the American and Asian Experiences*. Hong Kong: Chinese University Press. 1987.

Goodman, David, and Colin Chant. (eds.) *European Cities and Technology Reader: Industrial to Post-Industrial City*. Cities and Technology. London. 1999.

Hall, Peter. *Cities in Civilization*. New York. 1998.

Inoguchi, Takashi, Edward Newman, and Glen Paoletto. (eds). *Cities and the Environment: New Approaches for Eco-Societies*. Tokyo and New York. 1999.

Lee, Leo Ou-fan. *Shanghai Modern: The Flowering of a New Urban Culture in China, 1930-1945*. Cambridge: Harvard University Press. 1999.

Low, Nicholas, et al. (eds). *Consuming Cities: The Urban Environment In The Global Economy After The Rio Declaration*. London. 2000.

Marsh, George P. *The Earth Modified by Human Action. A New Edition of Man and Nature (1863).* New York. 1874.

Melosi, Martin V. *Garbage in the Cities: Refuse, Reform, and the Environment: 1880-1980.* Chicago. 1981.

Moe, Richard, and Carter Wilkie. *Changing Places: Rebuilding Community in the Age of Sprawl.* Henry Holt. 1997.

Mumford, Lewis. *The City in History: Its Origins, Its Transformations, And Its Prospects.* New York. 1961.

Newman, Peter, and Jeffrey Kenworthy. *Sustainability and Cities: Overcoming Automobile Dependence.* Washington. D.C., 1999.

Platt, Rutherford H., Rowan A. Rowntree, Pamela C. M[illegible]ick, eds. *The Ecological City: Preserving and Restoring Urban Biodiversity.* Amherst, Mass. 1994.

Reps, John William. *The Making of Urban America.* Princeton. 1992.

Rykwert, Joseph. *The Idea of a Town: The Anthropology of Urban Form in Rome, Italy and the Ancient World.* Cambridge. MA. 1988.

TeBrake, William H. "Air Pollution and Fuel Crises in Pre-Industrial London, 1250-1650." *Technology and Culture.* 16. July. 1975.

Logan, John R. (ed). *The New Chinese City: Globalization and Market Reform.* Studies in Urban and Social Change. Malden: Blackwell Publishers. 2002.

Thomas, William L., Jr., ed. *Man's Role in Changing the Face of the Earth.* 2 vols. Chicago. 1956.

Jones, Gavin W. (ed). *Urbanization in Large Developing Countries: China, Indonesia, Brazil and India.* New York: Oxford University Press. 1998.

Warner, Robin, John Dodson, and Howard Bridgman. *Urban Biophysical Environments. Meridian Australian Geographical Perspectives.* Oxford. 1996.

Index